# DOOM OF YOUTH

# DOOM OF YOUTH

## BY

## WYNDHAM LEWIS

HASKELL HOUSE PUBLISHERS Ltd.
*Publishers of Scarce Scholarly Books*
NEW YORK, N. Y. 10012
1973

**HASKELL HOUSE PUBLISHERS** Ltd.

*Publishers of Scarce Scholarly Books*

280 LAFAYETTE STREET

NEW YORK. N. Y. 10012

Library of Congress Cataloging in Publication Data

Lewis, Wyndham, 1886-1957.
  Doom of youth.

  Reprint of the 1932 ed.
  1. Youth.  I.  Title.
HQ796.L4 1973          301.43'15          72-2090
ISBN 0-8383-1475-9

Printed in the United States of America

**1763420**

# FOREWORD

## THE EVERYMANS

'THE education of the Young is for us a matter of life and death.' Those are the words of Trotsky. And that is the political principle at the heart of all 'Youth-politics.' But *all* politics to-day are, in one degree or another, 'Youth-politics.' This is very imperfectly understood. The Catholic Church has at all times directed all its energies to baby-snatching and youth-catching—that is well known: under the guise of providing 'a good education,' at moderate rates, or free of charge, even, to any child, of any communion, that wily Roman Papa has laid his nets: the 'good education' was of course also a *catholic* education. (And a very *good* education in every sense it has always been.) The Jesuits were obsessed with the idea of 'the Young.' These priests turned themselves into nannies, schoolmasters, mothersome and fathersome bodies, professional 'uncles' and good-natured aunts, nurses, and big-hearted big-brothers. The christian world became *a nursery* and *a schoolroom.*

That the masters of the Soviet should do the same thing is natural: for they have to turn back again, as it were, all these intensively-manufactured 'Christians' (emotionally byzantine into the bargain) into non-religious rough-material: also they have to convert the primitive moujik Hodge into an up-and-coming Modern American Man, all complete with mechanical mind. Hence highly-organized nursery-work and schoolroom-business for every one! So the 'Socialist State,' as seen in Russia, becomes a huge Nursery-governess and Pedagogue. And 'the education of the "Young" is for us a matter of life and death'—that is the view that all the Soviet takes of 'Youth-politics.'

But *all* politics are to-day, in one degree or another, 'Youth-politics,' I have said. In Italy the Roman Papa and Duce squabble from morning till night over boy-scouts and girl-guides. In Russia, morning, noon, and night, propaganda is being squirted under the skins of millions of infants by millions of trained propagandists, and they are taught to hate 'the Old' and to love 'the New.' But all this ferment does not stop at the frontiers of Russia and Italy.

In the great democracies of the West we live more or less under Press-government by *suggestion* and *education* of course, by absorption daily of column after column of gossip, breezy social articles, selected 'news,' 'controversial' special features, 'informative' pars., etc., plus Talkies. Whether openly or covertly, it is Press and Cinema hypnotism that rules Great Britain and America, not the conversazione at Westminster or the White House. But the spell-bound public, at the hands of the Popular Press or by way of the film, has notions and beliefs pumped into it that are the *reverse* of any recognized Tradition— either in Religion, Law, Government, or Ethics. In this sense it is 'revolutionary' propaganda—the propaganda of a power always *In Opposition*. Needless to say, I have no personal aversion to that side of the picture. I am not very impressed by the political institutions, legal practices, canons of art, architecture, or science of government bequeathed to the European by 'tradition.' I have a most revolutionary sort of mind: if I have an objection at all to these principles of indirect government in the democratic West, it is because, although revolutionary, it is purely destructive: and being 'democratic' it is destructive of what the lowest average 'low-brow' *Homme moyen sensuel* is disposed to hate and to destroy.

But the method of government here, just as it is elsewhere in openly socialized states, is pedagogic—the

politics are intensively 'Youth-politics.' **Mr. and Mrs.**
Everyman live in a *nursery*, above which smiles that
benevolent Uncle, Mr. Drage, and many another Smiler.
It is, in fact, a sort of *male-matriarchy*—if one can describe
a thing in that unnatural way. And it is the *technique* of
this government by picture-book (illustrated paper, cinema,
etc.) and elementary, 'gossipy' friendly instruction (the
controversial newspaper article) that I propose to study.
Taking you outside the walls of this vast nursery, I will
show you all the 'News' and 'controversy' kitchens, where
legislation by Public Opinion is prepared—a bird's-eye view
will be obtained of the subtle system whereby the old
European is to be turned into the 'New European.' But
because of the limitations imposed by Democracy—and
that is unfortunate—the old formulae are extremely well
smashed up, but really novel forms and modes of expression
are not taken on with an equal zeal and promptitude: the
true innovator is as badly off as ever he was, and he cannot
look to this enthusiastic smasher of the Old to help him with
his patents and inventions. Hence the 'New European'
is apt to be merely the old one turned inside out, or else a
sort of half-man emerges—or a Child-man, or a sort of rag
doll, more and more—composed of the bits left over, oddly
arranged. A sort of ill-favoured 'transitional' dummy
results.

The term 'Youth-politics' signifies the management of
this system of education and propaganda-politics, in which
Ma and Pa Everyman are two childlike persons, of course.
But the *Everymans*, as a family, are very decadent—they
in fact do become more infantile every day: and while
'Youth-politics' is in full blast all round us, measures of
disinfection, for the intelligent, are often necessary. Really
of course the Everymans, in their present condition (they
have reached the stage of dribbling and babbling, and
scarcely are to be trusted any more to attend to their

domestic slops and flush the drains of their natural offices)—
as things stand they *ought* to be isolated.  That would be
the only truly sanitary course.  But that is not an easy
matter—there are so many of them.

What is taken for granted in these pages is that the disintegration (a phase of the technique of which we are considering) cannot be arrested, even if we would.  And the
disintegration is bound to contradict many things that are
desirable, that goes without saying, for destruction cannot,
*in itself*, be good.  Meanwhile, as the old disintegrates,
the new does to some extent (in patches) *integrate*—that is,
of course (as things are at present), the trouble.  Much that
is purely destructive—indeed well-nigh imbecile—is bound
to get mixed into the integrating substance : and that
is bad.

Such an essay as this, with its radical exposure (rather
than criticism) of the processes of this integration taken as
ends in themselves, should serve (that is its object) to
prevent people from taking up more than is necessary of
purely destructive material into the brick-making for 'the
New Jerusalem.'

Our Western Society has entered upon, as is often pointed
out, 'a period of transition.'  So ours is *an interim world* as
it were.  Nothing is made in it that is intended to be more
than a make-shift.  Nothing really novel or decisive can be
undertaken, or can come to perfection, in this interregnum.

But the community which, going through its Transition,
does not sink *too* low in the scale of human values, will have
a distinct advantage (once the *Transition* closes) over those
communities which go pitiably to pieces, and embrace this
shadow, this interim *Scheinwelt*, as though it were the
substance and the reality.

Most that is being made mincemeat of was not certainly
so perfect as to cause us to long to perpetuate it, I suppose :
therefore, not too hysterically to regret it.  But, enfeebled

by repeated attacks over a long period of years, most of our institutions, and their symbolic representatives, have even become (whatever they may have been at the start, or at their zenith) entirely abject. On the other hand our *race*—the bed-rock of our aryan nature (or whatever term, 'aryan' or another, you care to use to describe that blood-related, fairly homogeneous type—whether Swiss, Scotch, Lombard, Irish, Bavarian or Breton)—*that* it is important to keep, as far as possible, intact. None of the institutions of that race, necessarily, but certainly something that is in a sense the soul of it. The hysterical wail of D. H. Lawrence—'We are doomed: the doom of our White Day: . . . Melville knew. He knew his race was doomed. His White Soul doomed. His great White Epoch doomed!'—*that* certainly we should not echo back. The whole world—and all its 'epochs'—black, yellow, white, and café-au-lait—are 'doomed' from that point of view. But the 'White Soul' is independent of its 'Epochs.'

The traditional European Family is 'doomed'—about that I do not think there is any occasion for us to argue. But 'Youth' in the european sense, that also is 'doomed.' It is the same purely economic consideration 'dooming' the Family which dooms 'Youth.'

The subject of this essay is the doom of 'Youth': by this I mean that the European generally has had a certain fixed conception with regard to the leisurely growing-up of a human being, and certain hard and fast ideas of what 'Youth' should feel like, behave like, and do with itself— as a *separate* communion, of a different clay to the adult world. If affluent, 'Youth' would be different (in this way) for a period of anything up to twenty-five years—or a quarter of a century. Then 'adult' life began. This segregation is at an end. At ten to-day the human being is a little 'adult.' 'Youth' in the old sense will tend more and more to disappear.

Meanwhile by means of 'Youth-politics' of the most highly-organized, astringent, and mechanical (rock-drill) type, 'Youth' is being broken up. It will be superseded by another, a far less sentimental, conception. The old 'Youth' is beyond any question 'doomed,' in that respect, it is going the same way as Sex—as the old over-emotional love-relationship.

All these ancient, fundamental, european concepts— 'Youth,' 'Woman,' 'Man,' 'Sex,' etc.—are being de-molished. The idea 'Woman' (with all the chivalrous and sensuous colours with which it has always been bathed and distorted—for the Celt, the Anglo-saxon, the German, the Provençal) that has long ago ceased to be intact. (A much more *masculine* contour is already transforming it beneath our eyes.) And the 'Man'—of the war-like, military, euro-pean tradition—the conception is for all practical purposes so out-of-date to-day that all that was 'manly' in the old sense is scarcely better than a laughing-stock, as it sur-vives among us (the footballer, 'strong-man,' cave-man, or police constable). Its *specific* time-honoured attributes are now tokens of inferiority.

'Youth' then will go the same way as 'Woman' and as 'Man.' And this book clearly indicates the methods, and the causes, of its translation.

# INTRODUCTION

## I. FOREWORD

**M**Y approach will be by way of the more immediate and emotional issues. I open upon the popular plane—where the music-hall joke of 'a lady and her age' or of the 'never say *forty* to a spinster' order flourishes. There I shall at once make contact with a considerable public, I feel sure. Having captured its attention, and stimulated its emotional interest, I shall lead it on to consider, bit by bit, the more fundamental issues involved; those that underlie the familiar, time-worn sensitiveness of everyday, where the question of the passage of years is concerned.

But, of course, to get to the bottom of the 'Politics-of-Youth,' you must in fact banish altogether the emotional, subjective conception of 'Youth.' As realized most intensely in the medium of the suffering feminine (or homosexual) vanity, Youth is one thing: in the mind of the politician another. Seen from the purely political end, Youth is not, fundamentally, a *being young*—or, rather, any sentimental attitude to a *being young*. The hardened old criminals who are responsible for 'Youth-politics' are far past, or are congenitally insensitive to, any considerations of a sentimental order. That goes without saying. 'Youth' is for them a label—or an army of peons (shouting *Giovenezza!*)—a stated quantity of ciphers, enregimented or not enregimented.

With this brief preliminary advertisement of how my argument is plotted, and of the plan of my campaign, I shall at once advance, and engage in a brisk general discussion. In this way I shall familiarize the reader, in these introductory pages, with the field chosen, the scope of the research, and the sort of difficulties he is likely to encounter.

## II. THE AGE-COMPLEX

A dispute occurred between two Frenchmen in a café in Marseilles last summer: I was not able to gather how it started, but the climax, which I witnessed, divided itself into three well-defined phases. First one of the men called the other a fool (an 'imbecile'). The man addressed in this way merely laughed pityingly. *Fool* had no effect whatever. Next the other called him 'an old' something-or-other. Result the same: he only gave a contemptuous sniff: the epithet 'old' was useless—that dart had no sting. Then the other man called him 'a dirty coward.' '*Coward' was the word required!* That had an instantaneous effect, and the 'coward' kicked the other man at once in the belly.

It is evident that a man's behaviour, in such a case, will depend upon his business interest, his vanity, his age, his sexual make-up, his profession, his class, his country, his race, his standing, and the qualities upon which it rests—a mass, in short, of very complex factors indeed. All of these three arrows—fool, old, coward—might be completely ineffective if directed against a member of a very sophisticated system, especially if the subject enjoyed a sheltered position near the top of it. But there are certain laws, I believe, that could be shown to control the major orders and classes of men at any given time.

There are three very simple persons known to me, their reactions I feel I could with some accuracy predict. With one of these I should bet on 'stupid' (or 'imbecile') as the word that would do the trick. With another I am sure that 'Old' would get nearest the bull's-eye (although both are of the same age). In a *behaviorist* experiment the figure would work at the word 'old.' I know only one person (and he is very simple, he belongs to a very primitive race) who would mind being called 'a coward.' He is half Corsican.

But of these three terms of opprobrium, there is no question at all which of the three would register most hits in a very complex society, such as ours. Indeed there is only one of the three that would do any execution at all. That is the word 'old.'

Let us consider the potentialities of the three words in question, one by one. First, no Everyman to-day needs to be 'brave.' Indeed it would be extremely foolhardy, after the experiences of fourteen years ago, to allow the fact to leak out, if by any chance he did happen to be that. On the other hand, as to 'intelligence,' it is a great handicap to be intelligent. It is far better to keep that to yourself too—unless you are in a sufficiently secure and privileged position to be able to afford to reveal it. But even the very rich to-day are compelled to give themselves out as being perfectly naïf and stupid.

The steam-roller of Big Business having gone over the democratic mass pretty thoroughly and achieved a mechanical 'levelling' (a uniform flatness never dreamed of before), no *exceptional* qualities are any advertisement at all for Mr. Everyman. No. The democratic average has nothing to gain by being 'clever': and the most conspicuous bravery, if not rewarded by death by shell-fire upon the field of battle, is apt to lead to a much-bemedalled beggar's tin-mug for coppers, and a fine view of the backsides of the prosperous passers-by from a position in the gutter.

But *age* is for the average man about the only value (in workshop, office, or factory) that survives, in a world from which all personal ambition has been banished, and in which there will soon be, in any fair-sized country, five or six million out of work. As a humble cog in the machinery

*b*

of Big Business  your *only* value is that you are fresh—and
of course, as a consequence, *cheap*.  So as cannon-fodder
for the great Peace Offensive of competitive Big Business
all exceptional qualities of brain or character are taboo: the
major asset is a fresh bodily machine—for machine-minding and mechanical tasks involving no responsibility there
can, logically, be no other value.

But if this is true, then it is not surprising if, in a general
way, 'old,' much more than 'fool' or 'coward,' would be
the word of the three—if indiscriminately discharged—
which must do most execution, say, in among a Post Office
or Banking Staff, or among a Railway personnel—on the
Permanent Way, or in the Offices and Workshops.

'Old,' of course, as an epithet of denigration, could only
be effective with a person already upon the borderline of
Youth and Not-Youth.  But this conventional limit is
to-day not much past the Thirty mark—the year when
Villon began his *Testament*.  And given circumstances of
intense sexual, or homosexual, competition, even twenty-
five may have a very nasty sound—in the course of my
field-work I have encountered great age-sensitiveness
(mainly, it is true, in homosexual quarters) around twenty-
two and twenty-three.  (In *Destins*, the well-known novel
by Mauriac, which I shall quote later on, such a case of
precocious age-complex plays a prominent part.)

In the *Evening Standard* (March 4, 1931) appeared a
piece of gossip about undergraduate life.  I will quote it
and then make my comment.

### UNDERGRADUATE DEBTS

Once every two years or so an agitation is engineered against
the monstrous methods of the University tradesmen.  These
shrewd but amiable merchants are accused of soliciting the
young to buy their wares without regard to the parents of the
said young nor yet to the fact that the credit system breeds
debts. . . .

FLATTERY

I remember that five and twenty years ago a certain
Oxford wine and cigar merchant had a habit of praising the
taste of undergraduates in their first year in order to sell them
expensive vintages and brands.

A youth of nineteen knows nothing, or next to nothing,
about such matters, yet often I have heard an eloquent sales-
man come out with some such rigmarole as 'Of course, sir, we
*have* a port at 48 shillings, but it would not suit a connoisseur
like yourself. Now *this* at 150 shillings we should like your
opinion on.'

And so forth. The silly young man was flattered (as most
young men would be), settlement of the bill was not pressed
for another two years, and then, when it was one of three
figures, father paid.

That is no doubt a true account of how the deal would
have been effected five and twenty years ago. But to-day
I think the really 'shrewd' wine-merchant would ad-
minister the flattery upon quite different lines—indeed his
strategy would be diametrically opposed to that of his
predecessor (or of himself) in 1905.

*To-day* he would address the 'youth of nineteen' as
follows: 'A bottle of port?' (he would be careful not to say
'sir' lest it might wake the reflex responding to *seniority*
rather than that of social eminence: also, one cannot say
'sir' to a kid). 'A bottle of *port*? What next—a bottle of
*milk* is what an infant like you should be requiring—it is
the *dairy* you want, not the *wineshop*, my little lad!'
Having paused to allow the pleased giggle of the 'youth of
nineteen' to escape and spend itself upon the academic air,
he would return to the charge. He would exclaim: 'What
would your mother say if she could see you asking for port,
I should like to know! Still, I daresay it is for somebody a
little *older* than you are, my little suckling. A bit of hos-
pitality, what! In that case, I have a reputation to keep
up in this University, and I shouldn't like any one to say

that I had taken advantage of a baby-in-arms and sold the poor kid an indifferent wine.  So it's up to me, I suppose! I couldn't sell *an old hardened connoisseur like yourself* ' (heaviest sarcasm and great sneers of infinite seniority) 'anything but this wine—and when I say it is 150 shillings a bottle, it is only that *for you*—I shall make nothing out of it at that price, I don't mind telling you!—but the price has to be tempered to the shorn lamb—even if you *have* been born with a silver spoon betwixt your ikkle toosie-pegs! One hundred and forty shillings—and if you tell any one what you paid for it I shall give you the best spanking you ever received, do you hear, my little fellow-me-lad!'

That (a little exaggerated, but not a great deal) is much nearer the mark, I think.  Certainly with fifty per cent. of his first-year undergraduate clientele the 'old connoisseur' approach would be not only out-of-date but disastrous. On the other hand, the method indicated above by me would ensure success.  Any manual of up-to-date salesmanship, having careful regard to the psychology of the young customer of the 'better classes,' would contain the most emphatic warnings on this head.  *Reverse all your technique of flattery*, or something to that effect, an important section would be headed.  And what would apply to the youngest boy, would (with certain obvious modifications) apply to the *oldest boy* in Britain.  The *white-bearded alone* may safely be credited with 'experience,' or the palate that comes only with experience and years, and even they will not thank you so much as all that.

If as a social historian I am unequalled, that isn't what I am here for in the present instance, and I must leave it to the reader to multiply the illustrations which—begging his pardon—his experience may suggest to him.  I am sure that, reviewed in the light of these novel remarks, his memory will disgorge a great variety of scenes and incidents calculated to bear me out in all that I have just asserted.

As a summary of this, I would suggest that it is in fact no obstacle to the ravages of the *age-complex* that a person should be extremely young. It is, of course, quite true that many people are quite untouched by this malady; but, on the other hand, it is surprising how many you may discover that are down with it. And it is one of the oldest symptoms of the suffering Zeitgeist that the truly 'young' should be infected with this obsession, one proper only to age; and, more curious still, at first sight, that the *male* should be infected by it even more than the female, although *age-complex* is traditionally a complaint of women, like the victorian 'vapours,' or cowardice in the face of mice.

### III. THE 'EX-YOUTH'

But intensive 'Youth-consciousness' (in the more high-brow fields this has been called 'Youngergeneration-consciousness') has its depressing side. Indeed it does tend to breed an entirely novel sort of 'inferiority-complex' in quarters where such a 'complex' does no good. The radical reversal of the 'Young' and 'Old' values—the 'experienced' and 'inexperienced' values—the insistence upon the value of all that is *primitive*, the contumelious propaganda directed against all that is *civilized* (that possessed of backgrounds, or possessed of any 'tradition,' as it is called) throws up a great variety of abortive growths. That is unavoidable. A political poisoner cannot guarantee to confine his destructive operations to the field selected for him.

The working of this system upon the emotional plane leads to many repulsive conventions and superstitions. And the *Age-snob* can be one of the most fantastic snobs that any caste-system has ever thrown up. In the vast museum of History he will be assured of a privileged place, as a first-class curiosity.

That upon social life as a whole the cult of the 'Youth-snob' must exercise an even more depressing influence than the cult of 'birth' or of rank, is evident—for there would be more of such anxious and unhappy snobs to the square mile with the former cult in vogue than with the latter.

Self-consciousness about 'Youth' produces ten years afterwards self-consciousness about *age*. That is inevitable —that follows like the night the day. And the more all-out the person goes, in his 'Youth,' for the *exclusive value* of Youth, the more, once his Youth is past, will he disseminate a dismal sense of the reverse, even at the expense of himself. Having committed himself to a doctrine (instinctively held only, perhaps) of 'Flaming Youth,' he must, when he can no longer call himself a 'Youth,' adhere to those values, and spectacularly enter into 'Eld.' As a fanatical adept of youth-mysticism there will be for him only Black and White: there can be no gradations. So, no longer 'young,' immediately he must jump into a precocious Old Age. He will become an 'Ex-Youth'—since 'Youth' of some sort he must be—there is no other value.

These movements apply, of course, not to the working-class, but to the 'educated,' or middle-class. The workman is too near the misery-line, and has more primitive pre-occupations, of hunger and of breeding, Woodbines and Work.

But my object has now been achieved, I think. The emotional backgrounds of this study have been opened up a little, and the reader has been given a glimpse of the sort of problems that are involved, upon the emotional plane. So I will now close this preamble and open the argument, in the first chapter of my book. For the guidance of the reader I have supplied a synopsis of the argument, chapter by chapter, which should I think be helpful, read in conjunction with these introductory pages.

# CONTENTS

## PART I

## PART II

## PART III

PART III is disposed in two chapters. It consists of what is called the 'Great Dossier.' It is a set of 40 'Exhibits.' There are the Headlines and Extracts of characteristic articles, showing the means employed to mobilize the Age-classes, for the *Age-war*, in the pages of the newspapers. It demonstrates, in as circumstantial a manner as possible, how this particular *class-war* is or-ganized, on the same lines as was formerly the 'Sex-war.'

The first forty numbered 'Exhibits' are examples of the propaganda employed for the *Age-war* as organized in Workshop, Office, or the Social world, mainly suburban. The forty

## PART IV

## PART V

# PART I

# THE BIG BUSINESS MIND HAS GAZED UPON 'YOUTH,' AND IT HAS FOUND IT, NOT *FAIR*, BUT *PROFITABLE*

THIS book should become a standard work upon the subject of which it treats. And that subject is 'Youth.' But it is necessary to give far more definition to the term than has been bestowed upon it in the Introduction, and describe the sort of 'Youth' involved. It is not the education of young persons of which this book treats—of graduate and post-graduate problems, for instance: nor does it refer to any moral corruption by which the young are supposed to be threatened. No Vamp, male or female, is to be exposed or discouraged in these pages. Nor is it a seductive meditation upon Love's Young Dream. It is merely the so-called *Politics of Youth* that is in question.

But are not Politics and Youth mutually-exclusive terms? It may never have occurred to the reader that there were any *politics* specifically related to young persons. Indeed, does not tender years preclude the idea of politics? Yet the reflective, in carrying a bouquet of violets to their noses, may, in sniffing, sometimes reflect that Monsieur Coty the Cosmetic King extracts from this delicious and modest plant certain delectable properties, which yearly he converts into a good many thousands of pounds.

There is a class of objects which, however ornamental, we are accustomed to regard as strictly useless. Yet many purely ornamental things are highly susceptible to exploitation. There is *nothing* that the Big Business mind does not see in terms of £. s. d. And it has gazed upon 'Youth'— and it has found it not *fair*, but *profitable*.

It requires imagination, in looking around a nursery, and observing this miniature world of innocent tots, to recognize how, upon a par with pig-iron, all this disarming human material would be turned to account by a really competent old harpy of a Big Business sleuth. Yet so it is. Even a beggar woman turns her howling offspring into gold, via shame and pity. And shall Big Business be outdone? It is not likely.—The oil-painter, when his professional eye falls upon you, is regarding you merely as a 'subject.' Your sole importance as far as he is concerned consists in whether you can be turned into a *picture*. Similarly the really first-class business man, upon whatever his eye alights, is solely concerned with how that object, whatever it may be, can be immediately transformed into hard cash, or may be put to do some profitable work.

It is the same with the politician. Only, with the politician you have to put *power* where with the business man you put *wealth* (or with the oil-painter, *paintableness*). And there has never been a time when business and politics were so nearly conjoined as to-day.

All contemporary political technique is upon the marxist model. All our politics are *class-politics*. Every system is based upon the 'Group' (or cell) technique of Marxism. The fundamental principle is that of universal '*Class-War*' (the war of Rich and Poor). But on top of that is built up an edifice of subsidiary 'Wars'—the 'Sex-War,' for instance, and the 'Age-War,' and the 'Politics-of-Youth,' as generally practised, is another word, merely, for Age-War.

During the next few years 'Youth-politics' is destined to be the pivot of all effective social movements. Therefore not 'youth'—the simple fact of adolescence and the earliest adult years—but the 'Mystics of Youth,' as it is termed on the Continent—'the Politics-of-Youth,' or 'Youth' as a political ideology, and lever or stalking-horse for political action—deserves special attention. And that is the study

to which you are invited in this unpretentious treatise. A
standard work, then, upon that important subject this
book shall be: but it does not set out to provide anything
more than the key to what otherwise would remain for
many a riddle.

Long ago the moderately observant must have noticed in
english public life—in the Press, in political addresses, in
fiction-books, films, the theatre, cartoons and so on—the
incessant recurrence of the 'Youth' *motif*. They will have
observed, for instance, recently, that the speed-king, Malcolm Campbell, not only gets knighted, but immediately
joins *The League of Youth* after his record at Daytona.
'Not too old at Fifty' one particularly hearty newspaper
shouts regarding the great motorist's feat. All this is apt
to puzzle Everyman: if fifty himself he will be apt to draw
in his belt a couple of holes, square his shoulders, and march
round to the nearest recruiting office of 'The League of
Youth'—or join this or that 'Crusade,' just to be on the
safe side. And in Germany, the home of 'Youth' in this
sense of a mobilized, class-conscious horde, *Jedermann*
betrays the same impulses, and goes bald-headed for the
same political bait.

The true significance of the surface disturbances resulting from the occult operations of a 'Politics-of-Youth'
escapes Everyman. Thus Feminisn was a political disturbance that remained, doubtless, a great puzzle to him.
'Ah, these women!' he would unquestionably bluster.
Just as now he would bluster, 'Ah, these youngsters, the
young devils!'

But for the Man-in-the-Street does not a war, like that
of 1914-18, appear in purely sentimental, 'nationalist'
terms? He really believes at the time that 'England' is
very angry with that great big bully, 'Germany' (and he
never looks behind these abstractions—America is 'Uncle
Sam,' a lean man of middle age in the costume of 1800,

'Russia' is a bearded Moujik, and so on): and when 'Old England' sees 'Germany' invading 'poor little Belgium,' well, 'she' gets very cross indeed and goes over into Flanders to put a stop to it! And Everyman, or the Man-in-the-Street, never quite gets these sentimental, national-ist values out of his simple head, or out of his blood, rather. That there is any intrigue of a mercenary or really cold-blooded political order behind such a calamity as the war he cannot steadily believe. If, in spite of himself, he should get a glimpse from time to time of such an un-romantic fact, his customary sentimentalism thrusts it quickly back into forgetfulness.

Now the 'Politics-of-Youth' usually takes the form of a 'Class-War,' namely, what may be termed the 'Age-War.' It consists in dividing the world into two rigid and hostile parts, and pitting them one against the other.—These are of course the Old and the Young. All these civil wars since the time of Marx we call *Class-Wars*. But they are, after all, *wars*. And one of the main difficulties that the writer of such a treatise as this has to contend against is that senti-mental standpoint towards *war* of the average man de-scribed above. But it is with a '*Class-War*' just as it is with a real war of cannon and bomb. For Everyman to be made to see that such *Class-Wars* are *not* spontaneous upheavals is very difficult indeed. Especially as the very intricate conditions of our complex civilization conspire to confuse him and blind him still further.

Say to him that the catch-words, or slogans, of *all* wars (such as the famous 'make the world safe for democracy') are humbug—that, if he has had his leg blown off he has been made a fool of merely, or if his sons who helped him in his business were all killed in Flanders that it was a sort of joke at the expense of his family, he will consider you mad and 'unpatriotic.' You will be for him a 'bolshie,' in fact.

In this way, regarding the 'Politics-of-Youth,' I find

myself at the very outset confronted with this identical obstacle. It would be the same with 'the Sex-war.' The issue, for Everyman, is a *sentimental* one. Thus the 'Sex-war' (in spite of the curious term 'war' and the other symptoms of organized *Class-Politics*)—that has been for him merely the age-old conflict between the 'Fair-sex' and the males of the species. The Age-war, the basis of the Politics-of-Youth, is for him merely the age-old conflict between the 'Young Idea' and 'Crabbed Age.' And Communism, of course, that he sees merely as a particularly violent and unreasonable form of the age-old conflict of Rich and Poor.

Why these 'age-old' antagonisms should suddenly take on a fanatical and even demented form—why they should be termed 'wars'—why the newspapers should print billions of words weekly upon the various phases of these conflicts (featuring champions first of one side, then of the other) and why these natural classes should suddenly have acquired this intensive organization, Mister Everyman does not stop to ask. When a bald-headed Press Magnate bawls at him fiercely 'Youth at the Helm!' it seems to Everyman a normal outburst of the 'cheeky' Spirit of Youth. Never does he stop to examine the portent of the bellowing Press Magnate, never to ask himself soberly what all this can be about, and why on earth this Magnate should be shouting that particular thing rather than another.

These, then, are the difficulties. There are many to whom the reasoning employed, here and there, in this popularly-written treatise, will appear harsh, and at other times 'bolshie.' That must be expected. For to deal with 'Youth,' as perforce I must seem to do throughout, a little as if it were an ideologic dummy, is unceremonious, and must appear to the sentimentalist untrue—and true youth is not of course that. Indeed the moment you begin to make use of youth in this 'power' way and cause it to use itself to ends that are not the specific ends of 'youth,' it ceases to be Youth, that is understood (either in the sense of the pure sentimentalist, the bonasse 'uncle of the Children's Hour,' or in the more noble sense of something ardent, native, and unspoiled). Youth turned into a 'class'—caused by every engine and device of the propagandist to become *self-conscious*—certainly the bloom is brushed off the traditional plum in the process. If you rationalize something that in its essence should be irrational, you banish for ever the Schoolgirl Complexion—no argument is possible upon that head. If that complexion really matters to you, you will be enraged by this book.

## CHAPTER II

# 'THE POWER-MATTER' AND 'THE BEAUTY-MATTER'

˙●

AT the outset we must make up our minds then, I think, to a loss of romance if we are going to *exploit* romance. And there is no question that in the technique of 'Youth-politics,' 'Youth' is considered simply as an abstraction—a mere natural force. For the 'Youth-politician' pure and simple 'Youth' is not a human thing at all, but something like water or wind—to drive a mill, or make electricity.

The 'harnessing' of water-power provides a large city with electric light. That is very useful. On the other hand it converts a mountain lake—of great romantic beauty— into a dull reservoir of water, stored energy to be tapped. Ruskin disliked these first triumphs of man over mountain-nature very much indeed. And it is open to any one to dislike those political engineers, whose eyes have detected the latent horse-power of 'Youth'-as-such, and have proceeded to 'harness' it. The malcontents may raise the cry 'Hands off Youth!' if they so choose. Like Ruskin, with his lovely mountain lakes turned into hideous cisterns, the person who feels about it in that way can wring his hands. He will not stop those engineers! There are, after all, more engineers in the world than there are artists: and then, the majority of men prefer electric light in the bathroom to a pretty picture of a lake, or a fine view of a glacier. In any case, I am nearly as bad, from that standpoint, as the engineer. What here I am explaining is simply how the torrent is dammed, the virgin waters trapped, and the hideous cisterns built. I am not considering this 'harnessed' force in its pristine and beautiful wildness at all. I am thinking of a typical Soviet,

9

a Fascist, a Nazi, 'boy-scout.' Mine is a repulsive task. I discourse matter-of-factly upon the most repulsive matters. But however ugly (and I have agreed that they are that), those things are quite *real*. It is only the person who refuses to believe in anything unpleasant, or unpretty, who will be able to deny that reality.

An involved international wrangle regarding Niagara Falls, that great beauty spot, has just been settled as follows by the United States Senate. The Hydro-Electric Power Commission of Ontario, and the Niagara Falls Power Company of New York, offered to carry out (I quote from *The Times*, Feb. 19, 1931),

> at their own expense, remedial work on the flanks of the Horseshoe Falls, and later the construction of a weir in Grass Island Pool, involving diversions of water—in excess of those permitted by the 1909 treaty—on either side, of 10,000 cubic feet per second, from October 1 to March 31, following each of the seven years of life of the instrument. This disturbance of the waters, it is said, would ensure 'unbroken crestlines' on both the American and Canadian Falls.
>
> The companies are given the use of the water thus diverted for power purposes, and the evidence before the Foreign Relations Committee disclosed that this would be worth to them 'something like $5,000,000 (£1,000,000).'

The Senate decided against these exploiters of Beauty—these water-power sharks, with their insidious guarantee of 'unbroken crestlines.' No! the Senate Commission favoured 'all reasonable action' by the United States to preserve the scenic beauty of the Falls, but 'desires to have the power matter' treated separately and 'that the United States bears the expense.'

So 'the power-matter' is to be separated from the 'beauty-matter.' But how, in the matter of Youth, and that of the Politics of Youth—which is a *Machtpolitik* or Power Politics—are we going to keep quite separate the matter of those 'crestlines' of Youth's curly brow, on the one hand,

and on the other the political uses of the deep-seated romantic mysticism involved? No parliamentary commission would be able to do that.

Yet there is no political party anywhere to-day who would not undertake to crimp, or to permanently wave, all the heads of all the voters under twenty given into its hands for political purposes, and 'ensure' as many blond or ebony 'crestlines' as they got votes!

The sentimentalist may be as right about 'youth' as Ruskin was about the virgin beauty of the mountain valleys. Indeed, the attitude of protest and disappointment is perfectly natural—just as the lake in the high mountains is *natural*—just as, certainly, the 'harnessing' of the torrent is *not*. It is the fell work of that civilized, that vandal, ant, Man! But Man is more powerful, in his roundabout way, than is Niagara. And (in the person of his politicians) Man, that born engineer, is at present everywhere eyeing 'Youth' —sizing up and measuring the length, breadth, and height of 'Youth.' 'Youth' is for him a technical problem. For, says Man, 'Youth' has quite long enough been merely ornamental—with his curly 'crestline' and all the rest of it. It is time 'Youth' *did work!* It is time 'Youth' was harnessed! So 'Youth-politics' ensue.

It was the same with 'Woman.' That crafty ant, Man, thought that it was high time that most women ceased to regard themselves as luxury-objects only. Even upon quite simple luxuries Big Business began to frown. Woman, the old sort of woman, was an absurd luxury. Woman must be made to *do work*. So their big crop of cumbersome romantic hair—'woman's crown of beauty' (away also with all crowns, of whatever sort, and what the hell *is* 'beauty,' anyway!)—that ridiculous handicap where *work* is concerned, must be cut off. Skirts (another hindrance where *work* is concerned) must be shortened: women must immediately be turned into little, cheap workmen. Men formerly wasted

endless time and money upon these absurd dressed-up dolls.
The Prohibition of alcoholic drinks (in intention) was a
great economic measure.   But that was nothing to what
would be saved if women could be prevented—by force or
persuasion—from dolling themselves up in that fantastic
way.   The sexual appetites of men (steamed up by all this
expensive femininity) had made the modern European the
most expensive wage-slave of all time, and his poor employer could stand it no longer.   So Prohibition and Feminism were put across,   And the 'Age-War' is a kindred war
to the 'Sex-War': it is entirely economic and political in
motive.

'Feminism' served the double purpose of cheapening the
labour of men, and of tapping an enormous, up-till-then-
unused, cheap labour market.   It must lead also to the
break-up of the individual home.   But to that I will return
a little later on.   Stated in this bare outline, as an interpretation of 'Feminism,' the above will seem extravagant
to some people.   And indeed that was not the whole of
'Feminism.'

In 1926 I wrote that 'short skirts were short for *work*—
not play, as is generally and very naïvely supposed.'   I also
predicted that long skirts for *the rich* would soon come back,
also long hair.—I am evidently a sort of Prophet.   But it
only comes of using a very little common sense.   My dearest
wish is to raise up as many prophets as possible.   Unlike
most prophets, I should experience no envy at all if they
simply swarmed on all hands.

It is important to remember, in connection with 'Youth-
politics,' just as much as with 'Feminism,' that the motives
for getting up, or for encouraging, such an agitation are
never stated.   Scarcely are they so much as hinted at.
When recruits were being called for in the War, threats
could be employed as well as Flattery (even then a great
deal of Flattery was used).   Also, 'To make the world safe

for democracy' and such fulsome phrases were liberally coined. It was not the methods of the Press-gang—we are democratic. But these class agitations, of *Sex-war* or of *Age-war*, occur at a normal time. No abnormal pressure therefore can be exerted. So nothing but Flattery is employed. Women were harangued to the effect that they were 'as good as men'! It was suggested that short skirts would enable them to display their legs, and that would be far more attractive—they were such lovely things and had for so long remained occulted by an obnoxious skirt. They were assured that it was only a lot of soured old maids and Mrs. Grundys who prevented skirts from going half-way up the thigh, and so on. It is very necessary to bear in mind that Flattery is the invariable instrument, in the case of a democratic and newspaper-run system, by which people are prevailed upon to undertake some 'crusade' (either to 'make the world safe for democracy,' or to 'assert their equality'). And that, once the trick is done, the cant is dropped.

## CHAPTER III

# 'THE FEW MAY WALK CARELESSLY, BUT THE MANY MUST BE DRILLED'

IN the emotional popular mind 'Youth' signifies something free and untrammelled. The question of natural versus *mechanical* 'Youth' is therefore an important one.

The politicization of 'Youth' is of course destructive of *the natural*, of necessity. All direct propaganda that tends to make very young persons begin to think of themselves (1) first and foremost as 'young,' and that (2) at the same time imbues them with the idea of an especial and superlative, almost mystical, *value* residing in the mere fact of youth (irrespective of gifts, training, or personal beauty)— such propaganda substitutes for the *natural* the *trained*. The cultivation of the mind in a definitely introspective direction (making 'Youth' think all the time of 'Youth') does rob 'Youth' of one of its traditional attributes— namely an expansive interest in things outside itself, in as it were a suspension of animal egotism. (The unselfish expansion is evolved in the interest, no doubt, of animal growth and adaption to future adult conditions.)

One hears often of the gloom that settles upon the undergraduate when his time at Oxford or Cambridge draws to a close. Even children of all classes to-day are so penetrated (in response to all they hear and read) with this notion of the uselessness of adult human life, that they are often heard to express themselves as anxious about the rate at which they are growing up. Soon they no longer will be 'children'! Soon the 'When we were very Young' of Mr. Milne will be read only with a pocket-handkerchief in the hand and gurgling sobs in the throat, in an atmosphere of

'Où sont les neiges d'antan?' Indeed, Shades of the Prison House begin to close around the post-war infant almost as soon as he or she is out of the nursery.

The sickly and dismal spirit of that terrible key-book, *Peter Pan*, has sunk into every tissue of the social life of England. Yet, of course, the devotee of Peter Panism is persuaded that Peter Panism is a beautiful glorification of all that is *natural* and unconscious in young life. Whereas, in fact, no book that was ever written has done so much to destroy all that is *natural*, native, and unconscious. Its vogue spelt the extinction of the traditional charm of young and unformed creatures. For what is more hideous than the *faux-naïf*? Affected simplicity, diffidence, and bashfulness are more unsightly, are they not, than slyness and effrontery? Far more unsightly than an early discipline, which results in an identification of 'Young' and 'Adult' values, thus putting an end to the old conception of Youth.

The few observers who are able to take the measure of these happenings are only waiting for one event (already overdue): they are daily expecting the first announcement in the morning newspaper that a small boy has committed suicide upon being asked to put on his first pair of trousers. (Every one is quite accustomed by now to undergraduates committing suicide, at the mere thought probably of no longer being an undergraduate, and having to work for a living in a grown-up world. It is the *horror at the thought of becoming an undergraduate* that should before many months are over provide us with an act of self-destruction on the part of a sensitive schoolboy of seventeen.)

The notion of 'Youth,' or 'the being a Child,' has some analogy with the notion of the Gentleman, in that both depend for their success upon a complete *unconsciousness*. A 'gentle' propagandist for the (also rather mystical) notion of 'the Gentleman' would be a most repulsive figure, and an adolescent propagandist for 'youngness' must seem slightly mad, and in some way ungraceful.

These are the extreme manifestations, of course, of an *unnaturalness* inherent in all things exploited by the politician. Do not make the mistake, however, of blaming the 'Youth.' Blame, if you must (and if all this artificiality, programmatic lack of ease and grace, is distasteful to you)— blame the old political ruffian who is at the bottom of the propaganda. Do not turn angrily upon the poor victim or instrument of it.

For those to whom the beauties of Nature mean much, who *will* have in spite of Mammon those 'crestlines' on Niagara—to them the political 'harnessing' of the power of Youth is, no doubt, a source of disappointment, if not of downright grief. The old original Wandervögel, the pioneers of the Youth-movement in Germany (we learn from Miss Cicely Hamilton's book, *Modern Germanies*), resent the dragooning of 'Youth' into a *mechanically* itinerant youthfulness (regulated by time and route-map) in the same way, rather.

I will venture to digress and to quote Miss Hamilton: in any case the Wandervögel—or what has come out of the Wandervögel—are an integral part of our subject :—

> The foreigner's ideas [Miss Hamilton writes] are frequently more picturesque than accurate: he imagines (the Wandervögel) wandering over forest and fen as irresponsibly as the birds their namesakes: strolling hither and thither as the spirit moves them, sharing pot-luck and finding shelter in barns! creatures of impulse and taking no thought for the morrow! Whereas, in reality, the goings and comings of these migratory young people . . . are systematized, very neatly and carefully systematized. . . . The accompanying forms were given me by the 'Hostel-Father,' or Manager, of one of the largest Youth Hostels. Application having been made by the responsible leader of a party of young people, he will be notified as follows:
> 'Your party will be welcome: we have noted its arrival

on—such and such a date. Will you kindly read the accompanying pamphlet carefully: it gives you full directions for reaching the Hostel, and also details with regard to our accommodation. Your arrival will only be considered definite when we receive the form enclosed, which we must beg you to despatch immediately. We must request you, further, to advise us promptly should there be any alteration in your arrangements.'

Not much bird-like irresponsibility about that: and that form which has to be despatched immediately is ruled for the day and hour of arrival, length of stay, number of party, whether boys or girls or both, nature of party—whether school-group or other form of association —and the number and kind of meals required.

And Miss Hamilton goes on to say, regarding the earlier and later style of Wandervögelism:—

What (the original Wandervögel) dreamed of was an unsophisticated pilgrimage, akin to the life of the gypsy. The very success of their movement deprived it of its gypsy character: *the few may walk carelessly but the many must be drilled,* and it stands to reason it would be impossible to run hostels by the thousand and guests by the million without definite rules and regulations. All the same, when the system started, there were difficulties with those who did not wish to be organized: amateur vagabonds in whose soul was the call of the wild, and who desired to turn their backs on civilization and all its works, even when those works spelt convenience. In an account of the rise and growth of Jugendherberge I read, without surprise, that Richards Schirrmann's project, when first it was made public, met with blank opposition from a section of the Wandervögel. Provision for shelter, the malcontents declared, was all very well and very comfortable, but it was not the vagrant life: and it was the vagrant life that brought them into touch with Nature, the village, the peasant and his field; they had far rather beg a night's lodging from a farmer, sleep in his barn or in the shelter of his stack, than lodge, however comfortably, in Jugendherberge— which were nothing more nor less than cheap hotels. And there was no romance about a holiday whose nights were

B

spent in cheap hotels—the charm and uncertainty of the gypsy life was gone. . . .

Here you see romantic 'Youth' become something else. It is like a figure of Lord Byron or of Shelley multiplying and turning beneath your eyes into a disciplined school-treat, in the neighbourhood of Spezzia or Rimini. Indeed this exercise to a time-table, in dense formation, becomes at once as matter-of-fact, and to the romantic mind as uninspiring, as the mere constitutional of the middle-aged upon a golf course, or is comparable to physical jerks or to a Boy-scout 'trek.'

Fundamentally it is a militarization. So the rebel 'Young' (like the rebel Woman of the Doll's House, the individual Norah) becomes a unit in an army. That is the price of 'Victory'—of politicization. 'What Price Glory!' —in 'Class-War' as in real war, if that is to be the end! But Glory is not the end, of course.

That is not at all the way to look at it, in fact. A poet wanders off by himself through the wild valleys, which no one else has ever shown any interest in: but if he supposes he is going to remain romantically *alone* for ever he is mistaken! Or Daughters of Eve by the billion spend all the money they can lay their hands on to make themselves romantic and attractive. But if they thought *that* was going to last, they, too, were in error. They *all* wanted to be luxury-objects. So (by means of a clever trick) they all had their Samson locks shorn and their skirts cut short. Now they are as practically 'rigged out' as possible: their *luxuriousness* has departed—and naturally a good deal of economically wasteful *luxure* too. *Le luxe* and *la luxure* exit arm-in-arm! Women have never been so cheap—for those who like 'a bit of skirt.'

## CHAPTER IV

# 'THE EXCLUSIVE VALUE OF YOUTH'
# IN TWO CONTINENTS

THE idea of 'Youth' we have now analysed into two values—namely, a something wild and unspoiled (and therefore *natural*) upon the one hand; and a something disciplined and given a stark definition—seen in terms of abstract *force*—upon the other.

The *natural* versus the *mechanical* (as that applies to 'Youth') is a crude statement of these values. But it will serve its turn in making clear what is at stake.

The Youth-sentimentalist, pure and simple, must be referred, without waste of time, to Sir James Barrie and to Mr. Milne. Those are his 'standard works' upon this subject.

The choice, as I see it, is between several well-defined types of the mechanical: not between the *natural* and the *mechanical* at all.

I am sure that ultimately (and if we really push beyond every sentimental value of both religion and aesthetics) only the *useful* is the *beautiful*, and vice versa, and that ugly and well-worn heresy is not only true but beautiful. All our mistakes arise from alienating these two terms: humanly they cannot be disconnected. The normal male of our species will always find the soft plump cheeks of a female bottom 'beautiful' or 'lovely': it is idle to suppose that such a term would ever have been conferred upon such an object if it were not for the instinct to reproduce our species.

> *Sin querer a una mujer*
> *es imposible vivir!*
> *Porque Dios, cuando nacem*
> *Nos incarna esse sentir!*

So it is. 'Beauty' is where the babies are, 'Beauty' is where the food is, or the sun and warmth—or, when we have fever, then where it is cold, and where the ice abounds.

In that way 'Youth' is good because it is *force*. A scientific brain must discover, must organize, and must direct that force. Then 'Youth' will be *used*. That is the first thing to understand. But it is equally important to grasp the fact that an evil brain will put it to evil uses (and by 'evil,' of course, I mean again, *not useful* to human life. I do not use the term in a theological or moral sense—the 'good' is the 'useful' in my vocabulary).

The 'Youth' of the anglo-saxon sentimentalist (who dribbled at the mouth and watered at the eyes, at the nursery sugar-sticks of Sir James Barrie's creation) is, as I see the matter, not *Youth* at all. The figure of Peter Pan symbolizes a formidable decadence—in which 'Youth' becomes a thing that-can-never-grow-up, is regarded as an end-in-itself—something entirely cut off from life: a strictly *useless beauty*. To such values we should deny 'beauty' and regard them for preference as 'disgusting,' just as we regard deformed persons. (If humps held babies, we should call humps 'Lovely.')

In the United States (where the ill-effects of the adoration of childhood are much further advanced even than in England) you see, at full blast, this nursery-philosophy in operation. No one is able any longer to come to a decision about anything: the most gigantic abuses thrive, while a curious lethargy and inactivity oppress all the mass of adult citizens, and an attitude of childish trustfulness endorses and allows the huge abuses practised by the only true 'he-men' in the country—namely, the Racketeers, and the Bosses behind the Rackets, who know that literally anything, *anything*, can be got away with, with such a mindless, gutless, riff-raff as the *Massenmensch*. Prohibition has shown them that. They have long ago taken the measure of that help-

less, spell-bound democracy—spoon-fed by Film, Newspaper, and standardized Fiction.

Let us listen to Count Keyserling. The european and the
american attitude to 'Youth' is fundamentally different
according to him. In his view, the American differs from
the European in being in fact childish, whereas the European is, as it were, a stage further on, chronologically—
'Undergraduate,' Adolescent or 'Post-adolescent,' where
the American is simply Baby-Boy. The european *Adolescent* is in the position of the american *Child*.

'Childhood and Youth,' writes Count Keyserling (*America
Set Free*), 'were not valued highly enough' a quarter of a
century ago (it is Western society of which he is speaking).
On the other hand, 'the high appreciation of the qualities of
youth' is a particular characteristic of the present period.
'As opposed to this, the young men of thirty years ago did
not develop this virtual beauty because they always looked
forward to being mature: and this, in its turn, led to a
voluntary exaggeration of the symptoms of maturity. Even
men of thirty were staid and grave then and took pride in
their heaviness: the women almost gloried in the early loss
of their figure, and did all they could—by wearing bonnets
and the like—to deprive their faces of all seductive charm.
How long did life under these circumstances really last? No
more, in the average, than thirty years, because a life fully
assented to and, therefore, really lived, only began after the
age of thirty. In post-war Europe youth alone counts: not
the earliest youth, though: but a youth fully developed,
both sexually and intellectually mature and conscious, with
the emphasis placed on intellectual wide-awakeness or sophis-
tication, a youth, therefore, in which nothing is left of the
stage of the bud. But this stage corresponds to the natural
stage of about thirty. Accordingly, even the youngest girls
of this generation are, psychologically speaking, thirty.
And since life beyond forty is no longer associated with any

values, human life really lasts, as far as its differentiated
contents are concerned, only ten years: that is to say, about
as long as the life of a dog.'

In the United States—which is, of course, the New
Europe—the emphasis is upon *The Child*, says Count Keyserling: the 'exclusive value' of 'Youth' '*is taken for
granted.*' I will quote the passage, however:—

> In the United States the case is different. There also no
> life beyond the age of forty-five is inwardly assented to. . . .
> But the nation does not really idealize youth, the exclusive
> value of which is taken for granted: it idealizes the child.
> America is fundamentally the land of the overrated child.
> This, then, is the deepest reason of that infantilism one so
> often observes in grown-up Americans. We found that re-
> juvenation to the degree of primitiveness is a fundamental
> trait of the nation as it stands out to-day: to that extent
> infantilism can be considered as a necessary stage of develop-
> ment. But there is another side to the question. Whatever
> belongs to the domain of psychology is subject to the influence
> of man's thoughts. If the American is infantile as a result of
> a natural process, he will soon grow out of it because child-
> hood never lasts long. If, however, over and above this, he
> idealizes this perpetual childhood, then he runs .the risk of
> never growing up.

America, Count Keyserling says, is 'the land of the over-
rated child.' Europe, on the other hand, he believes, is inclined to overrate its thirtieth year. And we know that the
patriarchal systems were disposed to overrate the eightieth
year. What the future will no doubt see is a merging of all
these exclusive values into *one* value—(called 'Youth,' *en
attendant*, because upon the popular plane the word 'Youth'
is the most convenient symbol of energy). This *one value*
will be, no doubt, energy, *tout court*. Nothing but *energy* (in
whatever form) will be recognized as worthy of life. (This
will be somewhat the Stendhalian ideal—that of Henri
Beyle, who always described himself as 'Professor of
Energy.')

## CHAPTER V

# ' SLIMMING ' AND ' THE PROFILE OF YOUTH '

THE 'High appreciation of the qualities of Youth,' referred to by Count Keyserling, dates from before the War. The Futurists, led by Marinetti, were fanatical Youth-politicians, and their successors of Fascism 'Youthed' away for all they were worth. But the world at large only settled down to intensive Youth-politics upon the conclusion of the War. And the phenomenon of 'Slimming' is one of the most obvious illustrations of this. It was the diagnostic of that central, pathologic impulse that still dominates our Society.

Where it was impossible to *be* 'a Youth,' it was at least possible to acquire 'the Profile of Youth.' The epidemic fashion of 'slimming' is an integral part of the 'Youth-movement'—since what the 'slimmer' aimed at, of course, was the condition its advertisement described as 'the profile of youth'—the silhouette if not the solid or unsolid fact. To many people (in northern countries at all events and especially England) it must have seemed rather an odd fashion. For the Englishwoman, upon the whole, tends to be boney. She does not need to be 'slimmed.' Often it is rather the contrary. The Englishwoman would not, spontaneously, have evolved such a fashion. But perhaps it originated in the South—or, as one ingenious acquaintance of mine even thought, the East.

This fellow insisted that it was in fact the great masses (*masses* in a twofold sense) of the womankind of the jewish New Rich who were responsible for all the fanatical 'slimming.' Who pays the piper (or dressmaker) calls the tune—and the traditional figure of Israel is on rather ample oriental lines, and further cursed with the thick ankle—so he argued. In short it was *Israel* that was slimming! The daughters of the Gentile had to follow suit, willy-nilly, whether they needed it or not.

There may have been some truth in this sardonic theory (certainly I have not seen a corpulent Rembrandtesque Jewess of the traditional type for some years—have they in fact all been 'slimmed' into a christian etherealness?—I hope not, for I favour the abundant asiatic hip—I prefer its volume for my pictures to the lean gothic flank of the Flemish or the English, though in other respects I am all for the northern type).

But the main reason for the 'slimming' dementia was the huge premium put on 'youth,' the War ended. Every one wished to be, as it were, *new-born*. To blot out the Past, especially the 'pre-war'—that was the idea. And it was, to start with, the Old and Fat for whom the technique of 'slimming' was invented, rather than the stumpy and fat-buttocked Daughters of Zion (old style).

Again, the earliest post-war psychology was frantically 'youthful.' A thousand influences contributed to this. First, as Bonaparte remarked, 'On vieillit vite sur les champs de bataille,' and the men who had survived the battles felt that they had aged in some inconceivable way. Many had coarsened and fattened too, from prolonged draughts of fresh air and a healthy regimen. The young woman as well had to get rid of the stains and corruptions of war. She was compelled to face increased competition, from hordes of sylphs of sixteen. In Berlin, for example, the average age of the prostitutes, of which there was a vast concourse in the first years of the Peace, cannot have been more than sixteen or seventeen. (They were advertised as 'from 5 upwards' in the arcade beside Cook's office.) And after the War's privations none but the elderly in Germany were fat. Thinness was, as a consequence, *de rigueur*. Thirty was old age for a woman, since seventeen was as cheap as dirt. Then Inflation, by throwing swarms of moderately 'well-born' german girls into the public love-market, further jacked up the standards. The assets of 'education' were super-added to those of extreme youth.

Every country that had been at war had millions of men for whom life had to be started all over again. But a handicap of not five, but ten, years had in fact been imposed on them. No women had been killed, on the other hand, so there were millions in excess, and the Old People were all there, too, so they, also, felt more *de trop* even than usual. Such were the most obvious reasons for the development of a universal *age-complex*.

## CHAPTER VI

# THE 'CHRONIC ADOLESCENCE' OF
# THE AMERICAN

THE shifting back of the spot-light, as it were, in the european consciousness brings the fixed centre nearer to adolescence, I think, than Count Keyserling's figures.

The crudely idealizing average mind is focussed not upon adult maturity as formerly, but upon adolescence, or a super-adolescent type of maturity—a semi-juvenile fixation.

But this would mean (in the light of what I have just been saying regarding 'Youth' seen as 'power') the erection of 'power' into an end-in-itself. A superphysical value would come to be associated with a merely physical thing—if 'Youth-politics' were to be taken too literally. And that they are so taken by the majority is certain. Count Keyserling is of course perfectly correct in his statement that a quarter of a century ago 'Youth's' only desire was to mature. It saw in the years of youth a preparatory period, in which to fit itself to become thoroughly adult, and 'experienced,' in whatever calling engaged. 'Youth' was the rough material—Man the finished thing.—'Youth' was, as well, its own engineer. It looked upon itself with the cold eye of science, rather than with the romantic eye of the sentimentalist (looking *back* upon his youth) or that of sexual love. And in contrast to that time, it is clear that to-day 'Youth' has no such confidence in the future (naturally enough, since the future is so much less certain) and looks forward to no time when it will wield mature power. Nor does it 'waste its youth' in preparing for such problematical future power. It seems to say to itself 'all I shall ever have is what I have got, I shall only get older—everything I shall

have *after* this will be less than this. I will spend all my
energy in simply *being* what I am, I will put all my eggs in
*that* basket, and spend the capital I have at once. After Me
the Deluge!'—All that is true enough.

As to Count Keyserling's remarks upon America, I will, in
order to endorse this foreign picture, quote a passage from
a book by Miss Suzanne La Follette (*Art in America*), which
in its turn I borrow from a review by Mr. Herbert Read.
Miss La Follette, who is an American (says Mr. Read), con-
cludes her survey with these words:—

> 'The want of a sound culture has had the unfortunate result
> of making a chronic adolescence the outstanding feature of our
> civilization: and a great art is the product of maturity, not
> adolescence. This country has the wealth necessary for a
> great art: it has the vitality. If it attains maturity in time,
> there may, indeed, await it one of those moments of equili-
> brium between the forces of civilization and those of destruc-
> tion—which are perpetually at war within the social organism
> —in which great art is born.'

Rousseau had the notion of the perfection of 'the natural
man.' And it is quite conceivable that some day there will
be a movement in favour of 'the natural Youth.' If there
were such a movement, it would undoubtedly run counter
to the romantic values of 'the natural man'; for it is those
values that have resulted in the mechanical youth—which
is a paradox.

The encouragement, indeed the enforcement (by propaganda and herd-hypnotism) of the notion of 'Youth' as an
end-in-itself, is a device, merely. The inveterate sentimentalism of the European, but especially of the Anglo-saxon,
can be dealt with in no other way. That christian sentimentalism is the *raw material*, with which the contemporary
politician has to work. Ultimately, it is however, I believe,
*an attack upon the standards of human life* (on the same principle as 'an attack on the standards of life of a community,'
such as is occurring on the grand scale in Australia at

present). But the whole principle of 'Youth' propaganda is in the nature of a bribe—as it were a *cash down* inducement. And the transaction is oiled and facilitated with a prodigal use of flattery. (The Omar 'Take the cash and let ‘.e credit go' spirit directs it.)

What it amounts to at bottom is a proposition *to shorten human life*—to shorten it to about ten years, 'the life of a dog.' (That the length of human life should be more in conformity with animal life, when it is lived in an animal fashion, is natural.) And what also it at the moment proposes, is to lay the emphasis upon, and endow with the supreme value, all that is purely animal, or mechanical, and to rob the average run of men of any pretension to anything else.

This is how it works out in terms of the raw material of european sentimentality, that is to say. But it is quite possible that human life will be permanently cut down, as a consequence of these operations. And—when you have thought that over—and should you come to the conclusion that there is some truth in it—what you next have to ask yourself is this—'Is average human life worth any more trouble than this mechanical, purely physical, standpoint implies? Is this *simplification* — this *curtailment* — not perhaps all to the good?' I am not suggesting that this should be your answer. I am merely showing you how this matter may be regarded from a rational standpoint.

## CHAPTER VII

# AN ' ATTACK UPON THE STANDARD OF LIFE ' OF MANKIND

IN the Labour Press, one of the commonest phrases to be met with is 'an attack upon the standard of life of the workers.' Attacks are always being made by 'Capital' upon 'the standards of life of the workers.' Some Captain of Industry will be interviewed, for instance; and he will proclaim that, in order to enable England to 'pull through,' or something of that sort, 'ECONOMY all round' is essential. That means *cuts in wages*. It means that the 'worker' is to be forced to work for less money—to do without this and do without that. So it has gone on ever since the War—with, of course, the vast background of Dole and Unemployment.

Is it *true* that 'attacks' are made in this way 'upon the standards of life of the workers'? Such concerted, carefully-planned 'attacks' are indeed made, and one attack follows another in quick succession: that seems to me plain enough. And in *that* respect, at least, I am not alone.

But when one goes on to say, as I am asserting in these pages, that, concurrently with these patent assaults upon the wages of the mass of people (a perpetual, ceaseless tendency to beat them down and force them to make do with less and less) a still more universal, abstract movement is for ever in progress (a less superficially palpable movement) to attack the very 'standards of life' of mankind at large—*then*, it is true, I cannot hope for by any means the same support. Yet that is what I am here asserting.

In the public mind 'Labour' is one thing—'Mankind' is another. This appears to me a short-sighted distinction. If a handful (an insignificant fraction compared to the multitude of Mankind) has the necessary power to do, and does not recoil from doing, all that is done to 'Labour' (there was the War, but the Peace is not, oh Unknown Soldier, a 'cushy' Peace!), why should the individual who does not label himself 'Labour' in fact suppose that this same Minority (which is at least as distinct from *him* as it is from Labour) should hesitate to lump him for all practical purposes in with Labour? It is very conceited of him! What happens to 'Labour' must also in the end happen to him. And if 'Labour' cannot equally be described as 'Mankind,' then by 'Mankind' must be meant a very minute fraction of all those men and women walking the earth to-day.

I hope that at least, in the light of this brief explanation, it will not be possible to dismiss at once my argument as founded upon conceptions at variance with the facts of life. There are roughly three classes in our Western Society—Labour, the Middle Class, and the Capitalist Class (the last consisting of the great Money-kings and their families). Since the War the Middle Class has suffered a profound change. In Germany most of it has sunk into the Proletariat, or 'Labour,' as a result of Inflation. At any moment the same may happen to us. The same tendency is at work here as it was there. The Middle Class is being taxed down into the Proletariat, except for that fraction of it that soars into the Super-tax Class.

At a not distant date there will be not Three Estates, but Two. There will be (1) the very small Super-Class, and (2) 'Labour.'

Unless you are in the Super-tax Class, therefore, it is absurd, so it seems to me, to imagine that you are not to all intents and purposes 'Labour.'

What is controversial, and what always has to be debated, in such a matter as this, is (1) whether any large-scale industrial conflict to-day is not *always* really a political conflict; (2) whether, as the organization of the Super-Class widens and becomes international, it is even possible for that Super-Class to legislate for a single industry, or a single nation, without also legislating for Mankind; and (3) whether the great international World-power of Finance is a *conscious* and intellectual power, or the reverse.

I have made clear the answer that I would give to these questions. There can, I believe, be no such thing as a purely 'business,' or a purely 'industrial,' conflict. Politics have become economics. There is an analogy between this and the state of Physics over against Metaphysics. The borderline of Physics and Metaphysics, in einsteinian theory, has been more or less obliterated. So it is with Economics and with Politics. Where one leaves off and the other begins it is impossible to decide.

And that those persons from whom, ultimately, the initiative comes, in all matters of large-scale, international business policy, and so political policy, are *unconscious*, appears to me a similar absurdity to that other often-repeated assertion—namely, that they are *stupid*.

Periodic 'attacks upon the standard of life of the workers' you would then probably be ready to allow. That would be localized usually to one trade, or a group of trades, and to one country. Such an 'attack' might even be thought out, carefully plotted, and launched at what was considered the psychological moment. What you *would not* be prepared to allow, in all likelihood, is the possibility of a grand-scale generalization. A tribal war—that may be hatched: but a world war, never. You refuse to these Big Business brains the power to think in World-terms. To apply to the destinies of great chains of people what they apply to national units—those are strategic heights of which they would be incapable!

Please do not imagine that I am *accusing* these powerful Magnates of being able and far-seeing. Oddly enough I do not regard it as an insult to be called able and far-seeing!

Please disabuse yourself of the belief that I consider them *wicked* because they wish to organize that gigantic business concern—The Earth Ltd.—according to sound economic principles! I am explaining an especial political technique —the technique of those so-called 'Youth-politics,' whereby they mobilize certain *classes* of the populations beneath their influence to acts of mutual hostility, whereby they weaken the individual resistance of these populations, and render them more easy to subjugate, one by one. Are we then so innocent of such tactics, in our small way? I do not regard that little sentimentalist, Mr. Everyman, as fundamentally *better* than his boss. And as to my personal interests, they lie neither with the one nor the other.

Hence, that there are people in control of vast capital interest (or people working in their shadow) who do *not*, in their essential processes, pass over from the *particular* to the *general*—that I find it hard to believe. It is, in fact, only a fairly stupid person who would imagine other people to be so stupid, so lacking in resource.

## CHAPTER VIII

# THE OLD AND THE NEW CAPITALISM

A T this point I must hold up my argument and eluci-
date one of the main contentions upon which it
turns. I am all along supposing the existence of a
*conscious* Force—a personal god *ex machina*. Up till now
I have contented myself with referring vaguely to it as
'Big Business.' But 'Big Business'—however 'abstract'
or impersonal' or 'soulless' a great Trust or Corpora-
tion may seem—signifies ultimately people of flesh and
blood.

'Big Business' does not depend upon the *personal*
initiative, energy, and resource of a *single person*: it
is a group-system: and to that extent, certainly, it is
more 'impersonal' than the old individualist industry.

Now at the heart of every Western Democracy at the
present time there are two principles at war, as I see it.
Indeed they are engaged in a life-and-death struggle. These
two protagonists are not anything so simple as 'Labour'
and 'Capital.' These are not the real protagonists. It is
rather two Masters that are in question—one, if you like, a
revolutionary Master, and one a conservative Master.

Of these two principles, one is the representative of the
old individualist system (shall we take that old pig-fancying
'Kulak,' Mr. Baldwin, as the representative of that *individualist* principle): and the other is what Mr. Baldwin calls
'an insolent plutocracy'—that is the other, more abstract,
principle. Mr. Baldwin, to use, as above, the jargon of the
Marxist, has the 'Kulak Soul': he stands for the 'personal,'
the 'human touch'—for the old bluff Master-and-Man,
parish-pump relationship. The other Capitalism (hostile to
this individualist-capitalism, of the Baldwin, Coty, Ford

type) is international, or imperialist, and is *dictator-minded*. It belongs to the same epoch as Lenin, Hitler, and Mussolini.

With much more fierceness than is manifested in the english political field (where all political 'scraps' are apt to terminate with a whisky-and-soda in a Club, or a round of golf) these two principles confront each other in Germany at this moment. But the issue is really rather different in the Reich to what it is in Britain. Even the principles themselves are not quite the same—and whereas in England the clever citizen would be very slightly disposed in favour of the *dictator-minded*, the same clever citizen in Germany, it is quite possible, might mildly prefer the passion and energy—the fine *dictator-mindedness*—of the Hitlerists. It is possible.

An interesting article in the *Forum* (April 1931) by S. M'Clatchie dealt in a popular way with this question, and I can save myself the trouble of finding a popular formula for what I wish to convey by quoting Mr. M'Clatchie. Writing of the Hitlerist attitude to *Capital*, he says:—

> The (German) workers are still at heart farmer's sons, with no understanding of the abstract economic force called capitalism. They feel themselves oppressed by industrialism, and they strike back blindly at what they sense to be the power behind the machine, which is the rule of gold. . . . How does it happen that a little band of bankers can sit in Paris and work out a Dawes Plan or a Young Plan which commits the German People to generations of servitude to foreign creditors? This race with the soul of the farmer cannot at heart accept such a transaction. It does not think in terms of capital and credits, but in terms of land and labour and goods. The reparation settlement is a bankers' settlement, which can be understood only by a nation of bankers. . . . The Germans have never played bankers to the world, as have England, France, and America. Money-mindedness is essentially foreign to them. They are a race still strongly rooted in the soil. To the land-minded, capitalism is always hateful. See how the westerner in this country distrusts, resents, and hates Wall Street. . . .

Our own Henry Ford is a beautiful example of a man after the German manner. He too thinks in terms of land and labour and goods, and not in terms of capital and credits. Some years ago he involved himself in the inconsistency of needing outside capital to carry on his business. He went to Wall Street, and promptly got into a quarrel with the bankers. This was inevitable. For no matter how many millions of dollars' worth of factories Ford may own, or how many billions of dollars' worth of goods he may produce, he is no capitalist. The banker's spirit is foreign to him.

As to the relative position of the Communist and the Nazi, Mr. M'Clatchie says:—

> Certainly Communism would go much farther in the socialization of land and industry than would Hitler, but the difference is one of degree. . . . Undoubtedly Communism favours the factory worker much more than does National Socialism. The interests of the latter are largely agrarian.

Now, I do not recommend you to regard all farmers as courteous, open-handed gentlemen, and all 'Credit-kings' (or 'Emperors of Debt') as diabolical villains—since in fact all men are fairly unpleasant, and normally there is not much to choose between them. But if it is six of one and half a dozen of the other in the matter of greed, brutalism, and low cunning, it is by no means the same thing when it comes to the *power* to do mischief or to do good. It is not true to say that a man with a lump of dynamite or a cylinder of poison-gas is no more harmful than a cave-man with a flint-axe. And the technique of Credit is an instrument of destruction in comparison with which every other known weapon of offence shrinks into insignificance.

Under these circumstances, were we dealing here in moralist-politics, we should certainly find no difficulty in pointing out the villain-of-the-piece. What is the villain but the person most *able* to do us harm? And there is no question to-day as to which of these two irreconcilably hostile principles possesses the more *power*.

But we are not dealing in moralist-politics. I am attempting here to supply you with a thoroughly opportunist political outfit. And 'opportunist' means every man for himself, does it not?—that is, of course, if he is not too much of an 'Everyman.' If there were two gunmen (one a gloved gunman and one an ungloved) it would be as well to know which had the bigger gun. All that we have to discover is where the true power lies and what is the nature of that power.

'Oh, you are an "opportunist," do you say? Then you are surely an *individualist*.' Somebody may ask me: and— How is it that under those circumstances, I do not favour that Party that stands for individualism (Baldwinism, for instance) against all that is dictator-minded. That is not difficult to answer. It is because, of course, such 'individualism' is of the wrong kind, and because it is so hopelessly incompetent that it would be unwise to rely too much upon it—though I do not agree with my communist friends that that 'old pig-fancying Kulak' is dishonest— that he puts up a smoke screen with his symbolic pipe, and so on.

Again: is the mass-midget person preferable to the 'free' Western *individual*? For myself, nothing interests me at all outside *the individual*. But since I do not mean by that *any* individual, I am open to conviction that the best way to protect the *best* individual is to eliminate the interference and futile competition *of all the myriad* 'individuals' of which the human herd is composed. The objectionable results of unchecked 'individualism' is apparent upon all hands.

The European, certainly, has demonstrated how hopeless it is to found a secure power upon the unlimited licence of individuals. Indeed, Europe (with its grotesque 'democracy') has shown up the average 'individual' Everyman, of late, in a startling manner. The history of the last 100 years seems to have been especially contrived for the purpose of rendering The Individual (as a political myth) completely ridiculous. But the U.S.A. (nothing if not a goer-one-better) appears bent upon still further *showing him up*, once and for all, and making all individualist life eternally foolish and the laughing-stock of the Ages. With its Bootleg Crime-kings, and blood-stained rat-emperors of the Underworld, we have a record-breaker in the U.S.A. and a likely claimant for the palm of democratic fatuity. The follies of Bootleg are the crowning insult to the Western notion of 'liberty,' and of democratic rule.

No: as regards all political leaders within sight I am of one mind with Mr. Mencken when he says, upon this painful subject, in a *Daily Express* article (April 10, 1931):—

> It is truly amazing that the human race, in managing this, its principal business on earth, has managed it so badly.
> Government, as it is run by the incompetents I have described, becomes the common enemy of all honest and well-disposed persons. Instead of protecting them against outrage and oppression, it becomes the chief agent of outrage and oppression upon them.
> They cannot trust their property to it, and they cannot trust their lives to it. The more diligent and admirable they are, and hence the more valuable to the race, the more cruelly it exploits them and grinds them down.
> In all other fields, man is the most inventive and ingenious of animals, but here he is left far behind by the anthropoid apes, and shamed beyond measure by the bees and ants.

An 'individualism' that merely conspires to put into the hands of any mediocrity opportunities for being mediocre to the top of his bent, unchecked and unchallenged, is worse, if anything, than an oppressive dictatorship, which makes war upon *all* individuals, irrespective of their importance to the species. For 'individualism' is not only useless, but it is not even 'individualism' if the best individuals are not found at the top, but at the bottom, and have no voice in the conduct of the State.

The old Capitalism, or its representatives (and the impoverished remnants of the great landed families is with the Old Capitalism)—that is referred to contemptuously upon all occasions as 'the old Gang' by the New Capitalism —of the *New Gang*.

But the *New Gang* claims that their party is *The Party of Youth*. And so, of course, we get back to our 'Youth-politics' once more. And 'Youth-politics' play a very important part (although not highly organised as yet) in these issues.

If one side could only succeed in creating the impression, in the public mind, that the other is an old, decrepit, 'moth-eaten,' moss-backed, out-of-date, old-fogeyish concern, that would certainly be a very great advantage. And in future we may expect both sides to compete on those principles. Cinema Stars *manqués*, fifth-rate Valentinos out of work, should throng our Parliament and Brighter Politics be the order of the day.

Although conservative by name, the New Imperialist capitalism is no more conservative than I am. But, unlike me, it is exceedingly low-brow, in technique hideously democratic—it is a great smiler on the Drage pattern, it is comfortable and nasty. That it is impossible not to say of it. The Popular Press is, of course, its chosen medium: it is a tremendously effective medium, a very brutalising vehicle. And, as it were, a pale (often an idiotic) reflection of the 'Youth-politics' of the great neighbouring revolutionary systems obtains in Anglo-saxony.

Meanwhile, all intelligent politics have been completely banished from the surface of the Popular Press. And I suppose we must agree that intelligent politics, or intelligent anything else, are not its business. Nothing but a great mass of Murder, Robbery with violence, Football, Racing, Radio and Cinema News, Gossip, Paris Modes, Weather and jokes remains. But, because politics have disappeared from view, that is not to say that they are in fact absent. In fact, they are always present, more insidiously they are even more present than formerly. The difference is that they are now, a few drops here, a few drops there, served up with everything: whereas before they were openly ladled out in great solid spoonfuls—in massive columns of argument. There is no *argument* now. All is done by suggestion. And that technique of suggestion is the specific technique we are studying here.

## CHAPTER IX

# THE ' YOUTHS ' AND ' HAS-BEENS ' OF SOVIET RUSSIA

IN the previous chapter I showed how at the heart of every Western democracy there are two principles, as it were, fundamentally at loggerheads. And one of these principles is disruptive (or 'revolutionary'), the other conservative. Without going into this any farther, it is sufficient to note that the policy of great interlocking Trusts—involved in world-wide colonizing and international undertakings—(1) cannot be narrowly nationalist or patriot: (2) are in their essence anti-individualist: (3) are Dictator-minded, rather than traditional and parliamentarian: (4) not being the ostensible and official Masters, they appear in the nature of a permanent, 'irresponsible' Opposition—always 'agin the Government'—they assume the character of a People's Party—always the champion of 'the People' against 'Authority': and (5) generally they control all the organs of popular publicity, through which they rule.

It is this very active and able, informal Directory that promotes and runs the various disruptive '*Class-wars*' (such as the 'Sex-war'): and their main motive in all such civil conflicts is an economic one. These economist-politicians, when they put their back behind a 'class-war' and push, it is (as with Prohibition, or Feminism, or what not) in order to manœuvre the 'worker' into an attitude of mind, or a direct wage-position, favourable to Big Business.

There is nothing particularly diabolical in the attempt to shorten human life. At all times the politician—or the king, or the priest, or the military leader—has regarded human life as an abstract material. We ourselves, of the 'conquering' anglo-saxon race, were formerly taught to regard a

40

million deaths among 'natives,' in a colony, from famine,
as a totally different thing to the death of one million
Europeans.  And even 'Dagos' might be wiped out in considerable numbers without it being a very vital matter.
'Human life,' in short, was *our* life.  Why should people be
surprised if one even of their own flesh and blood—in a
position of mastery over them—should not have more
humane views regarding them and their destiny than, say,
His Majesty King Henry the Eighth—or any great military
leader, disposing the various regimental units at his disposal
in battle-array, his mind set on a 'famous victoree'?

In this chapter and the next I shall proceed with the
study of the strategy of this vast civil-war, or congeries of
*class-wars,* and bring out further into the light the nature of
this attack upon the standard of human life.  Certain
selected beliefs, I think I shall be able to show, imposed
upon the public by means of Press, Film, Fiction, Popular
Science, Radio, etc., are calculated to *shorten* it.

In those attacks there are different phases.  At one
moment, for instance, the Press will be full of articles upon
the subject of 'monkey-gland': the Public will be taught
the wrong-headedness of monkey-gland—it will be pointed
out how to be full of years is to be full of sorrows: the most
aged member, no doubt, of the newspaper's permanent staff
will wax eloquent over the beauty of a 'short life and a
merry one,' and will probably remind his reader that 'those
whom the Gods love die young,' and insinuate a few menac-
ing words as to lethal chambers for the decrepit—alleging
a variety of ugly customs common in primitive societies—
such as the habit of the aborigines of Patagonia to hunt,
cook, and eat their grandparents.  He will darkly hint that
should he cling to life *too much,* the reader, perhaps, may yet
find himself poleaxed, filleted and eaten—for our society
does *not* become *more* civilized, does it?—with Capone
blazing away in the heart of Chicago, and the headmaster

of Eton the president of a 'Crime Club,' which it came to him (such a bright and schoolboyish idea) to found:—and with 'Murder parties' ending in actual homicide, so it is said, now and then—and wars that are no longer wars, but half a decade of massacre! No! Do not let the reader run away with the notion that the world into which he has been born is a soft one, benevolently prepared to support him gratis for *too* long past the bald pot-bellied line!

So for several weeks articles will be bursting forth everywhere in the popular newspapers, condemning and ridiculing that indecent, and at bottom unphilosophic, desire to prolong life (meanwhile the elderly editor, who is executively responsible for this pyrotechnic, is probably having daily injections of thyroid). The *anti-secretion offensive* may be followed by a series the nietzschean burden of which will be 'LIVE DANGEROUSLY'!—in brief, do everything you *can* to break your neck—emulate Malcolm Campbell and Amy Johnson, and if you *don't* get your neck broken you will join our 'League of Youth': and if you *do* there won't be a *three minutes silence* for you yearly, it is perfectly true, *but* you will have the satisfaction of knowing that you have been croaked in a glorious cause!

So the good work goes on.—At least this is evident, I think—that there is no tendency visible passionately to encourage the Public *to lengthen* its precious life: (nor, of course, to 'honour its father and its mother'—which, so Moses said, leads to our 'days being long in the land,' etc.). And I think that any fairly observant person will have noticed a drive definitely *away* from the 'three-score-and-ten' fetish of the Ancients. That was all very well for leisured Old Testament jewish patriarchs, but Everyman must take that with a grain of salt, like so much of the chaff and bluff to be found in the Scriptures.

The present masters of Russia foster, very systematically, a very great superstitious prejudice against all that is old enough to be 'experienced,' in favour of all that can lay claim to being, on account of youth, a clean slate—a *tabula rasa*. Upon all that is naïf, and hence teachable, there is a premium. My information upon this subject is derived from a very intelligent young Jew who has lived for over a year in Russia. People who were adult before the Revolution, especially those who were employed under the Czarist Regime, have a variety of insulting and discouraging nicknames invented for them. Everybody is taught to refer to such a person as ' a Has-Been.' The rulers of Russia in this way discount in advance any private criticism on the part of people who may be suspected, having been acquainted with non-communized Russia, of not relishing the New.

Talleyrand, who was a revolutionary, but a bad rebellious revolutionary, once said, I believe, that any one who had not lived in Europe before the French Revolution could not imagine how delightful the world could be. That is the sort of spirit that the word 'Has-Been,' of course, is coined to counteract and to paralyse. As I have remarked, the men in supreme control in Russia are anything but 'Youths,' but to be surprised at that would be entirely to misunderstand the significance of all 'Youth-movements.'

It is a tremendously carefully-worked-out technique. That particular 'class-war'—namely the 'Age-war'—is in the U.S.S.R. in full operation: but there is no occasion to outline the intricate measures undertaken by those able sovietic rulers to set the New against the Old. (Books upon Russia, abound.) I am only referring to the Russian situation as much as is necessary to show that Soviet Russia, that great model Collectivist State, is not *behindhand*, at least, in the implementing of intensive 'Youth-politics.' The propagandist-habits of the Soviet rulers remind one forcibly of those of Cato—that roman master never tired of making mischief among his slaves: it was his avowed policy to set them against each other, in order that they should not conspire against *him*. (Divide et Impera.) To-day it is still of the utmost importance for the newly-born russian oligarchy to blot out the Past. Their behaviour is a masterly piece of inhuman commonsense. The rulers who came before this dynasty of Lenin and Stahlin seem like emotional and petulant children compared to these machine-men, with their huge clock-work plans of wholesale enslavement, or, to use a milder word, enregimentation. Also, of course, the slavonic masses they have to handle are, strictly speaking, children—although prior to the Revolution, it is true, they had never been sedulously taught to regard themselves as exactly bright-eyed youngsters. That must be a new and delightful sensation, though in the long-run it will be very dearly bought, no doubt, according to democratic standards.

Upon the purely hard-boiled side there is a great deal to be said for 'Youth-politics.' And it is, of course, a game that especially amuses elderly people when they are the masters —when, that is, they are the people able to pull the strings and watch the Boy Scouts, Cubs, or Pioneers dance hither and thither. And there is nothing at all the matter with elderly people. Santa Claus must be three-score-years-and-ten.

## CHAPTER X

# A JESUIT MAXIM (THAT GOES TO THE HEART OF THE POLITICS-OF-YOUTH)

AN article entitled 'Marxism for Babes' (in *The Manchester Guardian*, Feb. 27, 1931) begins as follows:
'The future Russian national character is possibly
being determined in no small degree by the intensive training in Communist ideas which is being imparted to children
almost as soon as they have left the cradle.' Here the
famous jesuit maxim is seen in full operation—'give us a
child up to the age of six, and you can do what you like with
him after that.' Those who were twenty-five at the time of
the Revolution—and who therefore are now just on forty—
are (unless they be people of very marked character, and of
a character in consonance with marxist doctrine) eternally
suspect—they all now are Has-Beens. It would really only
be perfectly safe to have been born at the time of the
Revolution, and still better to have been born some years
after it.

'There are about three million members of the *Union of
Communist Youth*, young people ranging in age, as a rule,
from 16 to 23. Then there are, behind them, *The Young
Pioneers*—they are from 8 to 16. Still younger than this
age-class are the *Oktyabryati*. There are 800,000 of these
disciplined babies.'

One feature of the training of the *Young Pioneers*, says the
article—*Marxism for Babes*—'is the extraordinary precocity which it seems designed to inspire.' If one picks up
a copy of the 'Pioneer Pravda,' the newspaper of the
*Young Pioneers*, it looks very much like the senior 'Pravda.'
It is all politics: questions of alleged 'dumping' and of
'forced labour,' the communication of Fukien or Foochow,

and so forth. And with 'this same objective of turning children into conscious Communists as rapidly as possible, much attention is now being paid to the preparation of a properly industrialized, mechanistic and materialistic children's literature.'

So childhood is an earnest matter in the Union of Soviet Socialist Republics, both for the teacher and taught. There is no breathing space in which to kick your heels and dream in before life begins—certainly not a long procession of idle and irresponsible years. No waste. Time is money in that Economist's Utopia whose capital city is Moscow more than it ever has been in the democratic West.

The 'extraordinary precocity,' of which this writer speaks, is another feature of childhood and youth under a system dominated and obsessed by Youth-politics. And of course with us, too, in England and America, a great 'precocity' is everywhere observable. What distinguishes pre-war from post-war, as much as anything, is the sudden mental ageing of Youth. An absence of precocity—a prolonged, lazy, animal period of 'Growing-Up,' sheltered from the realities of life to a greater or less extent—is what has characterized the life of Western Man up till the present. The Asiatic always has been, in comparison with the European, 'extraordinarily precocious.' And the Russian of Europe, under the Czars, conformed to the european norm in that respect—except that our slavonic cousin tended to overdo it, and *never* to grow up at all. (He was the excitable and spluttering Peter Pan of Europe prior to the Revolution.)

The present masters of Russia soon put a stop to all that. And indeed this 'extraordinary precocity' suggests that the jewish Intelligence (which plays such a preponderating part in Soviet rule) is perhaps imposing a particular racial standard upon what in fact (outside the jewish Russians) is a backward and naturally indolent people. Is this a good thing or not for the Russian People? That is a matter of taste. To *read about* they were nicer before. But to be a good subject for Chekov is not necessarily synonymous with happiness.

But in all lands to-day the acuter, more intellectual, jewish nature has set the pace. In many ways it has given an alien colour and tempo to this period. Instinctively, it has shown itself impatient with this lengthy 'innocence' and tomboyishness, and felt that Youth should be treated more seriously. May not the jewish consciousness (that, of course, of a very ancient race) have set a quite unusual store by just that thing which formerly the European paid no heed to—mere freshness and Youth—in the way that an old person is attracted by the very young (or as King David procured virgins to warm up his old bones in bed)? The people of the Western Democracies certainly have been taught, as Count Keyserling says, to value their-up-till-then neglected Youth. Even *a new value* in this manner may have been erected for us—*youth-for-youth's-sake*, in short.

This, of course, would not be 'Youth-politics' at all (although it might quite well give the person with a high sense of Youth-values a predilection for a certain type of political technique—just as a woman-ruler, for that matter, would always be a little prone to over-indulgence in political values based upon the notion of 'Youth'—simply because traditionally the care of the Young has been hers.

But 'Youth-politics' pure and simple—and especially the more foolish manifestations of that technique, such as we meet with in anglo-saxon communities—are a specifically Western, even teutonic, or anglo-saxon thing.

The great civilizations of the East, indeed any fairly intelligent civilization whatever, would have under no circumstance admitted, or even dreamed of, a policy whose avowed aim it was to poison and destroy the tradition that was the

very principle of its being. It remained to the half-baked
—the ill-cooked—Western Man to indulge, in the first
instance, in this last suicidal sentimentality and egoism.
But everything has conspired to cause the European and
American to adopt such courses. The notion of *Progress*
leads naturally to the development of an attitude of disdain
and hostility for anything that is not the *latest model*. So
all human values end by imitating the conditions and
values of the constantly improving machines of the Machine
Age. Industrial Technique imposes its 'progressive' values
upon us. Our individual life is quite overshadowed by the
machine, which separates us from all human life that has
gone before us.

There is no new *human* entity present in the world. It
is the *machines* by means of which, or because of which,
the Great Revolutions are imposed upon us—and, of course,
the economic masters of the machines. Even more than
the Age of Machines, this is the age of the machine-guns.
Against *these* we are in the position of the 'Pore benighted
'eathen' of Kipling's day—absurdly brave, but all in vain.
It is a totally novel world-situation. (So few people realize
that it is a *world*-situation at all. They still talk in terms of
Thirty Years Wars and muzzle-loaders, or the tribal diplo-
macy of remote events, and local geographical interests
which are entirely obsolete.)

Going back to the question of an 'extraordinary precocity,' imposed upon an anything but 'precocious' herd,
it will be remembered that a few years ago an american lady-
tourist accused all Hindus of being extinct ('impotent,' she
said—thinking of It), of being 'Old Men' at twenty-five, as
a consequence of being bridegrooms at thirteen. And no
doubt the Indians are precocious; and no doubt it *does*
shorten life—for obviously the sooner you *begin* life the
sooner you *end* it—although in general the lady-tourist's
observations were highly open to question.

Nevertheless, if you focus your attention exclusively upon 'Youth,' and if you in any way 'force' it, and speed-up nature, will not you attain the same result? Would not the effect inevitably be to shorten life—to halve, say, the period occupied by a human being in making his leisurely progress from cradle to grave?

## CHAPTER XI

# ONE OF THE AIMS OF YOUTH-POLITICS
# IS TO SHORTEN HUMAN LIFE

SO far, I think, we have in fact arrived at this: that
Youth-propaganda, Youth-politics, *does* start life
earlier, as it were: that, as a consequence of that, it
does *shorten* life (in the manner indicated by Count Keyserling): and that it is just possible, to put it at its lowest, that
these results are perfectly well understood and have been
foreseen—since, after all, they are obvious enough, and it is
surely absurd to contend that the world is full of simpletons.

At least may we not suppose that in the matter of their
intensive Youth-propaganda it has been the conscious
object of those responsible for it *to put to some good use at
last*—to rescue from incompetent, extravagant Nature—
those twenty years supposed by the European to be necessary to allow the human being to grow up? Those vast
tracts of dreamy months and years at the beginning of life
must be put to account, these perhaps a little over-provi-
dent economist-rulers may have impatiently exclaimed.
And why not? It is a natural reflection. It is a reflection,
in fact, which less bustling and less interfering people must
often have made before them.

We know that 'the Family' (as it is understood in
the individualist systems of the West) is marked down for
destruction. But 'Youth'—in the old dreamy, useless-
but-ornamental, Western sense—that sentimental notion of
'Youth' is dependent upon the Western conception of the
Family. But if one is to be destroyed, then it is surely
inevitable that the other should go with it?

The european attitude to 'Youth'—based upon a long
and leisurely training, where the well-to-do were concerned

—did not allow of the conception of a Boy, or 'Youth,' being an independent, self-reliant being. He has always been a minor, and an inferior—an imperfect, because only half-formed, facsimile of Papa or Mama. He has been taught to depend implicitly upon the two people responsible for his birth. But all modernist training of the Young has tended to modify that notion, and to teach him to regard himself—much earlier than formerly—as a separate individual. Also, as a consequence of this, the Young have *started* life earlier.

The children of the Poor have always done this in any case. And, of course, we must not lose sight of the fact that revolutionary influences have everywhere been at work under the guise of 'Progress' and 'Modernity,' to break down *privilege* of every kind. And, of course, it would be regarded as a crying example of privilege to be given plenty of time and to spare to grow-up in.

At all events, the old european conception of 'Youth' is doomed to destruction, as much as is 'the Family.' And we may, if we keep our eyes open, remark upon every hand an inclination to curtail life at the hither end—that nearest birth.

Here, for instance, is an account of the conditions in a Welsh mining village—I take it from *The Sphere* (Feb. 28, 1931):—

> I gazed out of my hotel bedroom at P—— in South Wales. The sight . . . was one of the most doleful I had ever seen in my life. It consisted chiefly of this: Men—obviously dressed in their Sunday best—standing with their hands in their pockets along the street kerb. Just standing . . . I knew that if I asked some of them, they would tell me they were ' waiting for something to pass by '—a chance to run an errand, or to do something to earn a few pence. Others, especially the men over thirty-five (and they are becoming bitter realists now), would answer they were waiting for the Old Age Pension to come along.
> These were some of the 15,000 hale, hearty, and capable

miners of X (a population of about 164,000 people) who will probably never go down a mine shaft again in their lives. A problematical chance if improved markets will be met by rationalisation; and it was the conclusion of practically every one I talked with in that 'valley of despair' that, unless there is found some way to drain them off, there will always remain about that number of permanent unemployed. Of course, hope springs eternal—even after eight years—but many of these men have now resigned themselves to this fate. They have gone soft now, after four, six, or eight years: they say the owner's agents do not want them any more, especially with so many younger, stronger men clamouring at the pits: and one man when I asked him what he looked forward to said: 'I am just lingering.' That's it—lingering.

There is one question, especially after you have been among them for a time, that you will never ask these miners in South Wales; and that is whether they would rather work or live on the Dole. That peculiar dead-alive look in their faces as they stand in the streets is enough to save you from that.

If you make life too awful people will not *want* to live beyond a certain age. (As it is, the *average* life of the workman is not much over forty.) So what is there surprising if people should tend to curtail it at the other end: or, *making it start sooner*, bring it more quickly to a conclusion?

The 'Youth' agitation (I speak of the vulgar anglo-saxon form of it)—the arousing, *organizing*, rendering *self-conscious* of Youth—is in fact in every respect the same sort of operation as the Feminist Revolution. The Hausfrau—a Hausfrau *personally attached*, in considerable freedom and idleness, to *one* man—in a 'home' of his own (the European Family, in short) would be quite antediluvian in a perfectly mechanized Communist State. Formerly the horse-power (the cheap labour asset) of literally billions of such Hausfraus was lost to Industry. To-day there still remain vast numbers of such married body-servants (as Big Business sees it)—for the European Family is not dead, it is in process of breaking up only.

Well, bearing this parallel case in mind, must not the

same Super-Economic Intelligence (seeing everything in terms of power or of £. s. d.), surveying life as lived in the West and noting the unconscionable time that it takes any boy or girl hereabouts to *grow-up*—the interminable dawdling and tarrying of the 'Training for life' (then the shortness, the futility, of what it was all for)—have itched to reorganize it from top to bottom?  In looking round for cheap labour a hundred years ago, the Super-Economic brain would see Child-Labour as a solution.  Woman-Labour would be another.  (Cheap Black-Labour or Yellow-Labour, that would be a third solution, which the observant and far-seeing eye of a great economic prophet, of the Stature of Marx, would discern and make a note of.)

'Oh, how expensive,' he would fiercely sigh, 'this precious White Male Labour is!'

Because he is (1) White: because he is (2) Male—on account of those two arbitrary facts—this White Man (however inefficient, however stupid) asks a fancy-price for his precious day's work!—Then, what centuries he takes to grow up!  Years and years pass, and he is still 'a minor' as he calls it.  He is being (at enormous expense, and with an infinite squandering of time) *prepared* for this glorious 'manhood' (as he calls it)—where he will expect to be paid ten times as much as is strictly necessary for 'work' (so referred to by him) which his bitch of a wife could do sometimes twice as well as could he!  Why, even his children, by the time they are ten, could do about as much in a day and make less fuss about it!

So the Super-Economic Intelligence would, undoubtedly, cogitate.

## CHAPTER XII

## 'THE LIFE OF A DOG'

'ONE of the aims of the present Youth-politics is *to shorten life.*' Such was the title of the last chapter. But *to shorten life* is one only of its aims. It is a very important one. It could be described as *the principal of its purely economic aims.*

Before passing on to the other major objectives of the *Politics of Youth*, I will restate the main reasons that make it probable that the curtailment of human life is part of the super-economic programme. (Elsewhere, in my *Hitler* book for instance, a statement will be found to the same effect.)

In the present era of Big Business, vast, ' rationalized,' semi-State concerns have been evolved. They tend to engulf, more and more completely, all the smaller concerns with which they find themselves in competition. The conditions of work of the employee therein grow every day more analogous to those obtaining in the State Services. Individualism or initiative is, as far as the great majority of these employees is concerned, not only pointless, but actually undesirable, and so taboo.

The Machine takes the place increasingly of the Man. A bank clerk, a post-office employee, both perform work that requires no intelligence or particular training or skill. To receive and to check paying-in books, do invoicing, to sell a shilling's worth of three-halfpenny stamps, demands as little intelligence as that of which the least gifted Bushman or Australian Black Boy may boast. The *skin* of the person performing these miracles of intelligence is *white*, and he is remunerated, in consequence, more than would be a mere 'native.' If a civil servant, he gets on top of that a jolly little pension. Economically, how can this appear otherwise than all wrong to the really fanatical economic brain?

Now if, in addition to the fancy-price expected by the proud possessor of the white skin, there is a further complication on the score of *gender*—in short, if, because this expensive little White Fellow asks for still more because, in addition to being a White Fellow (rather than a Black Fellow) he is of the *male sex*—why, then, how can the business man pure and simple do otherwise than squirm with impotent rage! In the past especially he must have done so, before Feminism (which found itself, so to speak, during the War) corrected all that for Big Business and knocked on the head for its Patron all the 'gender'-nonsense. But even to-day the Business Lord still has to pay, on the average, his *male* wage-slave more than his *female* wage-slave. All along the line he feels that he pays through the nose. He pays (1) for the colour of the skin, he pays (2) for the sex, he pays (3) for beer and cigarettes, (4) for semi-detached, self-contained domiciles. But there is no end to what he has to pay for.

But there is something worse even than all that—a still greater affront to common sense. For, on top of everything else, a man actually has the effrontery to expect more and more, *the older he gets*. That is the last straw! For doing exactly the same thing, only not quite so efficiently (because he is more and more bored and henpecked, catches cold more easily, and moves about with less elasticity)! The cup of the sorely-tried Economic Magnate is indeed full to overflowing!

In the majority of cases these people who expect, the older they get, to have *more and more* money are nothing but a Postage-stamp-machine, or an Adding-machine, or a Sorting-machine. Only they are a machine that once was new, *but that is wearing out!* Ninety per cent. of these semi-automatons are anything but *indispensable*. A child of ten could do their work just as well, were child-labour not illegal.

Prior to the Machine Age such terms as 'seniority,' 'experience,' may have had some meaning. To-day they have absolutely none. All this clutter of obsolete notions, inherited from an individualist past (different in every respect from the era of the *Massenmensch*), have in some fashion to be got rid of. Desperately this pathetic little robot of a wage-slave clings to all the vestiges of Privilege—realities in another system, unreal in this one. Relentlessly his invisible, anonymous Boss, in a hundred ways, discourages and snubs him. In a hundred ways, likewise, this invisible person teaches and encourages the younger colleagues of Mr. Everyman to snub and discourage him. For, after all, he *has* to be taught somehow that his pretensions are absurd—preposterous claims such as no law of Economics or of common sense would be found to endorse.

And this, of course, is where the Age-war comes in handy. In the democratic West measures of drastic reform cannot be carried through quite so high-handedly as in Soviet Russia. The manager of the super-concern cannot send for the little Robot Tom Thumb in question, and address him as follows: 'You old bald adding-machine of forty odd—I admire your impudence—I am taken aback by your sheer neck! Do you realize that every year, for fifteen years now, you should have been getting *less* annually, not *more*, for your wretched services? Is it possible that you do not see that a boy of twenty is far better able than you are to perform the simple tasks for which we pay you so handsomely —better because he is twenty years more fresh than you— no other reason—ten years hence he'll be in the same class as you—but at least we are teaching him what to expect! His notions won't be so grand as yours: he knows that he will get less if anything, and will be very lucky if he *gets as much* for a time. But you—you are preposterous! You ask

for *a rise*—for *more and more money,* the older you get!
That is indeed the limit! There is many a good strong
youth of seventeen who would eat his hat for your job! Do
you know that? For two pins I'd give it to him! I love
Youth, I do—there's no nonsense about Youth—grateful
for whatever turns up, as hard as nails, and none of your
nonsense about "Experience"!—*Youth at the Helm* ! that's
what I say! You hop it—and don't let me hear again a
word about *higher* wages, see? From now on I drop you
4s. 6d.! And at the New Year out you go! We shall
require your services no longer!'

The corpulent and highly experienced manager would by
this time be quite out of breath, we will suppose. But
actually this justifiable tirade could never be uttered at all
—democracy precludes any such divine directness. But
*indirectly* it can be. The newspapers are the *propaganda-
department,* as it were, of Big Business. And they, in a
thousand 'chatty' or 'serious' (straight-from-the-shoulder)
articles, can say all this to Mr. Everyman—say this to him,
naturally, *for his own good*—in a friendly spirit, in a rather
joking way.

And then—still more effective—Young Mr. Everyman
can be steamed up (by hypnotic compulsion of Press and
other propaganda, and incessant hoarse whispers in his ear
that he is *young,* and that he should inherit the earth by all
rights): and Young Mr. Everyman will scowl or curl his lip
more and more at the sight of Old Mr. Everyman—until
eventually, upon any pretext, Young Mr. E. will be telling
Old Mr. E. over and over again all the disobliging things
that the strategic G.H.Q. of Big Business has had conveyed
(via Press and Film) into his otherwise not very well-
stocked or resourceful noddle. (It is the story of Cato and
his slaves over again—Divide et Impera.)

Again, Mrs. Everyman will be called upon to play her
part in this bitter and squalid comedy. She *also* will read

the daily bulletin of Big Business (which she calls 'my newspaper'): and (the passion of contentiousness and the desire to stab and wound far outweighing any considerations of common interest, much less of common humanity) unfurling the Banner of the Sex-war, she will *also* tell Mr. Everyman what she thinks of him and what Big Business thinks of him (or rather 'my newspaper')—and Mr. Everyman, what with one and another, will have what he would describe as 'a very thin time of it.' And if he does not learn at last what it is highly desirable that he should know, *re* his utter insignificance—well, then he is unteachable indeed!

There you have, I think, a true, if caricatural, picture of what is happening just beneath the surface, upon all hands, to-day. When you reflect that the 'Youth' of to-day will, in fifteen years' time, inevitably become the villain instead of the hero—only a villain who *knows* that he is a villain, as it were—then I think you will agree that what you may at first have regarded as 'a theory' of mine is in fact an accurate statement of the trend of events.

So an attack upon the standard of human life itself—of the life of almost the whole of mankind—is in progress. There *is* a considerable chance that the world is not big enough for both Man and his Machines: and it *is* quite true to say that the Economics of the Machine Age impose upon man either the need for a Neuter Sex (and such phenomena as homosexuality are tentatives in that direction), or else *a shortening of life*. As the social organization of our planet becomes closer and closer, and still more mechanically efficient, the wage-slave must be compelled to terminate his existence at thirty-nine or forty. ' Every man over forty is a scoundrel!' is one of Mr. Shaw's canny old sayings. If you put *robot* for *man*, that must come to be literally true —and Mr. Shaw to-day, were he a robot (as he is not), would of course be 'one of the oldest scoundrels unhung!'

But there is 'one law for the rich and one for the poor': in this matter as in any other that would be the case. And indeed, in the future, one of the distinguishing signs of the most absolute aristocracy might be a long white beard. 'Methuselah,' in fact, might be, in such a future social system, the reverse of the medal—upon the other side of which would be the Robot with his ten years of life—'the life of a dog' as Count Keyserling puts it.

## CHAPTER XIII

# THE POLITICAL ISSUES INHERENT IN ECONOMICS

THE most important uses of 'Youth-politics' in the purely economic field have now been set forth. It will be seen that they are almost identical, in that respect, with those of the Sex-war and the Black-versus-White-war. The advantage of the Sex-war to Big Business has been, as I have already pointed out, to procure cheap female labour. The uses of the Race-war (of coloured Peoples versus White) is exactly the same—a Black or Yellow Skin is *cheaper* than a White. In many cases, too, Coloured Labour is more efficient and can be bullied into working harder.

But even that bare statement of the purely economic motives suggests at once the corollaries of such a transformation. Many things of a purely political order, and of far wider significance, ensue from the economic conditions brought about by the successful management of the gigantic *class wars*.

In the first place, if as a result of the Sex-war Women and Men tend to draw apart into hostile camps or at least into distinct and self-sufficient classes, that must entail results of far-reaching political importance, altering the character of the family life, as practised in the political system of the Aryan World. This I have already touched upon. The relations and attitudes of children to parents will be altered, and of the Man and the Woman respectively to themselves.

As a consequence of this, the immense advantage that Europe and the United States of America possessed, imperialistically, at the beginning of this century, over the rest of the world, would be immediately affected. The

racial pride and self-assurance of the European was dependent upon technical superiority. That must rapidly wilt if
his standards of life are thrust down beneath feminine
competition. (The Women of Europe, whatever else they
may do, will not take the place of the Men of Europe as
'Masters of the World.') Further, if the microcosm of the
Family—with its father playing the part of responsible
chief and domestic legislator—is to a large extent dispersed,
that must react, too, very forcibly upon the European
Man. All responsibility whatever will thus be removed
from his shoulders. Outside the family circle (in the abstract world of Big Business) his individuality is denied any
effective expression. And if, at the same time, he is, *within*,
denied any further initiative in his private life, and if
responsibility is not required of him regarding his house-
hold, then an entire group of instinctive functions will be,
perforce, atrophied. A new group, of a quite different
order, will be called into being.

The *Coloured-versus-White-war*, taken to its ultimate
conclusion, must result in the same psychological im-
poverishment. For—however good a Christian, or con-
vinced an internationalist and communist—if he is forcibly
thrust down, in his standards of life, to the Coolie, Hottentot level, the White European will undergo a radical change
of character.

In brief, subjected to the same oppressive conditions and
influences, he will become like the Coolie and the Hottentot.
I am merely pointing out here what course things must
take. The European has my best wishes—I am a European.
But his helplessness is colossal. I fear he is destined to work
for an anna a day. Mr. Réné Guénon, in his book *Orient et
Occident* (p. 107), says, with perfect truth:—'Les peuples
eurcpéens, sans doute parce qu'ils sont formés d'éléments
hétérogènes et ne constituent pas une race à proprement
parler, sont ceux dont les caractères ethniques sont les moins

stables, et disparaissent les plus rapidement en se mêlant à d'autres races; partout ou il se produit de tels mélanges, c'est toujours l'Occidentel qui est absorbé, bien loin de pouvoir absorber les autres.' Not only are the European's racial and physical characteristics unstable and fragile— and in intermarriage, with Jew or Indian, it is the other race that absorbs the European, not the reverse—but with his borrowed religion (so ill-assorted with his aggressive personality) and his mongrel culture, a member of any race of a fixed cultural complexion and logically developed ethnical purpose can 'absorb' him spiritually within half an hour. And especially the democratic, americanized, european Tom Thumb of to-day is, over against a member of a race of fixed tradition and well-defined ethos, in the position of the average Hodge confronted with a hard-boiled and well-polished aristocrat. And it is in vain for M. Guénon to play with the idea of a 'European Élite' saving the situation. There is as much *esprit de corps* among the 'Élite' of Europe as there would be in a street where every other shop was a *cut-shop*. Each 'Élite'-person allows his vanity to be mobilized against every other 'Élite'-person upon the smallest provocation. Each makes himself (or allows himself to be made—still worse) into a 'class' all to himself; and hence class-war is as rampant at the top as at the bottom of the scale. No, it is not the 'Élite' who will save Mr. Everyman from Cooliefication.

Disintegrated into a thousand class-warring factions— analysed back into its composite cells, and incessantly stimulated to one huge destructive civil broil—the Occident is much too far gone ever to recover, upon its old lines, even if we desired it. We are here, therefore, taking Occidental disintegration for granted.

In the back of our minds it is admissible to entertain some picture of a future *integration*. And for my own part, the more novel it was the better I should like it. But the disintegration is already very far advanced: the new integration even has long ago begun. Such a book as this is primarily intended *to influence the integration*. (Certainly it is not intended to arrest the disintegration.) In what manner does it wish to influence the integration? Principally in such a manner as to prevent the mere destructive technique of the *transition* from being taken too seriously, and so to avoid a great many false and puerile passions and modes of thought—or unthought—from being taken up into the body of the new synthesis.

## CHAPTER XIV

# THE RAGE AGAINST 'YOUTH' OF A BAFFLED YOUTH-MASTER

THE *integration*—as opposed to the merely destructive 'class-warfare' of the Old World in violent dissolution—is more advanced in Russia than anywhere. But in the nature of things Russia cannot be a model to be slavishly followed all over the world. The German and the Italian, for instance, are a different *matière* to the Slav masses.

However, everywhere—if only by way of a pale reflection from the 'redness' all over the North of Europe and Asia—*integration* in one degree or another is in progress, side by side with disintegration. There are little novel patches *going hard*, even in England and America. And Germany is in a perfect ferment. I am not sure that eventually the German will not rival, and *modify*, the Russian. And Germany, of course, is the original home of Youth-Movements, and is therefore especially interesting from the point of view of this inquiry.

As to the directly political, as opposed to the economic, uses of which Youth is susceptible, and in the interest of which 'Youth'-propaganda is launched, the most obvious is war, and the preparation for war. There is no occasion to coax and flatter Youth into bearing arms once a war is started. Martial law settles all that. Military conscription in peace time is more difficult. But if it is to be imposed, it cannot be achieved so well through 'Youth' pyrotechnics as upon some other issue.

But it is *Social Revolution* which, in fact, offers the opportunity for a great 'Youth-politician.' For in any violent change it is always young, unformed persons who are the most readily inflamed; and who, because they have no groove or long-standing habits, are most willing to welcome violent changes and reversals of settled conditions. All these, and similar, considerations make Youth the chosen material for the revolutionary agitator.

An article appeared in *Harper's Magazine* (March 1930), and, although popularly written, it contained a very interesting confession, from any point of view worth studying. It was by an american political journalist, Mr. Seldes, and it dealt with present conditions in Germany. Now, Mr. Seldes would no doubt describe himself as 'independent.' But I suspect that, in fact, like most active-minded american correspondents, he is dogmatically communist in sympathy. Indeed, the internal evidence of this article proves as much, I think. At all events, he displays the greatest animosity for those german revolutionaries, the Nazis or Hitlerites.

I suppose you will agree that it would be a good thing for the Anglo-saxon to get a clear idea of what is occurring elsewhere; and I think you will agree also that if political Fashion-Plates *all* come from Muscovy, that a good deal of local distortion of anglo-saxon, german, or spanish character must ensue. We do not want in political ideas a snobbery to set in, which would lead to a muscovite monopoly —that would be worse than 'Paris Fashions' for dress.

Therefore, the conventional, snobbish, transatlantic 'radical' will really be an object-lesson for us, I think. But I will quote him at some length: and I think that Mr. Seldes' state of mind proves conclusively the extent to which the Hitlerites have disturbed the more orthodox 'radicals' of the West.

The indignant attitude of Mr. Seldes towards the disgusting exploitation of 'Youth' by wicked politicians is amusing and in the highest degree instructive. Had 'Youth' remained the monopoly of the political orthodoxy favoured

E

by Mr. Seldes, then we should never have heard so much as a whisper of all this groaning and grumbling over the unprincipled manner in which 'Youth' is got hold of and inflamed to political activities—instead of being left alone to make daisy chains, write Free Verse, or play Rugby Football.

Yes—Mr. Seldes opens his article upon a most portentous note. The way 'Youth' was bamboozled and dragooned before the War, oh, that was bad enough! says he: but 'not even in the most militaristic nations (prior to the War) was there systematic perversion of the mind of Youth, nor did Czars and Kaisers dare to begin physical training for war of children of six and eight, and to place knives and rifles in their hands at twelve and fourteen, and machine-guns when they were in the high schools and universities. That is what is happening now. The preparation of children for future wars is one of the most alarming facts of the present era of peacemaking in Europe.'

In the matter of the juvenile armaments complained of above, it is Russia, as always happens with a great revolutionary regime, eager to defend the Revolution, who is the principal offender. But Mr. Seldes rather suggests that it is 'the handsome Adolf' who slips machine-guns into the little innocent hands of german laddies of six. The reverse, in fact, is true: any National Socialist found in possession of firearms is expelled from the party.

'The education of the Young is for us a question of life and death,' said Trotsky (I quote Mr. Seldes). But in Russia 'the Young' have to have their souls altered from top to bottom. The children of the characters of Chekov will need a good deal of overhauling before they get properly machine-minded. But it is not Russia that worries Mr. Seldes. It is the way Youth is behaving elsewhere, that is the thing that really worries him. Indeed, at the end of his article he washes his hands of 'Youth' altogether.

'The Youth Movement, it seems to me,' exclaims the embittered Mr. Seldes, 'is now *so far corrupted* that little can be done with it. Even if we supposed that the Communist or the Fascist regime (in Germany) will give way to liberal government, *it will take a generation to undo* the evil of another generation.'

It is really the german, italian, and partly the french 'Youth,' that have let Mr. Seldes down. He would have wished them to have remained—like the anglo-saxon 'Youth'—an exclusively social, sporting, and sensationalist mass, pleasantly tinted a sunset 'pink.'

'Each of these desperate men '—Mr. Seldes is speaking of the present european dictators—'each of these desperate men has seen the success of the Roman Catholic Church founded on the principle of the training of Youth, and each has tried to add politics and machine-guns to a new sort of school education, frequently to the applause of democratic nations.'

Here follows Mr. Seldes' account of the rise to power of Adolf Hitler in Germany:—

If one looks at the past two years and the present state of the Youth Movement in Germany, one can see exactly what happened in Italy. For example, just before the Hitler victory (that of September 1930) there was a battle between the Berlin branch of the National Socialists, as the Hitlerites are known officially, and a group of Democrats holding a quiet meeting. The Berlin head of the Hitlerites, Herr Goebbels, led the young men. They had been challenged to a platform debate, but the National Socialists preferred clubs to propaganda. They declared they had no need for spiritual weapons when they could win the majority of voters by action of a determined, armed minority. (It was Italy all over again.) Youth gladly followed Goebbels. His boys of twenty and under beat up the Democrats.

Again, during a meeting of the Reichsbannerlokal in the Roentgenthal a telephone call alerted Branch 29 of the storm troops of the Hitler Youth; the National Socialists appeared in the dark, fired rifles and revolvers into the meeting, killed one boy, and disappeared into the darkness. Sixteen Hitler-ites were arrested, the youngest seventeen, the oldest twenty-four; one was tried for murder. He was seventeen, a member of a Hitler 'cell' in the Schliemann public school. In the first two months of 1930 there are police records of thirty-four such acts of violence committed by the Hitlerites. These little terrorisms are encouraged by the leaders. . . . The early days of Italian Fascism are being repeated in Germany in more ways than violence. It takes not only the leadership of crafty elder men, but a lot of money to turn an undisciplined mob of young men, who never saw military service and are forbidden conscription, into an organized, illegal political movement. For the owners of the Milan and Turin metal industries, the Genoa shippers, the Milan bankers, and the great estate owners of Italy who financed Mussolini's Youth-movement, we have in Germany the Berlin manufacturers, the Hanover potash makers, the Rhineland industrialists, and the group which with Doctor Hugenberg once owned the Nationalist Party and which now owns the Nazis. As in Italy, there is a large subsidized Press. It is Hugenberg's.

What happened in 1930 is, therefore, quite simple. Another 2,000,000 between the ages of twenty and twenty-three had become enfranchised between the elections, which, added to the 5,000,000 young men and women of the post-war generation already having the vote, produced an electoral reservoir of war-ignorant youth, 7,000,000 strong, a large number in semi-militaristic orders and fascinated by the Hitlerite stream with its violent, headlong, overwhelming flow. It was the end of the romantic pacifist Youth Movement.[1]

Alas! Hitler has turned 'Youth' sour upon the palate of Mr. Seldes! Indeed it *was* the end of a brief, artificial, internationalist wave that overcame the Youth of Germany at the conclusion of the War. But Mr. Seldes does not say, as he should, that internationalism, or 'pacificism,' was just as political, or could rapidly have been turned to ends just as unpacific, as that of the Hitler organization. Russia ten years ago was frantically 'pacifist' and is still 'international.' But that does not prevent Russia from training

[1] In the above passage I have altered the term 'fascist' used by Mr. Seldes into 'Hitlerite.'

children of twelve upwards, and also girls, to arms.  The
Russian Socialist Empire cannot be blamed for doing this—
every great revolutionary state has had to attend to its
defence.  But why should Germany, which is a very great
country too, be compelled to remain permanently unarmed,
with great states all round her feverishly arming?

However, Mr. Seldes is particularly unfair to the Nazis,
who are more characteristic of 'Young Germany' than any
other party: and Mr. Seldes is doing the english-speaking
public a disservice by this partisanship.

The Nazis say, 'Why, when we can get what we want by
way of the parliamentary electorate, use violence?'  For
many months now that has been their steadfast policy.  But
Mr. Seldes makes them say the opposite.  Again, he describes Nazi violence, but is studiously silent about the
violence and provocation of the Communist, or of the
Reichsbanner.  That is what one would expect.  In Lord
Rothermere's papers in England the Nazis received both
advertisement and sympathetic treatment.  But it is very
seldom that in a general way you find the reporting, for
the english or american Press, anything but ill-disposed
and prejudiced.  So the Hitlerite standpoint, in the interests merely of truth, must be insisted upon a little.  It
cannot be a good thing that England and America should
have nothing better than a counterfeit and unreal picture
of what is going on in Germany.  The great german Youth
Movement has become the Hitler Movement: you do not
need to be a keen Youth-politician to grasp the importance
of that fact.

But what really is interesting—and that is quite un-
usually enlightening from the point of view of the student
of 'Youth-politics'—is this *volte-face* of a political writer
with regard to the *Politics of Youth* altogether.  'Youth' is
a fine thing, in fact—a very fine thing—*but only so long* as
it serves the political end you have at heart.  It is a splendid

notion—'Youth—it is glorious' and should be 'at the
Helm.' Oh yes! But the moment 'Youth'—with all its
natural reckless idealism—turns about and attacks the
dogmas of your particular political faith—oh, then, you can
find no words too hot and strong to denounce 'Youth' and
all its works! 'Youth' then becomes, upon the spot, a
despicable tool of unworthy and scheming 'Older men.' It
is very odd, and a very significant fact, that we never hear
of these 'older men' when all is going well, and 'Youth'
behaving itself: you would think, indeed, that there were
nothing but 'Youths' in the world—when all is as it
should be!

For, listen again to Mr. Seldes—he deserves your closest
attention:—

> The history of the Youth Movement is the history of the
> success of governments, dictators, and political parties—the
> older men—in taking control and propagating their policies.
> The socialist-pacifistic-equal-economic-rights program of
> thirty years ago remains in the constitution of the clubs and
> leagues which follow the weakened parties of the middle road,
> but the main trend has been to the Left and has resulted in
> the Fascist-Hitler reaction to the Right. The middle road
> is pretty empty nowadays.

'Youth' is usually represented as an irresistible, independent, natural force—SPONTANEOUSLY erupting: but let
'Youth' but take the wrong turning (from the speaker's
standpoint) and lo! 'Youth-politics' become upon the spot
the disgusting manœuvres of the 'older men,' or of the
'crafty elder men'—stirring up 'Youth' in such a manner
that 'little can be done with it'—indeed 'corrupting' it
to such a degree that it will 'take a generation to undo
the evil.'

Poor Mr. Seldes! German Youth has let him down badly!
But we must not, in Anglo-saxony, take Mr. Seldes' cries of
despair too seriously, if we should overhear them. And he
is a godsend to the student of 'Youth-politics.'

PART II

## CHAPTER I

# THE DOSSIER

IT is difficult, out of the enormous welter of 'Youth' propaganda, to know what to choose and what to leave. For our argument it is necessary to demonstrate the incredible profusion of the material: it is not so much the intrinsic importance of this newspaper-cutting or of that, as the spectacle of this cataract of words, that it is desirable to bring out. For a decade this swollen torrent of verbiage has poured out of the great newspaper presses of England and America. It shows no signs of abating. So it is a sense of this colossal weight of *material* that you want to get first. Yet, short of simply reprinting, facsimile, pages on pages of it, it is difficult to expose its density and extent.

A mere enumeration of Headlines may do something towards it. So I will marshal a score of Headlines that will speak, in loud tones, for themselves. These Headlines could be carried on *ad infinitum*.

# WHEN A WOMAN'S THIRTY

By

### BARONESS FURNIVALL

# THIS WEARY GENERATION

## By CLEMENCE DANE

'Up to 25, and after 75, England is quite her hearty self,' says this brilliant analysis of the world to-day.

But what of the 35's to 60's, the people who saw the War through?

# The 'Come-Back' of Youth

## Pointed Replies to Sir MAX PEMBERTON

'The retort of Youth to Sir Max Pemberton has been tremendous in volume and pointed—sometimes very pointed—in its vehemence.'

*Childlike*
*Innocence At*
*40 Years*
*Of Age.*

*BATTLE OF THE*
*GENERATIONS*

*JOHN VAN DRUTEN'S*
*NEW PLAY.*

SUBURBIA AGAIN

*How Old Are You?*

A LITTLE ADDRESS
TO THE MIDDLE-AGED.

# When the Wine and the Kisses Pall.

*YOUTH'S SHAKEN FAITH:*
*THE NEED AND THE*
*REMEDY.*

## By C. E. M. JOAD.

---

# 'WHAT I THINK OF
## People Under 25,'

### By People Over 25.

Men and Women who are not
'modern youth,' here is your
opportunity! Youth now is
in the pillory: will the story
you tell fall at Youth's feet
like a bouquet, or will it crash
upon Youth's head like —
a Mills bomb?

# WHY YOUTH IS RESTLESS

Isn't the Mess of the World for Which Generations of Elders Are Responsible Enough to Make It?

*By SIR JOHN FOSTER FRASER.*

# The HUMAN PARENT and His Very MODERN SON.

By J. D. BERESFORD.

*VICTORIAN FATHERS WOULD SHUDDER AT THE CHANGE—BUT IT WORKS.*

# THE GALLERIES

## YOUNG PAINTERS IN EXCELSIS

JUDGEMENT OF YOUTH

# Einstein, the Child-like Master, Who is Mothered by His Wife.

# STRANGLING THE YOUNG IDEA

## Away with Old Men Who Lay Paralysing Hands Upon the Life of the Nation!

*By SIR BRUCE-PORTER, K.B.E., C.M.G., M.D.*

February 28, 1931     Family Herald

# THE BOOK-TASTER

## THE SORROWS OF THE YOUNG.

### 'Fools to Mourn Our Passing Youth.'

' The adolescent falls in love with cricket captains, with school teachers, companion adolescents, and other Olympian but unresponsive persons,' says Winifred Holtby in *Good Housekeeping.* 'Later he may find rapture in response, but the very intensity of his pre-occupations with personal emotions inevitably leads to sorrow.'

\*     \*     \*

The young woman who wishes to outrival Shakespeare flings curses to the sky when a local paper refuses her verses on the First Swallow. The future Florence Nightingale's humiliation is unmitigated when a ward-sister scolds her for leaving finger-marks on the brass steriliser. The ambitions of youth are of its few merits. But let no one think they are pleasant passions. 'We are fools to mourn our passing youth. We should congratulate ourselves. It is time that some one called the bluff of youth and revealed it as the touching, comfortless, self-conscious, uneasy, and preposterous period it really is. The sooner we are done with it the better.'

# The Boys and Girls To Put Things Right

*By Lt.-Comdr. the HON. J. M. KENWORTHY, M.P.*

## The Young Generation and the Younger Young Generation.

London Letter
By HUGH WALPOLE

## GIVE US OUR LATCHKEYS!

**Smug, Self-Satisfied and Out-of-date Middle-Age**

**As It Seems to the Twenties.**

By GODFREY WINN, Author of 'Dreams Fade,' etc.

## Dread Days.

'Twenty years ago to-morrow,' said a woman friend whom I met at supper last night, 'was my wedding night.'

## The Woman In The Middle Thirties.

The reader will get some idea, perhaps, from this parade of Headlines of the richness and grossness of the material. And, casting his mind back, he will recall, no doubt (his attention having thus been focused), the strange frequency of articles of this type. The Headlines are from every description of paper, from the *Family Herald* to the *Daily Telegraph*.

Of course, as you run your eye over this haphazard collection of Headlines of articles assembled for the purposes of this research, you will see at first more subject for mirth than for serious study. And the articles themselves, more often than not, make very entertaining reading: and (if I am right in my conjectures) they doubtless provide a great deal of innocent mirth likewise to the newspaper staffs entrusted with their manufacture—also to the various proprietors (mostly jolly fellows of sixty-odd, as fond of a hearty joke as the next). So, unlike many other serious branches of research, this one is not without its amenities, I am glad to say. But it is none the less important for that reason.

In the light of the analysis I have provided in Part I of this essay, the type of *Age-tournament*, as it might be called, staged by *The Evening News* is a good illustration with which to open the scrutiny of this mixed bag of Press-cuttings from the prodigious *Age-war* campaigning of the great and little newspapers. Upon the front page of *The Evening News* (June 20, 1930) the following announcement appeared—five guineas prize for the best five letters and half a guinea for all letters printed from the Over-Twenty-Fives. Here are the terms of the announcement:—

### WHAT I THINK
#### of
### MODERN YOUTH.

An Invitation by *The Evening News* to People over Twenty-Five. When Modern Youth was expressing its very frank opinions of People over Forty, we received letters, some caustic, some piteous, from its victims! They knew then that their letters, by virtue of the terms of the competition, could not be published, but there were many pleas for a hearing.

So now *The Evening News* invites letters containing true stories showing—

What I Think of

### PEOPLE UNDER 25,

by People Over 25.

\* \* \*

Men and women who are not 'modern youth,' here is your opportunity! Youth now is in the pillory: will the story you tell fall at Youth's feet like a bouquet, or will it crash upon Youth's head like—a Mills bomb?

\* \* \* \* \* \* \*

You will remember that while some of the young women found you more interesting and charming than their contemporaries, some found you bores and Mrs. Grundys—that some of the young men called you hypocrites, wet-blankets, envious of their youth, grasping: and some called you tolerant, helpful, and trustworthy.

*What do you think of them?*

We want the stories you tell to be your means of expressing *your* very frank opinions.

\* \* \* \* \* \* \*

Address to 'Youth,' *The Evening News*, Carmelite House, E.C. 4. Names and addresses must be given, preferably for publication. As in the case of the letters from Youth, £5, 5s. will be awarded for each of the best five letters, and 10s. 6d. will be paid for every letter printed.

Youth should know its best points and its worst. It has told you yours!

F

# *A COMPETITION FOR THE OVER-TWENTY-FIVES*.  THE MOBILIZING OF THE *AGE-CLASSES*, FOR THE *AGE-WAR*

**T**HERE is one thing that must always be borne in mind: namely, that such competitions as that announced by *The Evening News* and all such 'Youth' articles are strictly for the consumption of *crétins*.   The contest proposed between the OVER-TWENTY-FIVES and the UNDER-TWENTY-FIVES is for an enormous half-witted *sub-average*—or lower-average—of office and workshop.   That is the majority of the newspaper public, it is true.   Such a competition is designed to inflame and to influence uneducated herds of the small employee and machine-minding class—that class that in a civilization run upon slave-labour would be the *slaves*.   It is strictly a slave-literature, therefore, with which we are dealing (although, in a 'democratic' system, such attitudes of mind percolate *upwards*, just as does the sobbing slave-music of the plantations—jazzed by Berlin or by Gershwin).

The announcement reproduced at the end of the previous chapter, then, is by way of being a direct communication, made by the Boss—the 'Old Man'—to his salaried staff. Like everything written for the Popular Press, outside of 'news' pure and simple, this is veiled *instructions*, or orders of the day.   It is designed for the bringing up of Mr. and Mrs. Everyman—that is Mr. and Mrs. Worker—in the way that Mr. and Mrs. Worker are to go.   And it is the Boss who is (in his inimitable, chatty, chaffing, human-all-too-human way) addressing them.

The *Evening News* cutting is the only one I possess, I am

82

sorry to say, from that series: but it is evident from the
text that a number of real or imaginary 'Modern Youths'
had been 'telling off' their elders at the invitation of the
newspaper.  The readers who were Over-Twenty-Fives are
described as writhing beneath the lashing of the tongues of
the 'Youths': they wrote either raging or 'piteous' letters
to the editor, we are told, begging to be allowed to answer
back.  But no!  'They knew,' the inexorable editor sternly
tells us—they well knew, these Over-Twenty-Fives—'that
their letters, by virtue of the terms of the competition, could
not be published.'  Nevertheless, 'there were many pleas for
a hearing.'  Much 'piteous . . . pleading,' but, at the time,
*no redress*!  All they could do was to roar or mutter in their
homes or in neighbouring public-houses.

At last the ban is lifted!  All people Over Twenty-Five
can give full vent to their spleen and say *just what they
think* of the Young 'uns.  They may relieve their pent-up
feelings, and answer for their *Class*—their *age-class*, that of
the *Over-Twenty-Fives*.

The archness of the language in this announcement (with
its offer of five guineas for the most peppery and indignant
five epistles of *Over-Twenty-Fives*) is in the best tradition
of such propaganda.  It is the tone of the secondary schoolmaster, or scout-master, with his 'little charges'—*Men and
Women who are not 'modern Youth,'* stand up, please!  Here
is your opportunity!  Will your five-guinea letter smell like
a bouquet, or sting like a hornet?  (*I think I know which!*
with many a finger-wag and arch chuckle, this good Press-
uncle can be heard to exclaim.)  *Remember!* shrieks the
agitator—Remember how *they*—the other *Age-class* (the
*Under-Twenty-Fives*) called you a 'wet-blanket'—yes, and
'envious-of-their-youth.'  Give it 'Youth' hot and strong!
(All letters to be addressed 'Youth,' etc.)

This cutting is a very fine specimen.  I recommend the
reader to examine it carefully in the light of the arguments

of Part I of this book.   There is, of course, no occasion to
point out how this type of propaganda is calculated to create
peace and good-will among men.   How the enlistment,
disciplining and dragooning, of these *age-classes*—making
them class-conscious (where to be *age-conscious* is to be
*class-conscious* at the same time)—can be of the utmost use
to Big Business in the disciplining of the world at large,
will be plain enough, I hope, by now.

To assist the reader, however, to an understanding of
what lies beneath the surface of such an ostensibly jolly,
light-hearted little competition as the above, I will quote
a message from the New York Correspondent of the *Daily
Telegraph* (May 28, 1929).   In comparing these two cuttings
—the one I am about to quote and that from *The Evening
News* above—it should not be too difficult, for a quite
unobservant person, or one not accustomed to generalize
his experiences, to recognize the strong possibility that the
TOO OLD AT FIFTY cutting may throw some light upon the
WHAT I THINK OF PEOPLE UNDER TWENTY-FIVE cutting:—

# TOO OLD AT 50
# IN U.S.A.

—————◆—————

NEW YORK.   *Monday.*

'America is the richest country in the world,' said Representative Hamilton Fish, in the House of Representatives
to-day, 'but our wage-earners are left alone to worry and
suffer the humiliations of poverty in their declining years.'
Mr. Fish urged that the time had arrived when the United
States 'shall cease playing the ostrich act, and attempt to
solve the serious problem of old-age dependency.'   He proposes a special committee of five members, to be appointed
by the Speaker of the House of Representatives, 'to inquire
into old-age pension systems, and study modern methods, by
which practically all advanced nations of the world afford

constructive relief to the worthy aged poor.' 'American wage-earners of to-day,' he said, 'are thrown out on the industrial scrap heap at middle-age, due to high-pressure and to the super-efficiency methods of industrial plants, and the man or woman of 50 is unable to keep pace with younger workers. . . .'

In a recent message to the Legislature, the Governor of the State of New York condemned the present method of dealing with the aged by means of almshouses as antiquated, inefficient, expensive, and demoralizing.

If the 'wage-earner' . . . at middle-age—unable to keep pace with 'younger workers'—is bombarded in the Popular Press with abuse, purporting to come from 'Modern Youths' (that is to say, 'wage-earners' like himself, but twenty years younger), it is conceivable that these little competitions may strike him as impinging too plainly upon the issues of life and death, of bread and work, to be really amusing. Again, the welsh miners described in a cutting from the *Sphere* (p. 51, Part I) are experiencing at 35 years old a novel superannuation. They shake their heads, we have been told, when people talk to them of employment, and say that there are too many lads of eighteen wanting work too, and that these will always be chosen in their place. When asked by the reporter what their plans might be, they replied that they were 'waiting for the old-age pension.'

But it is the OVER-TWENTY-FIVES—it is as well to note the age selected for the 'class' dividing-line—in *The Evening News* competition who are involved, as against the 'Modern Youth.' That compresses the 'Youth' area: it being in addition the *pensionable* line, ten years nearer the cradle than usual.

## CHAPTER III

# 'PUT THIS DOWN IN YOUR TABLETS, HORATIO!'

ALL questions of age are involved with the traditional (not the actual) feminine psychology, and are
of the nature of a music-hall joke. In the past,
invariably *age* has been a masculine joke—at the expense of
the 'Fair Sex.' But to-day that attitude is not only out-of-
date (for women are, if anything, less sensitive than men
upon that subject): it is also an attitude that must be
transcended if we are to understand exactly what is in store
for the average citizen, or wage-slave, of the New Era. The
emotional issue—the rough pot-house malice at the expense
of womankind—obscures the *real* issue. And that is what
we are here attempting to lay bare. It is behind these
smoke-screens of faux-bonhommish laughter that the genial
agents of destruction work: was it not that way in the War,
when the inferno of the battlefield was represented as a
Bairnsfather cockney jest, of the '*If you know of a better 'ole*'
order? And did not the Freiherr von Buchwald—in other
words Remark—perpetuate the Bairnsfather joke, ten years
after 'Armageddon,' with an intermixture of the macabre
into that 'If you know of a better 'ole' pleasantry? All
that order of convenient and disarming mirth-to-order,
imposed by the *Faux-bonhomme* upon the *Brave-homme*, is
especially effective in the anglo-saxon world. English
'humour' is to blame. More here than anywhere, if it were
your intention to put every man upon his guard, it would
be necessary to expose the over-jolly and too-visibly 'Good-
natured' person. Shakespeare's saying 'A man may smile
and smile and be a villain' could never have been written by
any one but an Englishman. No Italian, for instance, would

86

have written it. The sense of *discovery* resulting in the Englishman making Hamlet's remark into a proverbial saying, affords us a glimpse of the fundamental simplicity of the english character. It is indeed *always* necessary to tell the Englishman to note this down in his 'tablets' or chalk it up on his wall! Never more so than to-day. But however often this memo. were committed to the 'tablets,' it would be next minute forgotten. So if, out of altruism, you proposed to play Hamlet to that blockhead, you would soon learn to spare your breath—especially as it would be *you* that he would suspect, at the end of the transaction, for being able even to imagine such tortuous and criminal habits of mind, for being so 'suspicious,' in fine. All this must be said, painful as it is to have to record it; for the technique of a politician is of necessity adapted to the medium in which his work is to be carried out: and reluctantly it must be admitted that, by and large, the Everyman in Anglo-saxony gets the Government he deserves—a Smiler, a hearty and facetious despot.

## CHAPTER IV

## ' CLASS-WARS '

**T**HE great roman maxim for government—*Divide et Impera*: to *divide* first, in order the better to *rule* afterwards, any given set of people—that is still and ever the golden rule. And the marxian *class* technique— that of cutting people up into hard-and-fast antagonistic classes—that is nothing else but a commonsense application of that roman political wisdom.

The classes must not, however, be *invented* entirely. It is better to take 'classes' that already exist. And human beings are roughly segmented by nature and accident into a great variety of categories. There is the *race* category— a person is a Celt or a Saxon, a Semite or a Slav, and so on. There is the *sex* category—a person is a man or woman. There is the *age* category—a person is young or old. There is the *social* category—a person is rich or poor. There is the *trade* category—a person is a plumber or a farmer.

*A house divided against itself cannot stand*—that is another maxim, a jewish one this time. And obviously a nation that could act as *one man* would be a very formidable nation, whatever it undertook. But a nation each member of which, on one ground or another—of vanity, or of ambition—was on bad terms with every other—that would be a very ineffective nation. It would represent less than the power of one man—for no single man would be able to act without interference on the part of some other man.— These exceedingly simple political truths are so obscured to-day by *class-invective* that they constantly need re-stating.

The fundamental, natural, classes—sex and age—are dual. Man and woman—old and young. But in practice these two great subdivisions are infinitely split up—according to the fancy, or will, of the splitter, also because of the inequality of nature. Two great neuter classes are in process of formation within the male and female wings of the normal sex duality. And within the main age-groups of young and old, many sub-groups are formed. Thus in the years immediately succeeding the War the Paris literary world was wittily and brutally chopped into the 'Under-Thirties' and the 'Over-Thirties.' As these groups aged, they became the 'Under-Forties' and the 'Over-Forties.' There has been a great deal of scuffling around the Forty line everywhere for some time. The Overs and Unders from either side of all these age-pales glare at each other coldly. The animosities of the Sixties for the Seventies is notorious. And the barrier-reef of Puberty-and-non-Puberty echoes with infant brawls.

So out of the fluid material of the two main groupings, of *sex* and of *age*, many sub-groups can be constructed. And of course, ever more so, *Poor* and *Rich*, remain relative terms, and are each subject to infinite divisions. *Trade* affords the 'class' politician unlimited opportunities for fomenting rivalry and conflict. It requires no superlative powers of persuasion to convince a Postman that he is a creature of a different clay from a Pearl-fisher. And an Airman and a Coal-miner are as far apart as bird and mole, or it is not difficult to make them feel so.

In *The Art of Being Ruled*, which was published in the spring of 1926, these problems were discussed in some detail. Rather than go over that ground again (and I cannot take it for granted that the reader has read that book), I will quote several passages. My first quotation is from p. 115, and the chapter is entitled 'Causes of European Decay':—

> But even if race were abolished by intermixture, it would still be possible, of course, to get your class-factor, and with it your organized war, by way of sex, age, occupational and

other categories. 'The intensity of organization is increased,' as Mr. Russell points out, 'when a man belongs to more organizations.' The more classes (of which, in their various functions, he is representative) that you can make him become regularly conscious of, the more you can control him, the more of an automaton he becomes. Thus, if a man can be made to feel himself acutely (*a*) an American; (*b*) a young American; (*c*) a middle-west young American; (*d*) a 'radical and enlightened' middle-west young American; (*e*) a 'college-educated,' etc., etc.; (*f*) a 'college-educated' dentist who is an etc., etc.; (*g*) a 'college-educated' dentist of such-and-such a school of dentistry, etc., etc.—the more inflexible each of these links is, the more powerful, naturally, is the chain. Or he can be locked into any of these compartments as though by magic by any one understanding the wires, in the way the jesuit studied those things.

Next I will quote a chapter entitled 'The Piecemealing of the Personality,' pp. 228-230 :—

Race is the queen of the 'classes': but in Europe to-day its power is very slight—for one reason, because it lacks all organization or even reality. But there are less fundamental ones, but usually far more present to our consciousness in everyday life, needing the greatest attention, and involving a variety of ritual. The other 'classes,' it is true, have never been recognized as of the same standing as *race*. As a *casus belli* they have been inferior to it. None of these other differences, or the membership of any of the other classes, was recognized as a pretext for taking life. Race or nationality, on the other hand, has, in the modern world, been recognized as a sanction for murder by every State. But this sanction usually had only 'nationality' to repose on, which was a very different thing to race. Marx, with his 'class war,' indirectly demonstrated the absurdity of these privileges of race—especially when it was not *race* at all. The success of his system has shown how easy it is to substitute, in a disorganized, non-racially founded society, any 'class' for the classical 'racial' unity of the State.

Once 'war' between classes started spreading, from the teaching of Marx, it did not stop at social 'class,' naturally. Schopenhauer, for instance, early in the last century, called women the 'short-legged race.' So women were thenceforth one *race* and men another. The idea of race substituted itself for that of sex. But where there are *races* there are *wars*. The 'sex-war' was soon in full swing. Schopenhauer himself, it is interesting to recall, was one of the first in the field. He early in life flung himself upon a strange woman whom he found conversing on the staircase of the house where he lived, and threw her downstairs. For this pioneer engagement, however, he was forced for the rest of his life to pay a crushing pension to this crippled member of the enemy 'race.'

Women are notoriously unamenable to strictly *racial* mysteries. The classical example of this is that of the Sabine women deciding, as it is supposed, to remain the property of the roman ravishers rather than return to the defeated men of their own race.

*The child* is the 'class' that is most nearly associated with the sex-classification: or rather, the age-difference it represents. 'The child is father to the man': and the child is, as primitive societies saw, actually a different being, in spite of physiological continuity, to the grown man into which he develops. It is the case of the worm and the butterfly—only in inverse order, the butterfly coming first. So Master Smith and Mister Smith are as different almost (when they are the same person at different ages of Smith's career) as though they were offspring and parent.

But the difference diminishes when you are dealing with Isaac Newton, or even with Clara Vere de Vere, in place of poor Smith. The more highly developed an individual is, or the more civilized a race, this *discontinuity* tends to disappear. The 'personality' is born. Continuity, in the individual as in the race, is the diagnostic of a civilized condition. If you can break this personal continuity in an individual, you can break *him*. For *he* is that continuity. It is against these *joints* and sutures of the personality that an able attack will always be directed. You can divide a person against himself, unless he is very well organized: as the two halves of a severed earwig become estranged and fight with each other when they meet.

A good demonstration of the rationale of this piecemealing of the personality for attack was given the other day by a caricaturist. He divided his celebrated victims into their Young and Old Selves: in this way he had them in half, like hydras, and made the angry tail discourse with the fiery head. But you can effect far more than this. You can with luck cut men up so thoroughly that they become almost 'six-months men,' as they might be called, rather than men of one continuous personal life—that is, 'life men.' It is only necessary to mention the central subject of the very effective and fashionable plays of Pirandello to show how, systematically presented in a dramatic form, this segregation of the 'selves' of which the personality is composed can affect the public mind.

But there is no way in which people differ, however minutely, that does not supply material for a 'war.' And the general contention throughout this essay is that they cannot have too much of 'class': that people's passion for 'class' and for reposing their personality in a network of conventional 'classification' is not often realized. Where war is concerned you must, of course, disregard entirely the humanitarian standpoint. *Passively* men may even enjoy war, as the bird enjoys being drawn irresistibly to the fang of the snake. The blowing off of heads and arms is a very secondary matter with the majority of people. But that does not justify you as a responsible ruler in abusing this insensitiveness.

When really well mixed into a good, strong group, men are so many automata: they hardly notice any disturbance, like a war. But that the conscious self (in so far as it remains part of the average human being) is terribly bloodthirsty and combative, much as I should like to, I find it difficult to credit. By *themselves* people are, every one admits, averse to fighting: it demands too much energy. Perhaps a really *perfect* group, or class, to prevent itself from dying of inanition, would favour war, as a stimulant. But I think the more the question is examined, the more certain it is that people *for themselves* (not for others—they enjoy seeing other people fighting, and dying, naturally), and *in the mass*, prefer eating, sleeping, fornicating, and playing games of skill to killing each other. And even if *the happiness of the greatest number* is not so individual a matter as Bentham supposed—even if the happiness of dying, let alone living, with a huge crowd of people must have a serious claim on our attention—nevertheless the individual, betrayed momentarily by some collapse or etiolation of the communistic medium, does object very strongly to dying. As *an individual* he is all for not dying or being crippled—that *is* the law of nature. And the ruler who bases his action on the stability of this Artificial Man of Communism constantly risks sinning against God.

That people *wish* to be *class-men* is beyond question, I think—by this I mean the great average. It requires a very great deal of energy to be an 'individual.' The mass of men ask nothing better than to be *Puppets* (the word used by Goethe). And in discussing these matters (in a discussion between Free Men, that is) the only thing at stake is *how far* people should be allowed to harden into classes (and so evade all responsibility)—how far, in brief, it is good for the Free Men that the mere political intriguing Power-glutton should be given *carte blanche* to herd them and ticket them.

My last quotation from *The Art of Being Ruled* is from pp. 167-168—a chapter entitled 'People's Happiness Found in Type-Life ':—

An *esprit de corps* can be worked up about anything; the *regiment* is the unit of discipline and romance, rather than the region from which it comes. And a 'proletarian' class obsession is essential to bind together the 'proletariat,' whatever that may be. Without such fictitious ('artificial,' as Sorel says) bond it would fall to pieces. And even the parade of objective science and historical paraphernalia is justified if it is understood by the director of the movement which it is seeking to save.

Actually, again, the more you specialize people, the more power you can obtain over them, the more helpless and in consequence the more obedient they are. To shut people up in a water-tight, syndicalized, occupational unit is like shutting them up on an island. Further, occupation, in a world of mixed races and traditions, is the most natural classification (though it could be said from another point of view, of course, to be the most unnatural).

The ideally 'free man' would be the man *least* specialized, the *least* stereotyped, the man approximating to the *fewest* classes, the *least* clamped into a system—in a word, the most individual. But a society of 'free men,' if such a thing could ever come about, which it certainly could not, would immediately collapse.

The chief thing to remember in such a discussion is that no one wants to be 'free ' in that sense. People ask nothing better than to be *types*—occupational types, social types, functional types of any sort. If you force them not to be, they are miserable, just as the savage grew miserable when the white man came and prevented him from living a life devoted to the forms and rituals he had made. And if so forced (by some interfering philanthropist or unintelligent reformer) to abandon some *cliché,* all men, whether white, yellow, or black, take the first opportunity to get their *cliché* back, or to find another one. For in the mass people wish to be *automata* : they wish to be *conventional* : they hate you teaching them or forcing them into 'freedom': they wish to be obedient, hard-working machines, as near dead as possible—as near dead (feelingless and thoughtless) as they can get, without actually dying.

## CHAPTER V

## 'THIS TREATISE IS A WORK OF SCIENCE. IT TREATS OF THE "INFINITELY LITTLE." DO NOT FOR THAT REASON DESPISE IT!'

THE preceding chapter dug down beneath the smiling surface of the flippant field of Youth-politics. Here and there it may have frightened the more indolent reader a little bit. But now we will emerge again: we will deal only with what is bright, bustling, and emotional. More newspaper strips from the 'Youth' dossier will be spread out for the reader's inspection in the next chapter. But first a commonly-heard objection must be answered.

From experience of this type of investigation I know perfectly well what must happen with every forward step we take. We shall be told that the material we are about to handle—with all the practised care bestowed by the biologist upon a grasshopper, or by the ornithologist upon an eccentric sparrow—we shall be assured that this material is '*not important*'! All the pains lavished by us upon these newspaper clippings could be better expended—so it will be argued—upon the more worthy and considerable objects of legitimate research. That must be answered, I suppose —and for the last time, in this essay. For, although that type of argument is always used to discourage such a research as this, it is too stupid, or when it is not that, it is merely an astute attempt at sabotage.

I claim, then, that this research we have undertaken is of the highest interest and moment. *I claim for it, upon an equal footing, the same title to be 'scientific' as any branch whatever of biology or chemistry.* If I were about to dissect an earwig, or to lay bare 'the guts of a louse' (to borrow a phrase from recent politics), no one would interfere with me, or protest that earwigs were 'unimportant' or lice beneath my notice. What I shall be analysing is of just as much 'scientific' importance as anything else in nature. *And it is very imperfectly understood!*

The heart of man is a dark forest, *and* it contains every variety of human, of super-human, of sub-human, shape. But the man of science, and I am a man of science, is not, and indeed could not be, a snob. To command him *only* to examine what is super-human—grandiosely diabolic, or gigantically intelligent—is to misunderstand the very function of science.

Or, again, the way it will be put is that the subjects of this research are all *small*, are indeed very small, and, therefore, *insignificant.* But that is the old deep-rooted fallacy, is it not, that attempted to head the earlier men of science off any microscopic research? It is the old sentimental view, am I not right, that a thing studied under a microscope cannot be of the same moment as a thing studied through an astronomical telescope?

Would one not have thought that the Science of the Infinitely Little, the history of the Atom, was to-day sufficiently recognized to be of as much value and importance as that of the Infinitely Great (and indeed the true meanings involved in the terms Great and Little sufficiently popularized) to prevent such an argument being used?

For human life the microbe is more important than the Nebula, is it not? And a person who occupies his time with atomic structure is not looked down upon because quantitatively his subject-matter is so *small*—compared with the astronomer, whose subject-matter is so *big*. Ah, but your subject-matter is human, it might then be objected. Well, what of it? It is none the less a legitimate material of scientific research for that reason. It is not vivisection—

I hurt no living thing with my instruments.   And if it is again objected that my subject-matter is simply *idiotic*, well then, I say, regard me as a mad-doctor, an Infirmary Consultant.   But do not call my occupation an unworthy one, or attempt to discredit these researches on the score that the human beings offered to the reader's inspection are not as *great* as Caesar, as *wise* as Plato, or that their words are not as worthy of immortality as those of Dante.   If they were anything of that kind, they would be beyond the reach of my analysis.   It is *analysis*, in fact, that you are objecting to.

Once more, this treatise is not a work of literature in any sense.   It is a work of science, pure and simple.   I merely bring in so much literary rhetorical artifice as is necessary to enable me to excite the reader's interest, arouse his attention, and direct it to what it has been my object to expose and to explain.

G

## CHAPTER VI

# WINN AND WAUGH

THREE or four years since, in New York City, I met a man who, when elated with 'hooch,' would strike himself upon the breast, and unburden himself boastfully of this smouldering incantation:—

'IT WAS I WHO MADE AMERICA—IT WAS *I* WHO MADE AMERICA—YOUNGER-GENERATION-CONSCIOUS!'

*Youngergenerationconscious* was of course one flamboyantly sung winged-word. But it was he who had done that thing, some years before, and he did not disguise the fact that he experienced some satisfaction at the thought that it was *he* and not another who had been responsible for it! It was an 'I killed Cock Robin!' sort of minstrelsy, and 'hooch' brought back the act. No longer young in any spectacular sense, he was an 'Ex-Youth,' in fact, newly passed out into the conventional gloom of premature middle-age. But it was in a good cause, a *great* cause, and he had used his great Ten Years to some effect— so he had the air of saying: With a mere cupidon's small bow and arrow, and though only a poor sparrow, he had slain the Old Man idea in the New World, and there would be no sighing and sobbing in the firmament over *that particular* Cock!—and 'hooch' brought it all back as though it had been but yesterday. So 'It was I who made America, etc.!' he would shout.

But in England nothing of that sort had happened, at that time, nor has it really occurred since. Old England had never been made *Youngergenerationconscious*. It is an Old Country—it is Old England: it has a 'Glorious

Past' that is an obstacle (happy is the country without a history): to be definitely made *Youngergenerationconscious* was not in England's line, and anyway nothing had been done about it.

And then Messrs. Winn and Waugh and some others thought that this citadel of Tradition, La Vieille Angleterre, in spite of all its history, in spite of Restoration Comedy and of Tudor masques, of the Metaphysics of Berkeley and the Clown's tears of Laurence Sterne, might be laid siege to and shaken up on the 'Youth' ticket, and they started a 'Youth' Racket. Even if Merry England might never return, a Brighter Britain at least could be brought about. 'Youth-politics' being anyhow in full blast, this was done— it was a cinch. And the Ancient Britons awoke one morning, like Baron Byron, and found themselves Bright (Bright Britain is not only better but more appropriate than Great Britain): the 'Youth' racket had come to London, in a mild form, the gang-war of the 'Old Gang' and of the 'New Gang'—but it had come.

Mr. Evelyn Waugh is very intelligent and a great wit— or a bright wit—and he has already written two or three books that are far funnier than those of anybody in England except perhaps a dozen people whether nineteen or ninety (his posthumous fame is assured). He is a new 'Max.' Under these circumstances I experience a certain regret in having to draw upon him in this connection.

But *Youngergenerationism* may be regarded, in such a case, as in the nature of an advertisement for *Wild Oats* (not Quaker Oats—the opposite sort), nothing more. Mr. Waugh, I am sure, is far too sensible to object to being used as a witness in a serious treatise of this kind about 'Youth-politics.' In the case of Mr. Winn, there is no occasion to apologize. Mr. Winn has no pretensions to posterity as has Mr. Waugh. Let us plunge, however, at once into *younger-*

*generationconsciousness*, as exposed by Mr. Winn. Mr. Winn is a wag—he sings:—

> *What are little girls made of?*
> *Slugs and snails and puppy dog's tails!*

So sang Mr. Winn (aged six)—chanted 'in a shrill voice, for hours on end,' he tells us. 'Slugs and snails'—we are plumb in the centre of the universe of Peter Pan. A little girl (aged six) had broken his heart. But that was when Mr. Winn was very young: *now* Mr. Winn 'wishes he had a sister.' But I glean all this from *Modern* (March 21, 1931) —a very instructive twopenny Weekly ('*Every Saturday*'). The article is headed as follows:—

---

MODERN

## A *MODERN YOUNG MAN MOANS:*

# I W*ish* I Had A S*ister*

By

GODFREY WINN

---

The moans of the 'Modern Young Man' are conveyed above, of course, by the italics in *Wish* and *Sister*. Mr. Winn *all by himself* does not feel 'equipped' to 'win a wife' —that is why, it appears, he *wishes* for a *sister* to assist him.

'It is only lately,' writes Mr. Winn, 'since I have reached (I hope!) years of discretion and wisdom, that I have changed my opinion (about girls).' The exclamatory *I Hope!* in brackets shows how very arch Mr. Winn is with the hired help or nursery governess who gets 'Every Saturday' her tuppence worth of Modernity—it is, in fact, a case of *Get-away-closer-Godfrey.*

The archness assumes an almost pathologic intentness towards the end of this 'I *wish* I had a *siss*!' article:—

> I have noticed, rather wistfully and bitterly, that boys who have sisters are usually much more successful in their love affairs than young men like myself, who have grown up in a monastic atmosphere.
>
> Thus, in later days, when he finds himself alone with a girl who is not his sister (very much not!) he is not tongue-tied, self-conscious, all hands and feet, and stammer, but a debonair, dashing man of the world. And the girl is instantly impressed—and the battle is more than half over.

### If I Had a Sister.

> Again, if I had a sister, she would be able to advise me on what sort of presents a girl likes. She would be able to choose scent for her, take me to the right shop and the right counter when I wanted to buy silk stockings, and protect me from the merriment of the assistant.
>
> In conclusion, I feel I must remind my readers that this wistful wail, this pæan of appreciation, has been written entirely about the real blood-relation type of sister: it is very definitely not intended to include the 'let-me-be-sister-to-you' type of girl, of whose help, alas! I have had many—too many—offers already. I need hardly add that I have declined them—without thanks!

In this fragment (it is characteristic—I had not space for the whole of this 'Sissy' article, as we can call it for short) you will be able to examine *youngergenerationconsciousness* in full operation. Mr. Winn is 'wistful and bitter' because he is not one of those 'boys who have sisters'—yet in conclusion he is a little unkind to the breathless nurserymaid in Barnes or Belsize who is on the point of dipping her pen in the ink and offering to 'sister' him—he 'feels that he must remind his readers' that his 'wistful wail' should not be taken as an invitation! Let the '*let-me-be-a-sister-to-you-type* of girl' take notice! He has been snowed under, 'alas!' with such offers already! Mr. Winn's cruel coyness casts a gloom over the close of the article.   Mr. Winn is tantamount to a tease—the reader is left with the feeling that he does not really wish for a 'Sissie!'.

Let us swiftly—our nostrils fully expanded to catch the very essence of this 'consciousness' that we are stalking—turn to that beautiful veteran, Ivor Novello. Ivor is an old hand at being 'young,' but that makes no difference, his advertisement is still the best of its kind on the market. Song-writer and cinema star, *il travaille bien, celui-là!* Winn has a long way to go yet.

If you make Fleet Street *Youngergenerationconscious*, there is nothing for it, each newspaper staff must have a corps of Matinée Idols. It is not by any means impossible that stage-door queues will yet be seen at the staff-entrance of the *Daily Express* or *Daily Mirror*—and *Miss Modern* may require a cordon of police if Mr. Winn goes on being arch and persists in driving the suburbs to distraction. I don't know what Godfrey becomes in little-language, but if 'God,' then we get this in place of Ivor (for this is a little rhyme forming part of the characteristic publicity material of Mr. Novello: and I think that by substituting the name of a journalist for that of an actor it will be seen how these two professions are tending to draw together and overlap):—

> Stay, my sweet God, stay, most agreeable boy!
> Nor, in thy nimble Apollonian car,
> Immure the gentle charms we would enjoy,
> The grace, the symmetry, surpassing far
> Helen herself, the Non-pareil of Troy.

But in the *Sunday Graphic* (March 17, 1929), Mr. Winn debated for the Sunday public the pros and cons of *Youngergenerationconsciousness*—still very arch, of course, but upon a higher plane of social argument—in his GIVE US OUR LATCHKEYS.

---

# GIVE US OUR LATCHKEYS!

---

Mr. Winn's 'Sissie' article began:—

 '*When I was six years old,*' etc.

This one (the 'Latchkey' article) begins:—

 '*When I was young* (really *young!*),' etc.

In the first line Mr. Winn is ogling the reader in brackets: but this is part of that 'consciousness' that is the object of our research, and as such is *de rigueur*: these are the only two cuttings I have of Mr. Winn's, but there is no question but that, had I a dozen, each would begin: 'If I had come of age,' or 'Alas for Youth, how shall I ever "pop the question"?' or 'I should like just to stay nineteen,' or simply, 'I am very, very young.'

'At that age' (i.e. when *really* young), says Mr. Winn, 'one was so oppressed by authority. It was always 'You must not do this, you must not do that.' My parents seemed for ever saying in the voice only parents possess, 'Remember you are still only a schoolboy.'

As if I didn't realize that already! As if it didn't make me . . . loathe school, regarding it as a prison, full of discipline, fixed hours, do's and don't's in profusion. No freedom . . . no liberty to make up one's mind for oneself.'

The reason that I have chosen Mr. Winn as the first exhibit will now perhaps be plain. In the highest degree he provides us with, side by side, the 'Latchkey' *motif* (the pouting, bridling, feminine Infantilism) *and* with the political-revolutionary romanticism that caused him to star his text with such words as (see above) LIBERTY, FREEDOM, DISCIPLINE, PRISON, AUTHORITY.

In the purest form you get here the revolutionary romanticism *à la* Rousseau, of the most old-fashioned type (old-fashioned in the sense that nothing might have happened since Brumaire or the Bastille to enlighten and to teach mankind, or to bring a touch of scepticism into the mouthing of these old catchwords—*Down with Discipline!* or *Freedom for Ever!*

I will not insult the splendid 'Youths' of the new militant sects in Germany by comparing them with such a 'Youth' as our Mr. Winn: but I will recall to the reader that, in place of the ogling of the 'Sissie' or 'Latchkey' order, which accompanies the 'Youth Movement' as run by the Popular Press in this country (the refrain of which invariably is 'Oh, I want to be free!' or 'I do so hate discipline!'), in place of that the german 'Youth' has abruptly turned his back upon childish things: he is, in fact, just as inclined to seize upon the masculine prerogatives, as is our Mr. Winn (who may well be for us a symbol) to insist upon the feminine prerogatives.

'Weg mit dem Weiben!' exclaim the 'Youth' of Germany—*Out of the way with Women!*—when our Mr. Winn is wishing he had a sister to assist him to 'win a wife,' as he puts it.

In dealing with such material as these pronouncements of Mr. Winn, of course, to point out that in adult life for the majority of people there are 'Fixed hours' of work, 'discipline,' do's and don't's in profusion, that would only confuse the issue. Such points will have occurred to you, no doubt, but I have not put this text under your nose for you to do that with it. The text of Mr. Winn has to be accepted *tel quel*—and very grateful the student of these things should be to have a Mr. Winn to assist him, without arguing with him.

'I am of age,' exclaims Mr. Winn again. And he tells us 'I make a living for myself—I manage to exist on my earnings.' He is 'independent.' And yet, for some strange reason, Mr. Winn has not got a LATCHKEY! There are a lot of 'cold-blooded devils' somewhere who prevent him from 'dancing all night'—who *will* not let him 'motor away beneath the fading stars to see the dawn emerge, rosy-tipped.' He cannot do those things, because although 'independent' and existing 'on his earnings,' he is not allowed 'a Latchkey.' One gathers that these 'cold-blooded devils' must be Mr. Winn's parents. But, if he is 'of age,' and if he 'earns his own living,' why does he not leave the parental roof, and take a flat?- -I know that all this is inexplicable: but do not for that reason conclude that Mr. Winn is not worth your notice. Mr. Winn is a member of a new profession—or a new branch of the journalistic profession—he 'earns his living' by being a 'Youth.' And if what he writes is inconsequent and con-tradictory, that is nothing, for most hack-work is that. The 'Youth' hack is not going to take more trouble than other hacks over his routine articles. It would be as absurd to pick them to pieces. On the contrary, they must be left quite intact, and taken very seriously indeed as human documents.

The Child-Parent-War was in full swing in Russia when Dostoievski wrote *The Brothers Karamasov*—a conscious, carefully-fomented, 'generation-conscious' campaign of the Children against the Male Parent, that is to say. *The Brothers Karamasov* is, of course, the great epic of that revolutionary conflict.

The break-up of the Aryan Family has been the objective of all Revolution in Europe for a century. The *Child-Parent War* is always merely another phase of the *Age-war* —the former coming first in time, and first in importance. It is essential not to be taken in by the triviality of all the class-conscious, generational invective—all the 'Latch-keys,' Dancings-all-night, and so forth. Mr. Winn is a much more serious person, with a much more respectable function, than the simpleton would suppose. With such a phenomenon as is Mr. Winn, if you went in fact to the heart of the matter, you are in the presence of a salaried revolu-tionary agent, just as much as with any other herd-agitator.

The function of the revolutionary agent is to stir up trouble and set some population by the ears, by the time-honoured means of arousing the envy and hatred of everybody for everybody else. But such work as Mr. Winn's is directed to similar ends—within the family circle, instead of outside, in the streets. The facetious and gossipy technique of *Youngergenerationconsciousness* is merely a mask for something not at all 'young' or especially attractive (not more than other political gadgets): it is the form in which, in Anglo-saxony, a revolutionary purpose is bound to clothe itself. You may say that that gives Mr. Winn too sinister an air altogether, and that in fact he is merely a money-maker, who has been up-and-coming enough to perceive that by saying with an arch lisp, over and over again, 'I am just of Age!' he can put money in his pocket. But it is not so much a question of what Mr. Winn feels about it, or how much Mr. Winn is able to gauge the true sources of his prosperity: it is the why and wherefore of this particular portent, and the nature of the political interests whose ends are served by the spectacle of Mr. Winn, that we are attempting to lay bare.

Now Mr. Waugh is not a Mr. Winn. Only as a journalist (in a quite separate capacity from that of the author of *Decline and Fall*) he does a bit of agitation of the same order as Mr. Winn—to turn an honest penny doubtless, too. Yet Mr. Waugh makes too good a 'class'-warrior, and plays his 'Youth' trumps with too much unction and delighted bluff, not to be a bit of a born revolutionary agent, and not to be perhaps a little *too* like Mr. Winn, as well.

I need only quote from his 'Matter-of-fact Mothers of the New Age' (*Evening Standard*, April 8, 1929) to show you how this must be, and what a confirmed 'class'-warrior he is—and how his particular sort of Western Marxism causes him to community-sing in chorus with Mr. Winn.

'The Attitude of Mind of the Younger Generation' was the subject of a former article of Mr. Waugh's—in response to which it seems whole Brigades of red-faced Old Colonels wrote threatening letters—with minatory gestures of great horsewhips in the direction of his naughty *Younger-generationconscious* b.t.m. And then, he says, as regards this 'younger generation,' whose views he voices, 'Loyalty to one's own age is the only really significant loyalty remaining to us.'

So the 'Mysticism of Youth' provides a kind of *temporal* substitute for the old *geographical* one of 'England, Home, and Beauty.' 'Youth,' in Mr. Waugh's view, is in fact a sort of *temporal Fatherland.* All merely racial aggregates have become shadowy and meaningless. There is no *esprit de corps* left in our civilization, because there is no *corps* left —a corpse if you like, but no living body. The only reality is a chronological reality. Time is Waugh's god. The 'philosophy of Time,' as I have called it elsewhere, is here revealed in full dogmatic operation.

An Elizabethan (upon this partisan chronologic ground) would shoot at sight (or run through with his sword), as a mortal enemy, a Victorian. They would be *Time-foes,* as it were. The fact that they were both Englishmen would mean nothing at all beside this all-important *temporal* fact. This is, of course, the chronological dogma *in excelsis.*

Similarly a Father and his child, or a Mother and her child, of necessity they are enemies—Time-foes: the child only owes allegiance, and 'loyalty,' to other Children. The fact that his Parent and himself inherit the same traditions, belong to the same race, are the closest blood-relations, is immaterial to a properly *generation-conscious* Child. Time is the great fact for the Time-philosopher.

I have exposed this 'chronological' dogma enough in other essays, and need not again, in these pages, state its pros and cons. I will content myself with referring the reader to *Time and Western Man* (pp. 218 etc. and pp. 434 etc.). And with that I must leave Messrs. Winn and Waugh —those militant 'Youths' engaged in a crusade not dissimilar to that of the Suffragette. Indeed their movement is so like the Suffragist Movement, that some months ago 'a young man in full evening dress' introduced himself at speech-time into the Guildhall while a banquet was in progress (the Prince of Wales was, I believe, the guest of honour), and having, unremarked, tied himself to a chair, he began vociferating 'Will you hear me! I am only Twenty-One! Will you listen to me or won't you! I am only Twenty-One!' until he was untied and removed from the banqueting hall and taken away to the Infirmary. Apparently all he was heard to shout was that—just that he was 'Only Twenty-One.' A weak-minded victim, it must be supposed, of the propaganda of the Winns and Waughs!

## CHAPTER VII

# THREE SCORE AND TEN

A S a 'Youth' agitator Mr. Evelyn Waugh is eclipsed by his brother, Mr. Alec Waugh. That there is, after all, something pathologic in the former's excursions into Youth-politics is proved by the record of the latter—it runs in the family, in fact. For while the gifted author of *Decline and Fall* was still in the nursery, his far less intelligent brother was busy with Youth-politics—he was writing his *Loom of Youth*, to start with, and since that time Mr. Alec Waugh has never looked back—or it would be more correct to say, he has never looked forward. That gentleman's obsession with the game of cricket, love's young dream, the romantic sensualism of big schoolboys and little schoolboys, the naked Public-schoolboy in his after-football tub, canings and birchings, 'prep.,' chapel, balls of twine, inky fingers, slate-pencils, pipeclay, bread and butter and jam, is surely phenomenal. It must indicate some warping of the adult mind—this clinging to cricket!

Were Mr. Alec Waugh (as I believe he is not) the offspring of some enriched cornish tin-miner, or galician fur-hawking emigrant, or sweated East-End tailor, who with a colossal effort had thrust himself up out of the dark Mine or the grim Ghetto—then such a fascinated fixation upon the well-washed, football-and-cricketing, spartan-aristocratic training of the Young Briton would be accounted for, and of course excused. For it would be by means of those processes (that preliminary purgation and lustration) that the transformation from a socially *lower* form of life into a socially *higher* would have been effected. As it is, the psycho-analyst would look elsewhere, I suppose. And indeed *Infantilism* is quite prevalent, even with those born in the purple, at this moment. The Girl-Guide and Boy-Scout movements are a natural outlet for such instincts. Under these circumstances it is small wonder, perhaps, that such extraordinary behaviour should be fairly common.

The truth about Mr. Alec Waugh was, I think, very well brought out in a review in *The New Statesman* (Sept. 21, 1929) dealing with his book *Three Score and Ten*. I will quote some passages from it :—

*Three Score and Ten*. By Alec Waugh. Chapman & Hall. 7s. 6d.

It is surprising how much of an air of immaturity seems to cling to everything that Mr. Alec Waugh does. At the age of seventeen he was, for his years, astonishingly mature. *The Loom of Youth* was not a great book, but in many ways, and especially in consistency of execution, it would have done credit to a very much older practitioner. As time has gone on, and as he has followed that with six other novels, his soundness of execution has been increased, but he has not shown any corresponding advance in thought or feeling or in the comprehension of the minds of others. One is still arrested at intervals in all his books by the conviction that this is what a clever schoolboy imagines the minds of grown-up persons to be.

He rather encouraged this conception of him by a manifest inability to drag himself away for long from the life of the public-school, and by seeming always more at home there than in any other life. This story opens with Hilary Cardew going to Fernhurst, and though the story of his school career is compressed into some forty-odd pages, it contains all the familiar incidents which Mr. Waugh seems incapable of casting out of his mind. Hilary, to be sure, leaves school, goes round the world, becomes a barrister and marries. But the inevitable result of his marriage is that on page 143 we find his son Godfrey going to school, and that for some fifty-odd pages more another school-boy is in the foreground of the picture. The book ends with the christening of Godfrey's son, and no doubt if it had gone on longer we should have reached the expression of Mr. Waugh's belief that public-school life will be the same fifteen years hence as it was fifteen years ago (he evidently believes, and perhaps with better reason), that it did not change much between the 'eighties and the years immediately preceding the war.

The subject of the book, its central thought (for it has one), is that, as the generations go on, fathers will continue to concentrate all their hopes on sons and will continue, no matter how much they desire the opposite, to come into conflict with them:

'He's a cute kid,' said Godfrey, 'he looks like a baby, not like a wizened old man. My word, but it gives one a feeling of responsibility! I wonder what he's going to become? I hope he will do something decent. It won't be my fault if he doesn't.'

In silence Hilary listened. There it was—the old talk again. The father losing interest in himself, centering his ambitions on his son. Just as he refused to take silk so that life should be safer for Godfrey, here was Godfrey abandoning his political beliefs, going to the papers he had sworn not to go to, playing for safety. And, whatever happened, the outcome would be the same. There would be the first years of happy intimacy; then there would be the drifting apart, the misunderstandings, the bitterness, and ultimately, consolingly, indifference.

But immediately after Hilary has made these reflections, certain words of gratitude to him fall from Godfrey, and 'they seemed to give a meaning to everything he had ever done.'

I do not deny that this theme has possibilities, but I do assert that Mr. Waugh's treatment of them is disappointingly *jejune*. And I would also venture to suggest that he has approached, and missed, a theme which would have given scope to his talents. He might have written to the proposition that the prevalent theory that the main duty of each succeeding generation is to produce and rear another is stultifying of all that is best in mankind and unworthy of creative masculine intelligences.

Hilary, in Mr. Waugh's book, ends as a failure, as a second-rate barrister who has never dared to take silk, with no achievements of any sort to his name, simply because he was not strong enough and had not a broad view enough of life to take the bringing-up of his son in his stride. A man full of intelligence and full appetite for living would regard this duty as only one, even if a main one, in a career which should have many interests. It would have been better for both Hilary and Godfrey if Hilary could have done this. It is no great fun for a son to be the apple of his father's eye, not a very good preparation for his own individual existence.

Mr. Alec Waugh's 'manifest inability to drag himself away for long from the life of the public-school,' and his always seeming 'more at home there than in any other life,' is matched by an abnormal sensitiveness to the age-relationship, and a tendency to explain everything in life according to a *chronological foot-rule*, as it were—or a twenty-four-year tape-measure.

There is little question, in fact, that had Mr. Alec Waugh been born a little later he would have been an even more active agent of 'chronologic' revolutionism, and been more prominent in 'Youth-politics,' than his brother. But he has done his bit indirectly, as it is, in a series of increasingly depressing magazine-story novels. He deserves some attention from the student of 'Youth-politics.' A little more hair on his head, and he might have found himself leading a group of insurgent 'Children.' As it is, he is a sympathetic young uncle, and no doubt incites his far more talented relative to the erection of 'class' barricades.

I will now turn to the text of Mr. Waugh.

I do not believe that any one dipping into *Three Score and Ten* would fail to detect a something rather odd at once. The characters Mr. Waugh creates are feminized, as it were, to an obsessional extent. On page one a small boy is going to school, and, as might be expected, his brother is warning him against homosexuality. But we are then given a reassuring picture of our hero—the most homosexual prefect would be baffled by our little Hilary. He (the elder brother) 'need not have been concerned!' we are told; for 'Hilary was a stocky urchin and a grubby one. His hair was invariably unbrushed. His collar was rarely clean. He could reduce any tie within a week to the condition of a piece of string. His clothes were dusty. His pockets were bulged out of shape with letters, knives, chestnuts, compasses. There was nothing feminine about him.'

Mr. Waugh must have the soul of a nannie more or less—for he can go on like this for pages. Indeed, if I had to say what I thought of the strange case of Mr. Alec Waugh, I should say that all the feminine, maternal attributes were excessively developed in him, and of course (Mr. Waugh being a man) were thwarted. They relieve themselves, no doubt, by means of these incessant literary compositions about small boys with sooty faces and bulging pockets. One feels that the outlet is critically necessary.

But it is when you get to the grown-up characters that the book becomes really peculiar. For there you find the same manias reappearing.

Mr. Cardew (the father of the small boy described above) is as crazy about small boys as is Mr. Waugh himself—and this must have something to do with the fact that Mr. Waugh is his creator. But here is how Mr. Waugh describes him (pp. 12-13) :—

> On Monday mornings he (Mr. Cardew) was invariably in the dining-room long before the post had arrived. He could not settle down to his reading of the paper till he had received and read Hilary's Sunday letter. When he reached his chambers his clerk would never fail to ask news of Hilary.
> 'Did you hear from Master Hilary this morning, sir?'
> 'Yes, I heard from him, Smith; I heard.'
> 'And how is he doing, sir?'
> 'Very well, Smith, thank you, very well. He was first this week.'
> 'Again, sir?'
> 'Six times in the last eight.'
> And at lunch in his club it was only with the exercise of the greatest self-control that Mr. Cardew restrained himself from beginning each conversation with the announcement, 'My boy was top of his form again this week.'
> When Hilary returned at Christmas with two prizes and a report of general eulogy culminating in the headmaster's testimony that it would have been impossible to have had a better first term, 'the report was copied and despatched to a godfather, three aunts, two uncles and the headmaster of his preparatory school. Hilary received a Christmas present

of three pounds, and was taken to five theatres. It was generally conceded that he was on the brink of a career of exceptional brilliance.

If Mr. Alec Waugh does *not* play marbles at home it can only be, one feels, 'with the exercise of the greatest self-control.' I do not wish to be offensive to Mr. Waugh, but I think it is fair to say that there is something of an obsessional nature at work; and I do think that psycho-analysis would reveal the fact that *motherhood* in its most opulent form was what Mr. Waugh had been destined for by nature, and that a cruel fate had in some way interfered, and so unhappily he became a man.

## CHAPTER VIII

# 'SICK OF ALL THESE GROWN-UPS'

THAT the author of *The Loom of Youth* was 'at the age of seventeen ... astonishingly mature' I can well believe. And that suggests a very interesting point about *youngergenerationconsciousness*. If you are conscious of being a schoolboy, and as it were fanatically *schoolboyish*, that does seem entirely to cancel or inhibit those very qualities about which you are making such an unusual fuss. The *fuss* again suggests rather the sentimental yearning of the aged for a distant Youth, than the contempt for Youth, and the envy for the adult life, of the normal child.

Once more one is reminded of the consciousness of the *outsider*—of some one not native and to the manner born, but in some way upstart. What somewhere else I said about the value one would expect an ancient racial organism like the hindu or the jewish to attach to youngness and freshness as such—to fall in love, a little painfully, with the angelic choir-boy youthfulness of the English, after the fashion of the roman bishop ('angels—not English'), while at the same time despising it—again one is reminded of such a situation as that to-day. For of course all 'Youth-politics' are not nothing but politics: there enters into it some strain of congenital predilection and appetite, and often something pathologic, too. Especially is this the case in our relaxing, maudlin, Western atmospheres. In Germany or Italy the 'Youth-politician' is masculine.

To be 'astonishingly mature,' again, almost fatally results afterwards, in the adult life, in a prolongation of adolescence, rather than a normal 'growing-up'—for the 'growing-up' having been virtually achieved in boyhood, there is no more growing up to be done.

As regards the question of 'precocity,' I will quote a couple of paragraphs intended to prove the correct *childishness* of the child to-day. What, in fact, I think it demonstrates is the reverse.

*'Sick of all these Grown-ups.'*

The modern schoolboy is not half so precocious as he is made out to be.

Often it is the fault of the parents, who force him to mix with his elders and to behave and live as they do.

They imagine that they are being indulgent parents, but in reality the boy would often be more content with simpler pleasures.

I once talked to a small Etonian at a large dinner-party. He told me that he came down to dinner every night.

'And do you really enjoy it?' I asked him.

'No,' he said. 'I get sick of all these grown-ups. I'd far rather be upstairs eating biscuits and milk in my dressing-gown.

*His Idea of a 'Binge.'*

Two nights ago I had on my hands a fifteen-year-old boy, on his way back to school, out for a 'binge' in London on his last night.

I asked him what was his idea of the perfect 'Binge.'

'I'd like,' he said, 'to go to a "thriller," then to go and drink a cocktail, and then to walk about the streets and see life.'

And he chose to spend yesterday at a museum in the morning and bathing at the R.A.C. in the afternoon.

I don't think you need worry that the coming generation is being spoilt or becoming over-sophisticated in its ideas.

The Etonian who visualized himself in his dressing-gown 'eating biscuits and milk' sounds to me on the Waughish side. A ring of *youngergenerationconsciousness* in the eton-collared syllables, if they are correctly transcribed, is to be detected. And 'Grown-ups' are so often saying that children do not like being with them but prefer creatures of their own size and age, that children do increasingly *say* what the Etonian said, as a mere matter of imitation.

## CHAPTER IX

# PRECOCITY, AND EUROPEAN
# BACKWARDNESS

IF it is a recognized theory or not, or only a personal one, I do not know: but I have heard it asserted that the famous 'Worship of Youth' of the Hellene was the result of the hellenic preoccupation with Death. Is not this a mere paradox, though? I mention the theory for what it is worth. Their sunlit youthfulness, and the extraordinary value they attached to male adolescent life, was, so the theory runs, in order to escape from the obsessing notion of our animal destiny, and the horror at the idea of mortal demise. 'Man is mortal. Socrates is a man, therefore Socrates is mortal'—even their syllogisms, I suppose it would be said, are preoccupied with mortality.

The egyptian fixed idea of demise, and the stern and hieratic images they set up to give expression to it, may perhaps be accounted for, on the other hand, by saying that the Egyptian desired to check and discipline the irrelevant pretensions of what is too fleeting and over-transitory, and therefore meaningless: the natural gaiety of the egyptian nature may have been such that some such measures were found imperative to damp it down. Whereas the Hellenes may have brought with them a cloud of gloom from the home of their origin, in the subarctic mists and snows. This would have been on the same principle as the dour puritanism of the Anglo-saxon—which, so their french neighbours contended, was necessary to check and discipline the violent egoism and brutal covetousness of their natures. There, at all events, are a group of paradoxes. Is it advisable to discard the picture of the 'gay light-hearted masters of the waves,' in favour of that of a frantically anxious, pathologically *Youth-conscious* civilization? It sounds to me like a facile freudian interpretation. It is the sort of interpretation you would get if the painful and uneasy, 'extraordinarily precocious,' *Youngergeneration-consciousness* of to-day were imposed upon the hellenic lay figure of history—whose accommodating 'repose' has invited so much speculative tailoring, of theorist after theorist.

The only one of the peoples of the Ancient World who is with us to tell the tale, and to offer himself as a living model for our curiosity, is the Jew. But the judaized Tartars have mingled so much with the Hittite-cum-Arab patriarchs that the contemporary Jew shows many contradictions. Thus in the jewish moralist we recognize our old friends of the Old Testament. But in the great jewish artists, in paint and stone, we see the Tartar peeping through, I think. And astonishing artists, technically, they are.

That the Jew, according to the standards of european masculinity—if put beside a Viking or the typical warlike types of Gaul or of Germany—is feminine—that is clear enough. The women tend to be mannish, and the men emotional and nervous, according to those germanic standards—of strong and silent, dominant manhood, and of weak, subservient (for preference not intelligent) womanhood. And, as Schopenhauer long ago pointed out, there is a great deal of the child in the woman, in the nature of things—since the woman is accustomed and intended to live with children all the time.

The jewish home, again, is certainly a place where the child can never have been told that it was expected to be 'seen but not heard.' The 'hard northern nature' has never made so much of its offspring, or regarded indeed marriage as a matter of vast religious significance—with that oppressive obligation to go on selflessly procreating, and bringing forth 'seed.' All this must be taken into account

—especially when, as is so often the case, we hear about the 'childish' strain in the jewish nature. That need not surprise us, in spite of the ancientness of the race. Indeed, that very racial longevity could scarcely have been compassed without a cultivation of all that was primitive, immature, and emotional in the human being.

As Mr. Hannen Swaffer points out in an interesting article (*Britannia and Eve*, Feb. 1931), we owe to this 'childishness' of the jewish nature much that is admirable and much that is the reverse. 'If there were no Jews there would be no theatre,' Mr. Swaffer writes. 'They are its patrons; they are its parasites. They endow it; they bleed it. They are in the forefront of its most daring experimentalism. Yet, at the other end, they have commercialized it even more than the Gentiles try to do . . . the Jews have given us most of our worst revues.'

And the sub-headlines of his article are as follows:—

> 'Somewhere in every Jew there is concealed a child—a child with eyes of wonder, with eyes of curiosity, and with eyes of hope. This child is always waiting for the curtain to go up.'

That child is, of course, always waiting for the curtain to go up *upon him* (in the middle of the stage), and small blame to that child: and we can neglect the note of lyrical insincerity in this account by Mr. Swaffer—it is, to begin with, rather an insult to the Jew. But we can, I think, agree, from personal observation, that a 'Child'—an optimistic, adventurous, and undampable creature of some sort—is concealed in even the most mournful of old Jews. And that

may be the physiological secret of the race—the secret
its longevity, as was remarked above. Call it a second—
a third—Childhood, if you like: but there it is—it is
essential sly buoyancy, beneath a traditional mask
oppressive gloom. And in fairness to the Jew it must
said that if they have 'given us our worst revues,' that
Public gets the revue it deserves, and that, if the maste
showmen had thought that the Public would pay for *bett*
revues, then he would have been better pleased to give
good revues than bad revues, for on the whole he is mo
artistic than we are.

Albert Einstein can throw some light upon the obscu
corner of the universe we are examining, oddly enoug
But I am bound to say that what I am about to quo
seems to me to have far more to do with Mr. S. J. Woolf, th
interviewer in this instance, than with Einstein. Einstei
is not only in fact a dignified figure, but also a charmin
one : and what Mr. Woolf describes is what is tradition
surely in the households of most professors (althoug
usually at a more advanced age than Einstein). Still, M
S. J. Woolf thinks that Einstein, his co-religionist, is '
Child,' so let us give a piece of his article for what it
worth:—

# Einstein, the Child-like Master, who is Mothered by His Wife.

It was Mrs. Einstein who greeted me. A sweet, lovable
motherly woman, whose attitude towards her distinguishe

husband is that of a doting parent towards a precocious child.

There was the sound of bare feet on the floor, and holding a black and white bathrobe about him, apparently oblivious of his surroundings, Einstein himself entered . . . about his entire manner there is a repressed and malleable quality that is almost childlike, and this is accentuated by his wife's attitude towards him.

As he stood there saying he would be ready in a few minutes, it was easy to understand why his home showed so little of his personality.  It is doubtful if he even knows what is in it. . . .  Patting him on the back, his wife told him to get dressed, and as he left the room, with a smile she said: ' He is terribly hard to manage.'

### Mother-like Care.

In a few minutes he returned.  His brown suit needed pressing, and on his feet he wore, over wool socks, a pair of open-work sandals.  His coat collar was half turned up at the back, and as we started to go upstairs, Mrs. Einstein went over to him, fixed his collar and arranged his hair, much as a mother sending her boy to school.

We came to the top floor. . . . I was in his study. . . . Before I had arranged my materials he had taken from his pockets some scraps of paper on which there were figures, and also a black fountain pen, and as if he were absolutely alone he began jotting down notes.  As far as he was concerned I was not there. . . . As I left I asked him what he considered the formula for success in life.  He smiled, that same awkward bashful smile.

That is the description of a graceful and diffident scholar —one who happens to have set the world by the ears with a great revolutionary theory.  But, if only for the sake of Mr. S. J. Woolf's interpretation, it was worth quoting.

Before leaving this subject of *precocity* in general, and especially as displayed in an ancient and exceptionally gifted race, it may be interesting to quote the following account from *The Observer* (April 28, 1929) relative to a typical jewish 'infant prodigy'—namely Jehudi Menuhin. Here are the main facts of the article:—

# A VIOLIN PRODIGY

## THE STRANGE CASE OF JEHUDI MENUHIN

## BABY AT A CONCERT

## PARENTAL PROBLEMS

*(From Our Own Correspondent)*

BERLIN, *April* 21, 1929.

A new genius has been hailed by a unanimous German verdict in the person of Jehudi Menuhin, who was aged twelve years last January.

The events which have led up to this estimate read like a fairy tale. A still very young and modest man relates how he and his wife, struggling students at San Francisco, wrapped their baby in a big shawl one Sunday afternoon, with an extra large bottle of milk, in hopes that he would keep quiet during a concert. There was nobody to leave him with at home, and they could afford no help. The father himself cannot play a note, and his wife very little, but they both loved music. Writers of romances are shamed and students of heredity bewildered by the result of that concert. The infant Jehudi, age fourteen months, discarded his shawl and ignored his bottle, sitting bolt upright on his mother's knee, watching the orchestra. It was conducted by Mr. Louis Persinger, who is well remembered in Europe as Kapellmeister under Nikisch.

At the age of three, Jehudi Menuhin, a persistent attendant of those San Francisco Sunday afternoon concerts, demanded a violin like Mr. Persinger's. His parents did not dream of spending their hard-earned money on anything of the kind. They bought a toy fiddle instead, which squeaked horribly and was immediately smashed by its new owner. It was a kindly grandmother who scraped together the dollars for a real first-size violin.

*Einstein's Congratulations.*

Jehudi was then four years old. Within two years Mr. Persinger declared him to be miraculous. The rest of the world is now discovering the same thing. At twelve this small fair-haired and still chubby boy has, so his severest critics say, 'nothing more to learn.'

It is Dresden which has set the seal on hopes already wakened in Berlin. Jehudi Menuhin's playing of the three great violin concertos, of the three great B's, was the challenge to German critics, and invasion of their own ground. After his rendering on one and the same evening of the Bach, Beethoven, and Brahms Concertos with the Berlin Philharmonic Orchestra, under Bruno Walter, it was Einstein himself who came up and said, with tears in his eyes, 'My dear little boy, it is many years since I have had the privilege of receiving a lesson such as you have taught me to-night. . . .' To add to their burden, there is evidence of more talent in their family. Hephzibah, aged eight, chubby, dimpled, and bobbed-haired—the children look oddly German—displays gifts for the piano which are being carefully restrained. 'We keep her back,' says the father firmly. 'We do all we can to promote games and healthy exercise. Our other little girl has the same craving to play.' . . . A parallel to Jehudi's favourite literature must be sought in the real-life story of the young Brontës devouring political articles. He reads all the 'Liberal' periodicals his father will let him have; he is an ardent champion of the oppressed. He has never owned a penny of his own as pocket money, but he asks for money to give away! He is fond of mathematics and good at languages. He does not like the cinema, but he loves Charlie Chaplin in person. He is a perfectly healthy little boy, with a fondness for his dinner and a passion for ice-cream sodas. . . . Pressed to explain him, if they can, the parents believe that the religious fervour of his grandfather, a rabbi of the strict Chassidic sect (his parents went to San Francisco from Palestine), may have been transmuted into musical genius in this, his descendant.

The following point is an extremely important one to bear in mind. *What we, in Europe, call an 'Infant Prodigy' is a perfectly normal thing in the East.* In a civilization older than ours, and in a climate in which the human fruit ripens quicker, a talent of any kind does not have to wait for twenty, or for thirty years, even, to realize itself. Like Jehudi Menuhin, it sits up and takes notice at the age of fourteen months. At the age of three it is clamouring for the necessary materials with which to express itself. At twelve it is a mature master.

What I am arguing here all along is that *Youngergenerationconsciousness*, or 'Youth-politics' in general, is, among other things, a movement in the West to *hurry up* and bring to fruit sooner (with a great saving of economically wasteful years) the prolonged european childhood. This inevitably must result (in the case of the average man-in-the-street— the employee whose only excuse for existing, from the point of view of the great employer, is his freshness) in a radical *shortening* of human life.

What we can, and must indeed, say *against* this tendency is that not only traditionally, but climatically, the European may be unsuited to this *old-master-at-twelve* programme. Further, it may quite well be that a gradually, and extremely prolonged, development does, in the few exceptional cases (of men of genius—rather than 'infant prodigies'—for all infants tend to be mildly 'prodigies' or at least 'promising'), result in a higher type of man. I do not say this is so, but I do not think that we can entirely rule it out as a possibility. If, as with me, those *exceptional natures* are the only ones that appear to you important, then you will not dismiss this with too rapid and comprehensive a shrug of the shoulder.

## CHAPTER X

# PROMISE' HAS BECOME AN INSTITUTION. IN THE FUTURE STATE EVERY ONE WILL, AS A MATTER OF COURSE, POSSESS 'GREAT PROMISE'

YESTERDAY in the 'Popular Press' it was 'Sex-War' articles — to-day it is Age-War articles. 'Youth' propaganda has succeeded to Feminist propaganda. And these two movements are very closely related to each other.

The relationship, indeed, is that of Mother and Child. First, the Mother broke away from the Father. Next, the Child broke away from the Father. That is the order. The male, the Father, is in all these revolutions, *the enemy*. It is he that has been cast to represent *authority*. Therefore in modern revolutionary Europe it was he, the male head-of-the-family, who has been aimed at in every insurrection. The break-up of the Family—the Family as conceived in the traditional system of the Aryan World—must begin and end with the eclipse of the Father-principle.

Whatever form of 'Youth-politics' you take, it is essentially an attack upon the 'Father' principle. It is also of necessity an exaltation of the feminine principle. The sex-cleavage comes first. The age-cleavage comes next. We are at present in the midst of that.

Now, under the old dispensation the son (the male child) was usually preparing to become a 'Father' himself. As soon as the hairs began to sprout upon his chin he began to prepare for 'manhood.' And 'manhood,' what is that, in a general way, but fatherhood? To be regarded as a 'mother's boy' did not please him any too well. He was hostile to all the feminine values. His was the masculine outlook. That was the old dispensation.

But in the revolutionary femino-'Youth-politics' directed against the Family, all that is changed. No adolescent male to-day is over-anxious to become a 'Father' in his turn—he understands too well how very arduous and uncomfortable that position may be. (Uneasy is the head that wears a crown—also the chin that sprouts a beard, and the sombre grown-up who has the misfortune to be called Daddy.) Nor does 'manhood,' for that matter, offer any overpowering inducements to speed up the rate of growth. He is not in any great hurry to grow up at all. Hence the widespread Peter-panism. The adolescent is not especially prone to-day to look forward to being a full-fledged *male*. To be an Adult Male is to be in danger of being a Father. And to be a Father is to have all the engines of revolutionary wrath and envy (of 'Youth'-propaganda and feminist propaganda) directed against your breast. So far better (so sagely reflects the budding Male) stop where he is as long as that is at all feasible. Far better to remain a *bud* as long as may be. And that is only common sense.

But it is not difficult to foresee what this state of mind must result in. An emasculation of the adolescent male must perforce ensue. He adopts the attitude of the mother-principle towards the adult and responsible male, or Father. He ceases even to admit to himself the notion of becoming that hated thing himself. In the present state of the world he knows in any case that his future is extremely problematic, beset with hardships and uncertainties, with no 'get rich quick' left for any one much, with Big Business encouraging less and less the individualist virtues. Hence nothing but 'young,' indeed super-young, values are admitted into his consciousness, and, in the end, he must even become unadapted to accommodate any others.

All that there is left for the average man is, to put it

frankly, *to be young.* 'The only loyalty left,' says Mr. Waugh, 'is generational *esprit de corps.*' But it is perfectly obvious that Mr. Waugh, when he is no longer a 'Youth,' will not be overburdened with 'loyalty' for all that is *old.* Hence he could with perfect truth have added that there is *nothing else at all*—except a 'generation-consciousness' of the absolutely Young. In its simplest terms, 'There is only Youth!'

But the farther he shrinks from that male-adult goal— with all its terrible handicaps in a revolutionary—feminist and feminized—world, the more the male adolescent of to-day must tend to approximate to some sort of Child. The sort of Child will be one of almost adult size (though for preference *not too big*—rather of the feminine than the masculine stature—also a virgin, of course, and not a mother-of-men), a Child of 'extraordinary precocity.' A precocious, full-sized, but not too big, child.

Under these circumstances the 'infant prodigy' (a Jehudi Menuhin) is not so far removed actually from what is aimed at. And, of course, it is generally accepted that such 'prodigies' never develop—what they achieve as 'prodigies' is in most cases all that ever need be expected of them. Their existence *terminates*—or their effective life termin-ates—when they attain an age at which people no longer are able to regard them as 'marvels'—as 'marvellous boys.' As soon as they become fully adult the game is up. So, naturally, the longer they can remain *Children* the better for them. And that is, of course, what they as far as possible do.

It is not necessary to point out how, regarded from that standpoint, the 'infant prodigy' has a great deal of bearing upon *the shortening of human life*—one of the things in the forefront of the programme of the 'Youth-politician.'

But supposing *every one* became, to some extent, 'infant prodigies'! However mildly 'marvellous' if *all* boys had *some* sort of pretension to being, each in his sphere, very mildly and modestly, a 'marvel ' : or if not quite a 'marvel,' then at least 'precocious' and 'gifted'! But with a race like the hindu or the jewish, the percentage of such 'infant prodigies' is very high. The most spectacular with the jewish people are the musical 'infant prodigies' of course. With any asiatic race or race possessing an ancient and continuous culture at all, this precocity or tendency to be what we call 'prodigies' would, I suppose, be the rule. But obviously if this principle could be extended considerably, if people were not too particular about the quality, or intensity, of the boyish 'marvel,' the development and organization of such precocity would tend to telescope life. And to telescope and curtail human life is one of the ends conspicuously in view.

Life beyond twenty-one is—in the old terminology—*major*: life before twenty-one is *minor*. In such a super-precocious world of mildly 'marvellous' Youthfulness—with every possibility of self-expression exhausted at twenty-one—the 'minor' would be the person *after* twenty-one, the major the person before twenty-one. It is only jejune and raw races like ours—the germanic, northern, european races—who would find it difficult to conform to these standards. Other, more mature, races, find it difficult (on the contrary) *not* to do so, if anything. Such a race as the hindu, or the jewish, would find no difficulty at all. They could easily bring back what we call 'middle-age' to twenty-one or twenty-five. And this will be the constant tendency of the future. 'Mother India,' of course, was all about this *precocity* of the Hindu ; and, with a super-european fatuity, indicted the entire hindu system upon the ground that that system made people *start life too soon*.

As a matter of fact, in a very watered-down or embryonic form, something resembling this asiatic precocity exists already in Europe. An advance-specimen of our future civilization is provided by the 'young man of promise.'

Ever since the world began people have naturally specu-
lated as to whether perhaps a child was not going to grow
up to be a very 'great man'—a 'great statesman,' a 'great
soldier,' or a 'great artist.'  And of course every mother has
dreamed those dreams;  and every one has always said to
every mother that they were persuaded that her little
Tommy was 'very promising' indeed, and has not hesitated
to predict 'a marvellous future' for him.

But to-day the 'young man of promise,' or the 'young
woman of promise,' notion has assumed a much more
organized form, and developed into something much more
conscious and elaborate.  It is no longer merely the light-
hearted wagging of avuncular heads.  It has got out of the
stage of easy compliments into that of practical politics.
'Promise' has become an '*institution*,' as it were.  And that
has led to some very significant results.

*CHAPTER XI*

# NOTHING ENVIABLE MUST BE POSSESSED *IN EXCESS.* BRAINS ARE AS WICKED TO THE FANATICAL COMMUNIST AS MONEY

THAT 'promise' should have become *an institution* is natural enough. For in a time when all *privilege* is taboo, it is inevitable that 'promise' (the state of being 'promising' and destined to 'greatness') should become common property. To be 'promising' is no longer, therefore, the privilege of the few—of those, namely, who are really promising. No—*Everybody* is 'promising.'

The old easy-going democracy of Europe is turning rapidly into a much more fanatical, highly-energized democracy—namely communism, or something approaching communism. And as it does so, it puts taboos more and more upon the 'aristocracy of intellect' and its natural privileges, as much as it does upon other (to the man-in-the-street more obvious) examples of merely social privilege. And it is here that a danger lies for the human race: it is a tendency of any form of communism, which has to be modified for all our sakes.

'Genius' is one of the most envied things in the world. To be a 'genius' is almost as much an object of common desire as to be rich.

But people are very stupid, even, about being rich—they mean by 'rich' usually something very different from what in fact to be rich is, as has been pointed out in an earlier chapter. Money is power. And marxist attacks upon money are not attacks upon a lot of bank-notes or metal tokens, but upon *power.* But 'genius,' that is also *power.*

And in a perfectly 'communized' state a 'man of genius' would be as great a monstrosity as a king. This dangerous dilemma has to be recognized and provided against.

The 'man of genius' in a communist state would of course hide his 'genius' as far as possible. It would be as important to do that as for a man with a ten-pound note in his pocket not to let on that he had a sum of that sort about him if he had to pass the night in a wood in the company of a band of vagrants.

The majority of people have their mind firmly fixed upon the concrete fact of *money*. Power, being abstract, is not seen by them, except fitfully. So it is difficult for them to see that if communism is (as we know it to be) a highly organized, semi-religious movement to deprive the *individual* of anything he possesses *in excess*, that it is not only *money* that he must not possess in excess. He must possess nothing enviable in excess. Brains *in excess* would be as bad as money *in excess*.

In fine, it is THE INDIVIDUAL, and his *individuality*, in whatever shape or form, that is marked down for extinction. And what is 'genius,' after all, but an excess of individuality? And what is an excess of individuality but an excess of power? And is not *power* substantially the same thing as money?

## CHAPTER XII

# THE STANDPOINT OF GENIUS

AFTER this elaborate analysis of 'genius,' it will not be difficult to see how it comes about that 'promise' should become in some sort (or should tend to become) *an institution* with us.

But first, there is one point that I may emphasize here and now. It is this: *The standpoint of 'genius'* must be a very rare thing: there can be few writers who write from that standpoint—most have a quite different standpoint—mostly their interests are not, in the nature of things, identical with those of 'genius.' Now I admit that I am writing here from *the standpoint of 'genius.'* But if (*a*) I am doing that without myself possessing the qualities popularly conveyed by that epithet, and hence *against* my personal interest, then that is very altruistic of me, and I should be applauded in consequence: or if I am doing that (*b*) possessing myself those qualities, and in consequence defending them, then that must be such a relatively rare event that, again, it should be well received, or at least accepted as the expression of a point of view too little considered.

## CHAPTER XIII

# 'PROMISE' AS AN INSTITUTION

IN our jargon there are two things—there is 'greatness,' as we call it, and there is 'promise.' 'Promise' obviously means that *some day* So-and-So will be 'very great' or just 'great.' But how long can 'promise' last? How long is it possible—in politics, literature, or whatever the field happens to be—to *do* nothing, but just go on 'promising,' and promoting the belief that if one were not so 'young' one would be very 'great'? *That it is certain* that, the moment that one ceases to be 'very young,' one will become upon the spot 'very great'?

The answer to that question will depend upon a variety of things. But there is one thing that is quite certain, and that is that a great number of people, long after they have ceased to be in any significant sense 'young,' go on calling themselves young and inducing other people to do so—either through cajolery, fellow-feeling, or sheer hypnotism—without being in the least discomforted by the fact that 'greatness' has not supervened with the passage of years. In fact, they often seem disposed to argue that, as they are clearly not yet 'great,' then they must obviously still be 'young,' since one or other of those things they *must* be, in order to *be* at all!

But, it may be objected, the habit of *encouragement* involved in the epithet 'promising,' although it may cause many people to pass themselves off for a while as something they are not, may nevertheless result in that rare bird, authentic 'genius,' getting the encouragement that it needs in those early critical years. In practice, however, that advantage is cancelled by the fact that (1) a swarming of pseudo-young-geniuses obscures the real young-genius; and (2) the universal *lowering of standards all round*

involved in the adjusting of this starry and superlative term
to fit a thousand and one aspirants is so destructive of all
those values upon which, in the nature of things, all 'genius'
depends, that the harm done far outweighs the good.

The art of advertisement, after the american manner, has
introduced into all our life such a lavish use of superlatives,
that no standard of value whatever is intact. And the
word 'genius' of our popular jargon has now become as
cheap as dirt, of course, commandeered for the productions
of not even a respectable second-rateness, but in the service
of the dullest extremity of vulgar nothingness, in order to
cause that great gull, the Public, to *buy, buy, buy!* Hence
there is no difficulty whatever in appropriating this term,
and any other that confers distinction upon everybody—
just as *everybody*, in a truly democratic state, might be
presented with the Legion of Honour, or the Order of Merit,
upon attaining the age of ten. And, of course, sometimes the
distinction may be merited. But to suppose that those superlative qualities for which such superlative distinctions were
invented can possibly benefit by this wholesale bestowal of
accolades, would, I am afraid, be naïf and groundless.

But there is something that is more important still.
When a bluff is pushed too far, even the very simple cease
to be taken in. And in the present case that point has been
reached. No one any longer, *in fact*, believes that the
world is swarming with embryo-'geniuses.' They accept
the formula. They do lip-service to the 'promise.' But
they have come to recognize that there is usually nothing
beyond the 'promise.'

The whole idea of 'fulfilment,' however, is alien to our
time. The Time-god of Professor Alexander, or of Bergson,
'a god-in-the-making,' does, upon the philosophic plane,
represent what people have in the mass come to feel about
all achievement.

Hence, gradually, every one is accommodating themselves to the view—or, better, to the *feeling*—that there is
*only* 'promise.' There is only immaturity. There is *only*
a desire, but, in fact, no consummation. They still speak
of 'promise,' in consequence, in a state of half-belief: they
respond to the word automatically; but it is at bottom *as
if* there were beyond something perfect and unassailable—
no more than that.

One reason for this attitude is the obsessing model of
natural science. With the spectacle of the physicist, ad-
vancing hypothesis after hypothesis, which one after the
other he tears up and begins again, it is natural to get into
the way of regarding personal values, too, as impermanent,
and to look upon the artist's work, or the religious or political belief, as fluid in the extreme. Yet of course we know
that, in fact, the human values possess a permanence for us
that the hypothetical machinery of the technique of the
physicist does not possess. Homer and Shakespeare remain
a human limit, and such persons are few and far between.

How 'Youth-politics' operate upon, and are responsible
for, this 'in-the-making' state of mind—which erects
'promise' into a sort of God—I have shown. The 'Youth-
politics' assert that to be young is to 'promise'; and the
Time-philosopher, who converts into philosophical theory
the politics of the masters of the material situation, he
asserts that 'to promise' is in fact 'to be.' If there were
also a religionist who was at the beck of this same political
Zeitgeist (Zeitgeist being the term we employ to indicate
whoever it may be possessing the political power and
wealth necessary to compel us to believe and do what he
wants, and so make of our 'Time' whatever he desires it
to be), then that religionist would set up the Great God
Flux in some form or other. And we should bow the knee
—however, murmuring (just one or two), 'Still it does *not*
move!'

## CHAPTER XIV

# THE ' GENTLEMAN ' AND THE ' GENIUS.'

**E**VERYMAN a 'gentleman'—that was the outstanding achievement of anglo-saxon democracy in the last century—or Everybody a 'lady.' We have *char-lady* as a typical monument to this Big Push. And I have the honour of the acquaintance of a certain 'Charlady' who, when she refers to the place of employment of one of the people she chars for, always says—'He works at Mr. Barker's.' By this I have discovered that she means *John Barker's*, the super-store in High Street, Kensington.

But *Everyman a 'genius,'* that may well be the outstanding achievement of the present century. That will only be democratic justice. It is intolerable that nature should so flout and run counter to man's high policies—especially to his crowning achievement in the political line, Western Democracy—as to endow an infinitesimal proportion of all our 'teeming millions' with some superlative gift! These aristocratic tendencies on the part of nature must be dealt with, and that promptly! Why, who can tell—nature may even be *a royalist*! There is absolutely *nothing* that nature may not be, in the matter of oppressiveness and favouritism!

Have you ever heard the expression 'Nature's Gentleman'? There is a disgusting expression if you like! Yes, there nature is seen at it again—*as usual* flying in the teeth of mankind (who has the right to make and remake 'gentlemen' surely). Going aside, nature simply ignores all rule and precedent, and goes and makes a 'gentleman' of her own! Ah, *ça c'est trop fort!* That is rich!—as our bewigged ancestors would have exclaimed.

And if mankind decided that *all* men should be gentlemen (as long ago, indeed, mankind has decided), there would be that preposterous nature again putting her spoke in as usual, and remaking, or never endorsing, or *deliberately withholding the requisite qualities from* all the billions of 'gentlemen' mankind had decreed should exist!

So doubtless it will be with *genius*! Man proposes, nature disposes—and it is not difficult to foresee that there will be a great deal of trouble—there is all the material for a first-class battle ahead between man and nature. For 'genius' is even more important than 'gentleman' in nature's economies: and intellect is a more ticklish matter than quarterings. Nature is bound to 'secure the decision.' She may put it into the head of some 'genius' to invent a new political theory, or she may smite with sudden imbecility all the phalanxes of upstart talent, or she may simply afflict with a bubonic plague of Black Boredom all those concerned—the myriad Stars upon the stage and the yawning audience alike.

## CHAPTER XV

# THE 'GROUP' *VERSUS* THE 'INDIVIDUAL'

AN integral part of 'Youth-politics' is 'the Group.' In politics, in art, and every sort of activity, you have the thing we have come to call 'the Group.' (I am especially competent, as it happens, to explain this curious feature of our world in process of communization, having belonged to a number of 'groups' myself.)

The word 'Group' dates from the period of post-Revolution ferment in Nineteenth-Century France. In painting there was, for instance, the 'Impressionist Group.' And ever since that time there have been, everywhere in Europe, 'Groups.'

A 'Group' is, of course, a small rebel 'cell' in the heart of the orthodox mass. A small number of people put their heads together and say that they will propagate theories diametrically opposed to the herd around them, and they (more or less officially) found a 'group.' (In politics to-day a new 'group' recently came into existence, for instance—the 'Mosley Group.')

In the present treatise, the only sort of 'group' we need consider is the 'Youth' group. How that works is as follows, in the case mainly of the literary or art 'group.' All 'Youths'—though all 'promising,' and all 'geniuses' more or less—are not all, unfortunately, very go-ahead. There are many very backward 'Youths.' Then, in point of fact, the average 'Youth' is still not so anxious (as things stand at present) to advertise himself as a 'Youth' until he is no longer a 'Youth.' And a characteristic of most post-war 'Youth' groups, it must be confessed, has been that most of its members have been a bit long in the tooth if considered in relation to the real article.

A desperate spasm of ambition seems to set in at about thirty or thirty-five—thirty-five is a more dangerous age than thirty from this point of view: and a little clot of bald-headed, wall-eyed 'Youths' get together and form themselves into a 'Youth-movement.' If a genuine 'Youth' of twenty tries to get into their 'group' (having heard that there is a 'Youth-movement' on foot, and desiring to pass into circulation a poem or two or a bit of fiction) he does not meet with so much encouragement as he might legitimately have expected.

However, having got the 'Group' under way, the assembled 'Youth'-cell announces that it will give the Public 'Youth's' view (the very authentic standpoint of the most 'advanced' and youthfulest 'Youth'!) of everything and everybody. And the dear old Public chuckles as it reads these burning words, and thinks to itself, 'Ah, these young devils! What little iconoclasts the little monkeys are, to be sure! But there you are—boys will be boys!'

But at this point it is necessary to discriminate a little. It must be insisted upon that this sort of chuckling, Aunt or Uncle-of-the-Children's-Hour, Public, is, above all, the anglo-saxon public. With such a Public the technique is very different to what it would be with, say, the german public—which is very much better educated, tougher-minded, less feminized, and also less romantic, in a chuckling, woolly-headed way, about all that is *rebel*.

Yes, there are more *Revolutionary Simpletons* to the square inch in Anglo-saxony (England or America) than there are to the square inch in the german Reich. The *nursery values* (of the anglo-saxon Peter Pan Nursery) propagated by means of the most vulgar and gaga Press-technique to be found anywhere in the world, has done its work in Great Britain. The Public is now little better than a droning Aunt (smiling and dozing beneath her earphones) —that I suppose we have to admit.

'Youth-politics' are in the nature of things revolutionary-politics: and any 'group' advertising itself (more or less directly or by implication) in its prospectuses as a 'Youth-group' is vowed to a dashing and conventionally 'subversive' policy. (In America there could be no such thing as a 'Youth-group' that was not 'radical,' as there it is called.)

So we arrive at another characteristic of the 'Youth-group' as it exists in Anglo-saxony to-day. I know of no militant, professional 'Youth' to-day in England (whether of fifteen or fifty) who is not militantly 'radical.' And the solitary and unique way of being 'radical' that the Anglo-saxon has (or instead of being energetic at all) is to be communist: Communist, more or less, he must perforce be —for there is no other organization in sight. In France or Germany and, of course, Italy, and in all the smaller countries of the north and centre of Europe, there *is* an alternative to communism (though not always a particularly intelligent one). And it is an alternative road that, to-day, the greater number of the active young men have taken. But in England or America there are only these two things: (1) the *status quo* (namely, just not ever to think politically at all), or else (2) Russian Communism (*i.e.* Marxism).

Now there is no 'Youth-group' in existence in England to-day the majority of whose numbers are not *communizing* if not communist. There is nothing necessarily wrong in that, only it does mean that it colours all their attitude very strongly towards the Individual. For Communism, or Marxism, whether right or wrong, is unquestionably the most fanatical anti-individualist creed that has ever seen the light.

But the very idea of 'the Group' is an essentially *communist* notion—in the literal sense of 'communism.' It is (ideally) a disciplined unit, a band of people *sharing* the same views, *pooling* their resources and interests, recognizing each other as peers and equals, fighting for 'the common cause,' and so on.

I am not against 'Group'-making—any more than I consider 'Youth-politics' a bad thing—the reader, I trust, will
have grasped that fact. It depends, for me (as no doubt for
everybody—unless the whole idea of 'Youth-politics' or
of 'group' technique is abhorrent to them) what ideas pre-
side at the formation of the 'group,' and in what cause
'Youth' is to be mobilized.

Myself I happen to be an individual (not, however, an
'individualist'): and as such I am not a 'group' person.
That goes almost without saying. But a communizing,
pseudo-'Youth' Group—and there are one or two such in
London at present—*that* does seem to me an abortion of a
'Group': for (as indeed happens) they will be prone to
attack and attempt to discredit every value that is not an
anti-individualist value. Further, they will of necessity
attack every value that is not a strictly political (*i.e.* strictly
utilitarian) value. This policy they will describe as a
'criticism' of 'intellectualism.' To any individual who does
not care to participate in their sly, bastard christianity—
their antagonism to every value that postulates an *excess*
of personality above the normal communist quota—their
plans, and their crooked recipes, for enabling the average
man (brushed up to a bright cunning and equipped with an
intellectualist training to enable him to 'fight' the Intellect
—in the good old *class-war* of the low-brow *versus* the high-
brow) for assuring him success at the expense of his more
gifted neighbour—*no one* not adhering to all this wretched
chicanery and plotting to abolish that *excess* of life we call
'genius'—he will be called an 'intellectual' on the spot—
and a communist class-war will be declared upon *him*!

So here you see what I should regard as the *bad* 'group.'
And it is usually more 'youthful' in name than in anything
else—as 'Youth' it is generally bogus, as policy it is anti-
mankind. If you wished to think out a reform for that sort
of 'group-making,' I should say that the first step would be

to have 'groups' of authentic young men of twenty or less:
and second, abolish the obsession of anti-individualist
values.  If you do not, what must result is this.  Imagine
Jehudi Menuhin (to take a handy figure who has appeared
upon our stage), imagine the 'infant prodigy,' no longer an
'infant' but a disillusioned adult—past his infantile prime.
Imagine him combining (since there is strength in numbers)
with other ex-infant-prodigies and ex-'youths.'  What
would the policy of this Menuhin-'group' be?  It would be
much the same as the policy of the sort of anglo-saxon
'groups' I have been describing—who are not even so
anglo-saxon as all that—one that I know of contains three
Welshmen, three Jews, a Swede, and a Cornish gypsy, who
boasts that he is the bastard of a turkish Rabbi and no
'Creeping Saxon' at all.

But I think that I have said enough to reveal the danger
to 'genius' (and, as I have said, I am writing *From the
standpoint of genius*) that must reside in a too fanatically
communizing, bogus (literally or politically) 'Youth-group.'
And I have shown, too, how the very notion of the 'group'
must be suspect, unless it is integrated on behalf of mankind, and not against mankind—on behalf of exceptional
talents, and not in order to enable a small herd of talented
persons to masquerade as 'geniuses,' under the wing of
some Zeitgeist.

The radical curtailment of human life, which is part of
the unavowed programme of the 'Youth-politicians' responsible for the propaganda in the West, is based upon an
attitude that is too definitely anti-mankind.  It is too personal.  And to limit 'genius' to a class (or a Party) and to
forbid the possession of personality (or of its highest expression, 'genius') to any one outside the class, or Party, in
question, that is too anti-social a principle to be admitted
—at all events at present.

# PART III

## THE ' DOSSIER '

WE will come back now, once more, to our 'dossier.' It is a great pity that the format of this book precludes anything in the shape of a facsimile reproduction of my exhibits. Further, there is the difficulty of obtaining permission for literal transcription of entire articles, with the accompanying photographs and so forth. The best I can do is to show, in as large a type as may be, the Headlines, and then give beneath them typical extracts.

As in the OVER-TWENTY-FIVE *Evening News* cutting, the first batch I will assemble will be the ordinary routine stuff of the perpetual propaganda for the class-war of 'Young and Old.' These are the paragraphs and articles of the *pro-and-con* approach. First a 'Youth' is selected, and he is commissioned to say what he thinks of (*a*) the 'Old Gang' (this means the leaders of all the political parties to-day in England), or (*b*) 'Men over Forty,' of 'My Elders,' or 'The Last Generation,' or 'just Middle-age.' After that there is a brisk correspondence in the correspondence column of the newspaper. Those 'attacked' are supposed to answer, heatedly, and with much fist-shaking. These letters are signed:

> '40—*but still going strong !*
> *Twickenham.*'

or　　'*FIFTY Last Week.*
> *Are we down-hearted ?　No !*
> *Crouch End.*'

or　　'*Forty and Proud of it.*
> *East Lynn.*'

Many of such letters are, it is legitimate to suspect, composed in the offices of the newspaper. The same expert

'letter-writer' who is responsible for the letter signed
'*Forty—but still going strong*' in the Wednesday issue,
would also be entrusted probably with the post-haste
response of Thursday's date, signed:

> '*Nineteen and nine months.*
> *Linlithgow.*'

or          '*Only a Kid.*
> *The Isle of Man.*'

To show how widely the paper is read, the towns chosen
would generally be—when London addresses are not used—a
considerable distance apart.  The idea is, of course, to suggest
that all Cornwall Over Forty is in a ferment, and all Argyll-
shire Under Twenty-One is arming for the fray, and that there
will soon be a Massacre of the Innocents, or a Saint Bartholo-
mew, for the Time-sect of the communion of the Aged.

In the following exhibits, I have not attempted to intro-
duce any particular order into those chosen.  Attack and
Counter-attack—Cry of Triumph and Snarl of Hate—
Porty and Gouty Grumble, and Curly-headed, Milk-and-
Biscuit, pasquinade—are not put down in pairs.  One
reason for that is that I do not always possess *a pair*—I
only own one of one pair and one of another, and they do
not always fit, or afford the correct contrast.

Among my exhibits the conventional *Scolding* article is
not included.  That is the article 'denouncing Modern
Youth': they are all the same.  The real, or imaginary,
'Old 'Un,' in a gruff porty voice, admonishes 'the Younger
Generation' for their 'spinelessness'—for 'the Cocktail
Habit'—for 'lack of manners,' and so forth.  That article
we can take for granted.  Hundreds of thousands of such
have been concocted in the last ten years in England alone.

I will number this batch of exhibits: and at the end I
will provide a comment, with the reference number of the
exhibit attached.

# EXHIBITS

Numbered—1 to 39

From *Sunday Graphic*                    *Exhibit No.* 1

# OPEN THE DOOR TO YOUTH

### Let's Stop This Perpetual Girding at the Lubbardliness of the Young Man! The Impertinence of Age

*By SIR JOHN FOSTER FRASER*

Youth is beginning to find us out . . . so let us stop this perpetual girding at the lubbardliness of the young men of to-day. Let them adventure. Let them bring forth their ideas, asinine though many of them may be. Stop this dole coddling of our artisan youth, so they have no need to get in and make good or go under. You will not see the motto, 'I will either find a way or make one,' over the doors of many fellows who can draw twelve bob a week as dole.

Our staple industries are shaky because they are run by prematurely defunct men, who think they are progressive when they are mentally muscle-bound. The successful businesses of to-day, motor-making, for example, are in the hands of young men. Imagination is more valuable than experience. And pay men according to their worth and not according to their years of service.

I've so often heard nice old gentlemen tell eager young fellows what is wrong with them that I'm looking forward, one of these days, to hearing a chisel-faced youngster address a meeting of septuagenarian limpets with a vast experience: 'Now I'll tell you exactly why Britain has not been holding its own. It's because such as you——' and so on.

Anyway, Youth is once more knocking at the door, and if there is no swift answer that door will be kicked in. Better open it.

From *Sunday Graphic*, June 9, 1929　　　　*Exhibit No. 2*

---

# THE NEW DULL YOUNG MAN

———◆———

## Bad Manners of 1929 and Bolshevism in the Drawing Room.　An Uncensored Opinion

———

### By COSMO HAMILTON (*the Novelist*)

---

Between her hard, dry sobs she (the modern hostess) said that one of the young men who had graciously consented to decorate the proceedings the previous night had invented a new pastime of which he seemed quite proud.

Overwhelmed with boredom or feeling whimsical, he had withdrawn from the mob, dragged himself wearily up the famous staircase and prowled about the house until he had come with a glow of triumph to the room in which Mrs. Midas dreams of social conquests and marriages of her daughters to the sons of dukes.

Into this he locked himself and spent an entranced and curious hour placing all her frocks and stockings, underwear and furs, hats, gloves, shoes, hair-brushes, tooth-brushes, scent-bottles, and face creams, in a most elaborate pattern on the floor.　Whereupon, exhausted by this brain-work, he had gone forth into the night.

---

From *Arts and Crafts*, June 1929　　　　*Exhibit No. 3*

---

It is hoped the first of an important series of articles will appear in the July issue of *Arts and Crafts*.　Under the title *Scrutinies* it is proposed that some of the younger critics examine the work of older living painters in relation to contemporary aesthetics.　The first of a series of articles by Mr. W. J. Clement and Mr. Frederick W. Carter, dealing with contemporary French industrial art, will also appear in that issue.

From *Sunday Graphic*, Nov. 23, 1930          *Exhibit No. 4*

# STRANGLING THE YOUNG IDEA

### By SIR BRUCE BRUCE-PORTER

I am of opinion that the curse of England to-day is the paralysing hand of old age which is strangling the efforts of the young and enthusiastic in many walks of life.

It applies to almost every profession and trade. The older men insist on their views being dominant, with the result that the young men of spirit and enterprise become disgusted and despondent. . . . it is quite impossible for the old men to possess a real appreciation of the conditions of the immediate present and the very near past.

## TIRED OUT.

We hear a great deal about the value of experience, but this is a matter of degree and much of it is fallacious. I wonder how many men lie buried in Flanders because older men in command could not realize that the lessons and experience of the South African campaign were not applicable to trench-warfare in Flanders?

We know only too well that new ideas are not readily accepted by the generation in which they are introduced, but by one which grows up with them; and to this fact may be attributed the loss of success which has recently been so obvious in many departments of life.

.          .          .          .          .          .

## AN AGE-LIMIT NEEDED.

. . . There is an age-limit for the officials in practically every State department (an earlier one for those who do not attain certain ranks), but no age-limit for the men who control the whole show! . . .

There should be an age-limit for Members of Parliament; say twenty-five to fifty-five—and, as the principle of payment of members has been accepted, and the amount paid to various Ministers and Under-Secretaries is not small, a reduction in the number of M.P.'s should secure a livelihood for those who wish and are fit to enter the profession of politics.

---

From *The Evening News*, May 22, 1929        *Exhibit No. 5*

---

*A Great Law Lord writes an*

# OPEN LETTER
## TO TO-DAY'S
# YOUNG MEN

*My friends,*

I am almost an octogenarian.  You naturally ask me how I dare write this letter to you.  Well, I make free to say that it is the old, like myself, who feel with you far more and understand you far better than do the mere grown-ups.

When I was but a child, a big great-sounding word to me was Sebastopol.  You are the children both of a time of War and of its aftermath.  Perils by land and sea, the upheaval and the downfall of States, new shocks and new wonders in history and in science—amidst all this you were born and brought up.

You are our only hope for the future; and your enfranchisement draws near.  And yet the mere grown-ups hardly seem to care.

From *The Evening News*, May 23, 1929     *Exhibit No. 6*

---

**LORD CRAIGMYLE,** the great Law Lord, writes an
## OPEN LETTER

## *TO  TO-DAY'S*
# *YOUNG  WOMEN*

> 'You will be surprised to hear me
> say that I trust the young women
> more than the old . . . Society
> waits upon your act and word . . .'

*My friends,*

You may have read what I wrote yesterday to the young
men, and I beg of you not to consider that you were being
neglected even in thought.  For you, too, live in a generation in which the faculties of women have been evoked by
the unspeakable necessities of War and by the emergence of
new ideas not only as to women's rights but women's powers.
I realise, however, that with you the sense of guardianship
and of trusteeship seems to enter your life more naturally
and quickly than in the case of men.

.         .         .         .

In my heart I do not believe that, emotional as many
women are, their judgment on the lines of civil policy will
ever incline them towards armed conflict among the nations
of the world.

But that is high politics, and we must avoid that.

.         .         .         .

So much do I value the enormous social leverage of your
influence for good, that I shall for a moment venture to speak
frankly on another topic.  It is vulgarly known as the cocktail habit, a totally useless propensity induced by affectation and going under the name, in the infatuated woman's
vocabulary, of 'living her own life.'

# *Mr. Van Druten's Play About Parents and Children*

It is in the nature of things that parents should devour their children, and also in the nature of things, I suppose, that the meal should be a slow, contemplative, unhurried one, extending over a period of many years, rather than a rapid gulp and a swallow. . . . In the beginning of the new play the author of *Young Woodley* shows us a young man and a young woman oppressed by their parents.

They are not violently bullied, but mildly nagged and thwarted, and as much of better nature as they have taken advantage of. The father does it with blustering, the mother with tears. . . . A little later the father dies, driven to death, as is half-suggested, by the worry of his children. The mother lives on, and cries more than ever. . . .

Later . . . sister and brother, coming together, look back through mists of sentiment and rose-tinted memory on their childhood's days. The hands of the parents are still strong on them in death. It is suggested that their own children will probably be brought up in the same atmosphere of strictness and subordination. . . . It is suggested at one time that the son had his chances of artistic eminence knocked out of him by subservience to his family. But Mr. Van Druten cannot really mean this: artistic eminence comes out anyhow.

The people in the play are amazingly life-like to suburban life.

From *Everyman*, Sept. 5, 1929    *Exhibit No.* 8

# OLD FORMS OR NEW?
## By MAX PLOWMAN

*This week we print a contribution by a poet to our series on 'A Religion for the Young.' A selection from the correspondence received on the subject will be found on page 141.*

.    .    .    .    .    .

Do *young* people need a religion? Personally I am not so sure. I know that middle-aged and old people are destitute without one; but the best young people I know have not grown to the need, though it will come to them all in good time. If living religion is the fruit of experience, what has it to do with young people who have yet to gain the experience out of which to form a vital religion? Let us apply the question to even wider issues. Is not the whole of Western civilization suffering from the weight and burden of traditional dogma that has oppressed religion into forms which are now actually deterrents to the understanding and practice of true religion? This church and chapel stuff and all these rites and ceremonies are like sedan chairs being piously carried along the Great North Road.

Because Shakespeare has understood life more fully than I, because he has given expression to his understanding to a degree I shall never even attempt to emulate, must all literature stop at Shakespeare? Must I for ever be attempting to live in the reign of Queen Elizabeth? Must all literature ape the manners and conform to the customs of his age? And is religion a thing of less living growth than literature? Because religious experience has found expression in the past in forms whose beauty and expressiveness call forth our admiration, are we to accept these forms as the permanent expressions of religious faith and cast our experiences into these ancient moulds? Or are we to trust to the power of religious experience continually to be making fresh forms which shall be expressive of the truth in the day and generation that brought them into being?

From *Sunday Graphic*, March 15, 1931          *Exhibit No. 9*

# WHY YOUTH IS RESTLESS

## By SIR JOHN FOSTER FRASER

Whenever a bunch of parsons get together in conference they raise their eyes and wail 'Woe, woe; we are living in a terribly degraded age!' Instead of hymns of praise they sound perpetual pibrochs. Which seems strange because most parsons, individually, are cheerful, have an understanding of life, and are therefore charitable.

The annual Assembly of the National Council of Evangelical Free Churches, held last week at a jolly seaside place with bracing breezes, Weston-super-Mare, was composed of worthy men. They were, however, restless over the restlessness of the new generation. Youth is in a very, very bad way.

Without being impertinent, I suggest to these nice-conditioned ministers of religion, and other lecturers of budding manhood, that next year they debate how far they themselves—complacently confident that they have got hold of the right end of the stick in belief, faith and conduct—are responsible for the bad way into which youth has declined?

We lambaste our heads of industry for the wretched state into which trade has fallen: why shouldn't our spiritual leaders do a little personal scourging for their failure to keep us from falling from grace?

There is much that is wrong that needs righting; but as an ordinary sinner I cannot help noticing that while these parsons blame the Press, cinemas, novels, dance halls, and whatnot for our laxity, they apparently rarely ever put the question: 'But are we doing our own job in the winning way?'

From *The Evening News*       *Exhibit No.* 10

## 'PSHAW!'

*To the Editor of* 'The Evening News.'

May I congratulate you on the leading article 'PSHAW!' It was the finest attempt to show a blind England the real George Bernard Shaw that has ever appeared in a British newspaper. Would that it could be written in letters of fire against a darkening sky as a warning to those who believe Shaw to be a god instead of a foolish old man who was once famous and clever!—*Arthur Groom,* 404b, *Richmond-road, East Twickenham.*

From *A Daily Newspaper*       *Exhibit No.* 11

# MEN of 40 years and over

**Do You Suffer:—**

**FOOT AND LEG PAINS**
**BLADDER TROUBLE**
**BACKACHE**
**FREQUENT URINATION**
**LOSS OF VITALITY**
**NERVOUSNESS**
**SLEEPLESSNESS**

*THESE ARE SIGNS OF PROSTATE DISORDER*

## Learn the Truth about the Vital Prostate
### Get this Free Book NOW

Two out of three men, past a certain middle age, suffer with prostate gland trouble, say many medical scientists. If you are troubled with any of the symptoms mentioned above, you should send at once for our Free Book, 'Why Many Men Are Old At 40,' which describes a new method of drugless gland stimulation that has already proved a blessing to thousands of men. Send at once for this Free book to Electro Thermal Company (Dept. 5931), 130, Regent Street, London, W.1.

From *The Daily Sketch*                    *Exhibit No.* 12

---

# LEAGUERS ABROAD

### Recruit of 60 From Far-off Zululand

Not only are the four corners of Great Britain and Ireland already represented in the membership of the *Daily Sketch* League of Youth, but applications to join and messages of goodwill are being received from all parts of the world.

Latest recruits include Patrick Daly (24), from Saskatchewan, who seeks to become a Leaguer and mentions that he 'sure enjoys' the *Daily Sketch* and that it 'sure tickles these Canadian people I work for, so here's luck and success to your League.'

Yesterday also a bright young man named Charles Vejarano (16) sent a 10-franc note for his membership book and badge from St. Jean-de-Luz, France, while another young man from Oporto, in Portugal, also joined up.

Even Turkey must be represented in our League. Not only did Captain James G. Peters send from Galata, Istanbul, Turkey, his shilling entry fee, but also an additional 10s. 6d. for the 'Good Deeds' Fund.

But one of the most interesting recruits to the Senior Section yesterday was W. A. J. Burt, who is 60. He looks after planters' accounts and income-tax returns at Empangeri, in Zululand, South Africa.

### 'As a Kid of 60'

'Without any intention to flatter,' writes Mr. Burt to the Editor, 'it appears to me that the brains and initiative of

he daily illustrated press are concentrated in the offices of
he *Daily Sketch.*

'The League of Youth is an inspiration. May I, as a
*:id of 60,* be permitted to join the Senior Section—that is
f the extension of the League beyond the British Isles is
:ontemplated; if not, the "bob" can go to the Good Deeds
'und.'

Let them all come. Have you joined yet? There is a
Junior Section for all up to 15 and a Senior Section for all
over 15. Many valuable free privileges are available to
members. Join to-day. Membership form on page 15.

From *Sunday Express,* Jan. 18, 1931       *Exhibit No.* 13

By WILLIAM GERHARDI, the brilliant young novelist

# *What I Think Of The Men I Know*

### The Old, Old Story

It has been said that there is to-day no outstanding young
man under forty in literature. But this was said before—
and will be said again. For if there is no outstanding man
in literature under forty it is because, in literature, a man
does not properly stand out till he is past forty, when,
ceasing to be 'promising,' he becomes 'outstanding' on the
strength of work done at the age of twenty and thirty.

Mr. Bennett might go on to-day writing books as good as
*Riceyman Steps* only to be reproached indefinitely with *The
Old Wives' Tale.* And though *Riceyman Steps* is certainly
just as good as the much earlier *Old Wives' Tale* he cannot
hope to get the credit for it in his lifetime.

On the contrary, all fastidious critics will sigh for the
'young Bennett,' for that *Old Wives' Tale* apparently not
good enough to have procured Mr. Bennett before he was
forty the position he has attained at sixty. By inviting

unfavourable comparison with *The Old Wives' Tale, Riceyman Steps* establishes him in old age as a master novelist in his prime.

And in the same way Mr. Wells will have *Mr. Polly* thrown at him till he dies—though he may write a dozen *Mr. Blettsworthys* and *Christina Albertas*. D. H. Lawrence had his *Sons and Lovers* chucked at him till he died—as Mr. Aldous Huxley, when he is eighty, will only hear of *Crome Yellow*, and I of *Futility* by the time I am ninety.

After the death of an artist the position is reversed, and it is the latest works which are deemed subtle, difficult, profound, incomprehensible, while the early works become the 'Rienzis' and 'Lohengrins'—schoolboy fare!

Already so it is with Lawrence, who has not been dead nine months. . . .

Aldous Huxley is not bad; but diluted, over-intellectualised, not really creative or original—a younger kind of Galsworthy.

I have been driven—not unwillingly—to the conclusion that Hugh Kingsmill and myself, through sheer abundance and concentration of talent, must eventually, when Wells and Bennett are dead, have the field of serious fiction pretty well to ourselves.

From *Sunday Express*, Jan. 21, 1931     *Exhibit No.* 14

---

# *What I Think of . . .*
# THE YOUNG
# MEN I KNOW

### *By*
### *ETHEL MANNIN*

ETHEL MANNIN *is a young woman whose works have aroused acrimonious controversy. Her 'Confessions' at the age of thirty, which were published last year, were attacked violently.*

*In this article she points the accusing finger at most of our young novelists, and says fearlessly the things which she feels ought to be said.*

A lot of us are getting very tired of these conceited young men of to-day. There are such a lot of them . . .

And all the distinguished men of letters who have not acclaimed their genius they 'put in their place.' Thus we get young Mr. Evelyn Waugh pitching into his elders and betters, having no end of quiet fun, and getting paid for it into the bargain; and young Gerhardi declaring that Aldous Huxley is 'not bad,' patronising Hugh Walpole and Somerset Maugham, and linking up *Futility*, his own pretentious little 'novel on Russian themes,' with that tremendous work, *Sons and Lovers*. Not that Lawrence would have minded. . . .

*       *       *

### 'A Lovely Person'

. . . Beverley Nichols is one of the few talented young men of to-day who can truthfully be described as 'a lovely person.' Now there, I should say, is a young man who really *has* a streak of genius in him. I have a greater admiration and liking for Beverley Nichols than for any of my male contemporaries in the literary and artistic world. . . .

### Van Druten

John Van Druten I have met only once, and then had no opportunity of talking to him. If first impressions of a person one has not had opportunity of talking to count for anything, I should say that he is perhaps a little conceited; but if that really is so, it is a conceit alleviated by a sense of humour. I like his amused eyes, and freely forgive him for saying in his review of my book *Crescendo* that all I had done was to make a dishonest woman of Ethel M. Dell. One would have to forgive the artist who wrote *Young Woodley* anything, I think.

Benn Levy strikes me as a young man with a near-genius

L

that never quite arrives. *This Woman Business* was as
cynical as *Mud and Treacle* and *Mrs. Moonlight* were senti
mental. He is an enigmatic young man, shy and unassum
ing—and elusive. And for some obscure reason he likes his
name pronounced 'Lev-vy.'

Paul Tankeray would be another Cecil Beaton if he were
less sensitive and shy.

.      .      .      .      .      .

Unhesitatingly I place Aldous Huxley as the most im
portant, the greatest intellect, and the most serious artist
of my male contemporaries.

From *The Sunday Graphic*          *Exhibit No. 15*

| | |
|---|---|
| # THE SPINELESS YOUNG PEOPLE | *By the* *MARQUESS OF DONEGALL* |

This will never do! A reader has written and thanked
me, on behalf of the younger generation, for 'putting our
point of view and showing the world.' What I have 'shown
the world' is not quite clear, but I seem to detect a note of
self-satisfied smugness in the letter. As I say, this will
never do, so here goes!

There are many things wrong with us.

Perhaps Professor Einstein has a lot to answer for. By
the time that he has finished telling us that straight lines
are really crooked and that nothing is really as it seems,
one begins to wonder whether we exist at all or whether the
whole thing is a trick of imagination.

'Nobody seems to be certain about anything!' That is
the philosophy with which we leave school. It is reflected
in our everyday lives, and it will go on unless we take ourselves in hand.

# 'THIS PERIOD OF LICENCE'

———◆———

## STRIKING ADDRESS BY DEAN INGE

## LITERATURE DEEPLY CORRUPTED

## SACREDNESS OF FAMILY LIFE

Dean Inge, preaching before the University of Cambridge yesterday, uttered an indictment of 'this period of licence.'

Our imaginative literature was now deeply corrupted; in the new books the element of sex was much more exaggerated than in the romantic movement and degraded to rank sensuality.

'But listen,' said the Dean, 'to the instructions given by an American editor to his authors: "Here's a man and his wife and another man. Write about them and let the shadow of the bed be on every page, but never let the bed appear."'

From *The Evening News*, June 11, 1929     *Exhibit No.* 17

# SIR MAX IS ANSWERED—

**'We Cannot Break Through to Command,' complains Youth—Vain Parents Treat Us as Grown-Ups Too Soon—Talk at the 'Rugger' Club—My Brilliant Friends, by an Oxford Man.**

*To-day again Youth has its fling at Sir Max Pemberton and his opinion of Youth. Sir Max wrote in* The Evening News *of the Inferiority Complex he finds in the modern young man, who, he thinks, lacking ambition, is too ready to say, 'Give me something to do, and I will do it—if you will show me how.'*

*'Thirty years ago,' wrote Sir Max Pemberton, 'they would have been showing us!'*

### '*I am 25*'

Sir Max Pemberton singles out a section and magnifies it into a cosmos. Ambition is the prerogative of the poor. The young man chosen by Sir Max as a specimen possesses a two-seater car, finds time to pen odes and plot plots, and is obviously not compelled to earn his own living.

\*          \*          \*

### '*Sir Max is Right . . .*'

Sir Max Pemberton is undoubtedly right, but is it youth's fault entirely that it lacks ambition? Ambition is in the newly-born babe of to-day in the same degree as it was when our fathers and grandfathers first saw the light; but so long as present-day parents continue to treat their boys and girls as grown-ups and allow them the same freedom and latitude that they themselves enjoy, before they have taught them that they have got to *earn* the right to be treated so, mothers and fathers have only themselves to thank for 'line-of-least-resistance' specimens of youthful humanity.  Youth wants trainers, not critics.

My parents brought me up in the right way.  'You've got to earn your own bread and butter,' they said, 'and that's not always easy.'  I am doing that.  Now I am aiming at the jam to go with it.        ERIC S. HUTCHENCE.

Lindholm, York-road, Woking.

### And What of Middle Age?

We are told by Sir Max Pemberton of the degeneracy of modern youth, but he omits to mention that this charge can always be countered by an attack on Middle Age. Never, so it seems to me, has Middle Age been more slack and spineless, and so full of cheap sentiment.  Golf clubs and dance halls are filled with middle-aged people mad on doing nothing!  They are an incubus upon the country; and it is to them that youth is being sacrificed.

Youth appears indifferent and casual, I think, because it never gets a chance.  Of all the brilliant friends I had at Oxford, most are still struggling.  True, there are Mr. Bernays, who is fighting Rugby, and a few other political successes such as Mr. Malcolm MacDonald and Mr. Edward Marjoribanks.  But most are still bearing the 'hopeless burden' as parsons or schoolmasters, and they will continue to do so till the selfishness and indifference of Middle Age disappears.

You cannot have fire without fuel, and youthful enthusiasm wilts without patronage.  Unfortunately, the sensitiveness of youth covers itself over with an armour of what is taken for indifference.    T. C. STANLEY LITTLE.

Chichele, Parkstone, Dorset.

### That Answer!

Has Sir Max never heard the phrase: '*I* built up this business, my boy, and *I* know how to run it'?

CHAS. H. KINGSTON.

'Myrtle Lodge,' Windsor-road, West Norwood.

*Proud Parents!*

I will tell you, Sir Max, what is wrong with the young men of my generation: we have been ruined by the vanity and stupidity of parents who have educated us beyond our stations in life.    We have been sent to expensive schools so that our good grown-ups could boast of them—with the idea, etc.

From *The Evening News*, June 10, 1929     *Exhibit No.* 18

---

# The 'Come-Back' of Youth

## Pointed Replies to Sir Max Pemberton

THE retort of Youth to Sir Max Pemberton has been tremendous in volume and pointed—sometimes very pointed—in its vehemence.

Sir Max wrote in *The Evening News* an article 'Youth Without Ambition,' in which he vowed that to-day's youth has the Inferiority Complex—that it will say, in taking on a job, not 'I will now show you how to do it' but instead, 'Give me something to do, and show me how'—that the young man nowadays 'does not want leadership at any price.'   Thus Sir Max.

We printed on Saturday one considered reply by a man just down from Oxford.   To-day again we let Youth have its say—as we said we would—in a few out of some hundreds of letters we have received.

### Only a Mask

Let Sir Max consider our position.   Our education came at a time when the world was in an uproar.   Our fathers and elder brothers were in the trenches.   Only the old men remained in their clubs, boasting of the number of grandsons they had 'given' to the War.   We passed our most impressionable years in an atmosphere of confusion and doubt.

Now the growth of large combines has made it more difficult for a young man to get clear of the mob.   Other things being equal, it is obviously ten times as difficult for the youth of to-day to reach the top of a business employing

1000 men as it was for the youth of Sir Max's generation in a business with only 100 employees.

Has Sir Max been deceived by our outward show? Youth to-day does not strike an attitude and say, ' I will be Prime Minister'; nor is it so foolish as to think that in four months it can learn enough about a business to teach one who has been in it forty years. Youth has its own fashions, and the present one is to treat life with a mask of indifference. It may be a foolish fashion—if it gives the onlooker the wrong impression, it certainly is—but Sir Max, as a novelist, should be able to probe beneath the surface.

We have a difficult task. A world smashed by the weakness and foolishness of Old Age has to be repaired; but, in our own way, we are settling down to work. We shall not do it in a night.                                    C. B. JONES.

17 Argyll-mansions, W. 14.


### ——Ambition Without Youth !

The eclipse of young men in business is not due to their own lack of ambition: it is more often due to the ambition of their elders. Business is *cluttered* with old men. There should be a law compelling business men who have (a) reached the age of sixty and (b) garnered-in a reasonable fortune—having, say, an income of £1000—to retire forthwith.

Why *do* elderly men cling to their posts long after their most useful days are past, and in many cases long after they have amassed more money than they need? It is partly because their predecessors did so before them—and so one generation of old men, sticking to the fatter jobs, keeps its successors waiting until they in turn become old, and sometimes ineffective, before they are allowed to take up the reins.

The result is that often the hard work is being done by young men—not boys, but men with brains and enough experience to make decisions and avoid mistakes—while above their heads, in a kind of semi-detached Valhalla, sit the old men of the tribe.

Sometimes, with solemn and studied irony, one of these 'elders and betters' will totter to his feet and deliver a sermon to the 'young men,' will bewail the scarcity of £10,000-a-year men. *There are no £10,000-a-year men because there are no £10,000-a-year jobs open.* When the old man preaches 'industry' he is perfectly sincere: of course he wants the younger men to work hard. But when he preaches initiative, he is usually not so honest: the old brigade distrust initiative in younger men employed by them. They *don't want* a departmental manager, for instance, to get the bit between his teeth and run his own show.

\*          \*          \*

\*          \*          \*

(3) Thirty years ago no Great War had happened, to leave its mark on the impressionable minds of boys who have now become young men, but remember enough to ask themselves, 'Is it worth while my struggling and striving, only to end, perhaps, like that?'

From *The Evening News*, Sept. 30, 1930      *Exhibit No.* 19

---

*Words With the ' Moderns '—I.*

# I  LIKE  THIS NEW  GENERATION!

### By
### ELINOR GLYN

*The Moderns of 1930, particularly the Young of the species, have been criticized and criticized until, we believe, they are tired of it.*

*The series of 'Evening News' articles, of which this is the first, will for a change give them helpful counsel, and some praise, which, we may be sure, will not turn their sensible young heads.*

*Mrs. Elinor Glyn (who has been studying Youth, as such, for a number of years now, since she rather startled the elders with her book 'Three Weeks') especially praises them. She is delighted with the very newest generation, and says so.*

From *The Evening Standard*, May 24, 1930    *Exhibit No.* 20

# *This* TALK *about the* YOUNGER GENERATION

## THEY ARE FUNDAMENTALLY SOUND

*By GUY KENDALL,*    *Headmaster of University College School, Hampstead*

**Criticism of our Modern Youth has received a new impetus from the comments made by Dr. Temple, the Archbishop of York, this week. Here Youth finds a vigorous defender in the headmaster of a well-known London public school.**

Much has been written lately about the Victorian and Georgian parent and their respective progeny. One would almost gather, from the language of some, that Nature, in the last thirty years, had suddenly thrown up some new and monstrous species, one of her ironical freaks, without motive or final object.

It is true that, according to the latest biological theory, some whole species, or at least whole families of plants and animals, do sometimes produce sudden and simultaneous variations, and it is not inconceivable that such a revolutionary change may have taken place in the mentality of the human species. If so, it is not wholly a development of recent years. For the greatest environmental change of late, the change of social conditions which has resulted from the War, was not the beginning of the new outlook on life.

It was observable in this country at the beginning of the century and was already in full blast in the Suffragist movement about 1910. The disillusionment of the Boer War began it. The Great War only brought it on in full flood.

. . . . . .

### Schoolboys and Sex.

In *Young Woodley* we were given a picture of the up-to-date schoolboy and his conversation. Mr. Van Druten (an old pupil of mine) . . . has assured me that the conversation in the 'Prefects' room in his play is true to what he remembers. I do not think it is very different from what was talked at Public Schools in the 'nineties. The schoolboy of that day was less serious about it: and he did not talk about Sex with a large S (*pace* Mr. Van Druten, I doubt if he does now)—rather about sexual things.

. . . . . .

Yes, I believe the younger generation of boys to be thoroughly sound. A good deal of their more spectacular rebelliousness is superficial 'swank' and no more.

From *The Graphic*, Sept. 27, 1930                *Exhibit No. 21*

---

**WE MODERNS—AND AFTER : No. 1**

# YOUTH AT THE WHEEL
## By PHOEBE FENWICK-GAYE

A successful young writer begins a many-sided analysis
of her own generation and of what is likely to succeed it

Being 'exclusive to' this century myself (in the sense that I was born within its limits), perhaps I am prepared to consider whatever pattern it may have with an unbiased mind!

The human mind . . . has a passion for simplification and standardization which expresses itself pathetically in calling certain passages of time 'eras' and 'ages'—almost as if each age and era were a little village on the long road of time, completely cut off from the rest of the world.

.    .    .    .    .    .

It is, indeed, this speeding-up of everything in life which fills some minds with apprehension. 'What do they want to go so fast for?'

Alas—the answer is so simple that it savours of cheekiness: *to get somewhere*. Don't be misled by the tousled hair and flushed faces of Youth at the wheel. It enjoys the exhilaration of speed—and maybe at the moment the speed is all that counts. . . . But there was first an urge, a longing, which led men to discover that speed, and train it to their will.

.    .    .    .    .    .

That is the lesson which this century has to teach. It is necessity which makes things beautiful. Ring out the old— as fast as you like—and ring in the new. There is nothing to regret in such a step. The stream that ran by the cottage door has gone, but only into the newest streamline models. Horses grow as rare as Pegasus—but their horse-power still roars along the road.

So let us hope that the new generation—the Youth of 1930, when it steps into the place of post-war Youth, will ignore with contempt all such atrocities as 'Ye Olde Petrol Pump.' For they know, as nobody else does, that new petrol—like new wine—must go into new bottles.

And that the new century is worthy of its own environment.

From *The Queen,* July 2, 1930                    *Exhibit No. 22*

*Ursula Bloom asks—*

# 'Is Forty ✧ ✧ Frightening?'

*' Forty,' says Ursula Bloom in this Very Wise and*
*Thoughtful Article, ' ought to be the Perfect Age.'*

### When I am Forty

Men have no time-limit set upon their loving.  A woman
has.  When I am forty, I shall realize that never again can I
indulge in a madly glorious love affair.

I should enjoy a glittering romance far more than I did at
twenty, because I should know how to handle it better, and
therefore should derive more from it.  But romance is not
for me then. . . . Yet men at forty are in their prime.  It
never seems to me to be quite fair.

### A Hot Bath or a Good Meal

. . . how greatly the simple joys attract one . . . at forty
I shall dare to admit it.  What is more rapturous than a hot
bath when one is tired?  Than a good meal served before an
open window at the end of a tiring day?  Than a garden on
a June day?  A husband returning at eventide, and a son
saying with joyous enthusiasm, 'Mum, you are a good
sport? sport!'?

### The Latchkey to Happiness

If you have staked your all on giddiness and chance, on
fun and froth, then forty will be frightening.  It is good-bye
to much of that.  If you are a serious thinker and look forward to a time when you will have the leisure to appreciate
good books, the best music, art, and higher thought, then
forty will be the latchkey to all that life holds best for you.

To me forty is not frightening.          URSULA BLOOM.

From *A Daily Newspaper*          *Exhibit No.* 23

# DO YOU FEAR FORTY?

*By ROSITA FORBES*

**She Will Mind.**

Would I mind being forty? I consulted a woman of thirty-three who has to go on looking twenty-five because she is a Beauty, which in 1930 is a permanent profession.

'Will you mind?' I asked. . . .

'Yes, I think I shall,' she said, and I was immensely surprised.

I thought being forty had ceased to be important, or for that matter, being fifty either. I thought age was one of the dragons slain by common sense, and here was a practical young woman with a brain and what passes for a career troubling about tradition, for being forty in the Victorian sense is no more than a habit of mind. . . .

My last effort was with a Personage, who dances every night and gets through more work in between whiles than any Cabinet would consider respectable in a whole session.

'Will you mind being forty?' I asked, and wondered whether anybody had ever thought of resisting her.

'I should find it odd,' she said. '*You see, I was fifty-two last birthday.*'

.     .     .     .     .     .

For our grandmothers the world stopped at thirty, and for our mothers at forty, but for us it is likely to go on as long as we keep a sense of humour and a state of fitness—on which modern life appears to depend. Being forty is an incident, not an event. One of the very young said to me the other day, 'we don't think any more in terms of age.' And to a certain extent this is true.

### Rebellious ' Buds.'

The 'Buds' have a set of their own, and stern mothers tell them, 'My dear, she's twenty-four. What would be the use of asking her to stay? You'd have nothing in common.'

And the 'Buds' rebel, wishing perhaps that they were twenty-four; but, once married, all social relationships are measured by tastes, habits, and modes of thought, not by these relentless years which mark decades.

All the same, I am sufficiently old-fashioned to think it would be rather awful to wake up and find oneself forty without anything to show for it. I would like to be able to say proudly, 'I am forty, and this is what I've done.'

It seems to me that it is the wasted years which brand one. The more one does, the less it matters growing old.

I remember wondering what life could possibly hold for me when I should no longer be excited by the imminence of Christmas or the possibility of paddling. But one can't paddle all the years between six and sixty. One doesn't want to.

### Thinking Dangerously.

.        .        .        .        .        .

As long as one can think dangerously and put one's thoughts into immediate action without counting cost, without trying to insure against failure, the years have nothing on one.

Time can be defeated by a venturous spirit, because in 1930 all we want is to be amused, interested, carried away by the new, the swift, and the unexpected.

That is why Beauty is at a discount, unless it is reinforced by charm or wit or enterprise.

From *Everyman*, July 3, 1930      *Exhibit No.* 24

# THE REVOLT OF YOUTH

*For many weeks past large numbers of our readers have taken part in this interesting correspondence. To-day we close it with a letter from our original correspondent, and an announcement. We regret that we shall not be able to find room for further letters.*

## A Suggestion

The primary aim that we have before us is to make the spirit of youth a power in the world—the spirit that is in revolt against the present state of the world, its social conditions, political creeds, religious dogmas, sexual humbug, materialism, hypocrisy, blindness, cowardice and ugliness.

Our ideal is to form a loose association of small groups and even of single individuals, supplemented and co-ordinated by postal correspondence. Members are united for exchange of views, for the acquirement and interchange of specialist knowledge in various subjects, and for strength in action.

All who are interested are asked to send their names and addresses to us at the address given below, and to send a nominal fee of one shilling to cover postal expenses. They will, if they wish it, be put into touch with their nearest co-members, or, if they prefer, with members in any part of the country who are interested in the same problems or subjects as themselves.

       \*             \*             \*

       \*             \*             \*

From *The Daily Mail*                    *Exhibit No. 25*

---

# BATTLE OF THE GENERATIONS

——◆——

## JOHN VAN DRUTEN'S NEW PLAY

---

## SUBURBIA AGAIN

---

*The Manchester Guardian*, Nov. 20, 1929     *Exhibit No. 26*

---

# YOUTH AND HUMOUR
## A MODERN GROWTH

It is always useful, if not always encouraging, to learn
how the young are looking at life: and our view of the
ballot taken recently by the Students' Union of the
Universities of England and Wales will depend to some
extent upon the way we others of more advanced age
are looking at life.

.          .          .          .          .

By admitting, then, that a sense of humour is a
modern product we appear to imply that human nature
is becoming more kindly, less ready to sacrifice our
neighbour's feelings to personal display, more aware of
our mystic membership of one another. If that is so,
the ballot of youth in its favour is a hopeful phenomenon.
But probably every one of the students who voted
cherished a different idea of humour.

EVELYN SHARP.

From *The Saturday Review*, Oct. 4, 1930    *Exhibit No.* 27

# IS LITERATURE DYING?

\*          \*          \*

For our part, we believe there are as good fish in the sea as ever came out.  We are ready to salute Galsworthy and Walpole as worthy successors of Meredith and Trollope;  and we go further and express the conviction that there are young men who are unknown to-day who will yet rival the fame of the author of *The Forsytes* and *The Cathedral*.

From *The Sunday Dispatch*, 1928    *Exhibit No.* 28

# YOUTHS WHO REALLY MATTER

## MR. MICHAEL ARLEN IN 'THE DAILY MAIL'

### SCHUBERT IN LOVE

Throughout last week 24-page *Daily Mails* appeared each day.  Again to-morrow there will be a big issue packed with all the news as well as with exclusive pictures and many special features.

*Of outstanding interest to-morrow will be the special contribution by Mr. Michael Arlen on 'The Young Men,' in which he discusses, with many a flash of satire, those who really matter in these days.*

M

From *The Evening Standard*, May 1, 1930     *Exhibit No.* 29

# THIS *COWARDLY* AGE

### By MARY AGNES HAMILTON, M.P.

*GROWING OLD, PUTTING ON WEIGHT, THINKING—*

### Never Was There a Time of So Many Fears

. . . there never was an age afraid of so many things.

·    ·    ·    ·    ·

#### Governed by Fear

I am going to ask the reader . . . whether he can think of anybody (himself, of course, excluded) who is not afraid of something, and so much afraid that the fear is the governor of his action?

·    ·    ·    ·    ·

#### No Longer Young !

Or there are the Joneses, both—low be it spoken—well past forty, who wear their nerves to a frazzle by going out nightly to dances. They say, of course, that 'dancing is such splendid exercise,' but the real motive is that they are desperately apprehensive of growing old.

For the same reason they spend fatiguing and expensive holidays playing golf badly, and sun-bathing, for which their figures are ill-suited. To refuse to grow old is sensible, you may say. Within limits it is, but to-day the notion is being pushed beyond all limits, and the cause is the insane fear that rides men and women that they may be put down as no longer young.

We are in a period of the worship of youth.  In dress, in habits, in speech, mature men and women ape their juniors.

Every one seeks to be young: if not really young, at least younger than he really is.

### Peril of Thought

Where are the middle-aged nowadays?  They only survive in the House of Commons.  There one may have left youth behind without having to face responsibility.  And responsibility, above all the responsibility of doing some thinking of our own, we avoid like the plague.  It is our darkest fear, and the parent of all the other fears we harbour.

---

From *The Daily Herald, Aug. 25, 1930*        *Exhibit No. 30*

# YOUTH Must Make Its Own CHANCES

*By*

*ANDREW SOUTAR*

I do not believe that the modern young man is too lazy, too fond of pleasure, too devoted to relaxation of every kind to make headway.

The young man of to-day is said by his cynical critics to be satisfied so long as he can find a leaning-post in the shape of a parent or a relative.

Indeed, everybody who likes to see his (or her) name in print seems to think that they have only to attack youth in order to command a sympathetic public.

Shall I startle you by saying that, compared with the youth of my day, thirty or forty years ago, the modern youth is a much finer specimen?  But he appears to lack appreciation of the greatest gift that can be conferred on any one—individuality.

There never was a time, at least during the years I have lived, when chances for young men were so few as they are to-day.  In the bitterness of our heart because of the demands made on us by taxation, we are disposed to say harsh things about, and make false accusations against, young men who find themselves compelled to accept unemployment benefit.

---

From

*The Manchester Guardian*, **March 6, 1931**     *Exhibit No.* 31

# How  Old  Are  You ?

## A LITTLE ADDRESS
## TO THE MIDDLE-AGED

A census year in the days of Queen Victoria.

The elderly lady was calling on her next-door neighbour, a white-bearded old Scotsman.  She would not, she insisted, give her age.

'All that sleep in the house must put their ages down cor-r-ectly,' rasped the aged neighbour.

'Very well,' replied Miss Clementina, with finality, 'I'll not sleep indoors;  I'll go out and sleep in the hen-house.'

'Ay, but that'll not make ye a chicken,' was the answer.

When the census year comes round with its probing papers it well becomes middle-aged people to sit down and to reflect that they are no longer chickens, whatever imaginary hen-houses they roost in. . . .

We should really take ourselves firmly in hand about this. If it be indeed the case that most women of, say, fifty, look forty, our opinion of what women of fifty ought to look like must be revised. There can't be more exceptions than the rule, or where's the rule? . . .

From the middle-aged point of view the above, though possibly salutary, is a little depressing. What are we to do about it? Well, even though we don't look 'young for our age' we may perhaps look 'nice for our age.' . . .

As regards the 'young in spirit' delusion, far be it from me to say that there is no possibility of friendship between the young and the middle-aged, or even the old. But the young must make the advances and lay down the conditions. It is for us to accept humbly what they offer, and for us to be prepared, if necessary, to do without them. After all, if we have lived our lives wisely, we shall still have kept in touch with many of our own contemporaries, like ourselves getting 'a little older, a little fatter, a little duller.' With them we shall have memories in common, and perhaps, with luck, we may not have changed much, even outwardly, to their indulgent eyes. And suppose the very worst, suppose the young are neglectful, and the old friends are removed beyond reach of word or pen. Well, have we not learned by now to be friends with ourselves? If one has not learned to live at fifty one ought to have done so.—C. C. F.

From *The Evening Standard*                    *Exhibit No.* 32

---

**Safe Slimming for Men.—No. 2**

# *FIGHT YOUR WEIGHT*

---

### Over-Eating, the Vice of Middle-Age

.        .        .        .        .

Any undue breathlessness or fatigue after the simple exercises indicated should prompt a general overhaul by the family physician, not with the idea that anything wrong will be found, but rather to make sure that there is nothing organically unsound.

In any case, for the middle-aged man, this is a procedure well worth doing at regular intervals.

*(**To be continued on Monday***)*

---

From *A Daily Newspaper*                    *Exhibit No.* 33

---

# *The* WRINKLE MENACE

*Showing that a Woman can*
*at FORTY still be HAPPY*

---

. . . The majority of us still go in dread of the wrinkle: we talk age, think age. The very hoardings blaze with recipes for postponing the horrid contingency . . . we are far from sane on the subject.

From *A Daily Newspaper*                    *Exhibit No. 34*

# The Woman
## In The
# Middle Thirties

We women who are approaching the middle thirties . . . cannot forget that almost as soon as we have reached the zenith of our career we are, in many respects, on the downward path. . . . We have to make up our minds that many of the younger generation, who are yet too newly fledged to feel the increasing speed of the clock-hands, begin to look upon women of thirty-five as dowagers of the morrow.

Surely our souls should rise superior to the pitying looks, however veiled they may be, of our younger sisters.

From *The Sunday Express*, Nov. 9, 1930    *Exhibit No. 35*

By **LADY DUFF GORDON,** London's Greatest Fashion Expert

# THE WOMAN OF 45—

*and those*
*22-inch*
*waists*

**Thank Goodness there is a Revolt— for her sake!**

From *A Daily Newspaper*　　　*Exhibit No.* 36

# WHEN A WOMAN'S THIRTY

### By
### BARONESS FURNIVALL

A fierce discussion was raging concerning the important question whether 'a woman is terrified of reaching thirty or not.' The general consensus of opinion appeared to be that this age marked a milestone in life's mileage, and most women were terrified at the prospect of attaining it.

Now being myself well on the way to this so-called 'terrifying' age, this verdict gave me furiously to think.

.　　.　　.　　.　　.　　.

**I look forward to it**

.　　.　　.　　.　　.　　.

Personally, I am looking forward to my thirtieth birthday. I rejoice to think that my 'danger point' of eighteen is past.

From *Sunday Dispatch*, Oct. 5, 1930        *Exhibit No. 37*

# Mocking The Moderns

### Slaughter the Old!

Now *The Breadwinner* is highly provocative.  It will make people argue for months, especially on account of the clash between modern middle-age and modern youth.  Neither side comes through with many honours, but youth with least of all.

Mr. Maugham's young people have ingenious and quite sincere theories, such as:

*All middle-aged people should be killed painlessly off to make room for us.*

*Nobody over forty can find any joy in life.*

*Parents are naturally fond of us, but you can't expect us to be crazy over them.  That's different.*

*We didn't ask to be brought into the world.  You had us for your own pleasure, and a very good time you had, too.*

No wonder the father of these trite young people decided that in the future he would seek his destiny alone.

From

*The Evening Standard*, Oct. 11, 1930     *Exhibit No.* 38

# DON'T FEAR
# OLD AGE

## By Dr.
## BERNARD
## HOLLANDER

### Keep Cheerful

One essential is the practice of contentment. We must not get disturbed by the smaller worries of life, have no vain regrets for opportunities gone by, no jealous envy or carping criticism of the younger generation. Altogether we should try to avoid depressing emotions, for they are apt to disturb the functions of the body; but should keep a cheerful outlook on life, a kindly interest in new methods and ideas, and make it our aim to spread happiness around, for there is truth in the saying that 'those keep young longest who love most.'

From *The Evening News*, June 21, 1930     *Exhibit No.* 39

---

# This Is What I Think
## Of
# MODERN YOUTH

By——

**People Over 25**

---

*THE EVENING NEWS,* **having allowed Youth its fling at its seniors, now invites anyone over 25 to send in a true-life story to show what is his or her opinion of Modern Youth, the young man and young woman of to-day. Youth did not mince matters : its seniors may be as frank.**

.     .     .     .

**Five Guineas will be awarded for each of the five best letters we receive, and 10s. 6d. will be paid for every letter published.**

### Letter A.

## Those Cockney War Stories.

In a crowded tube train one evening I was eagerly devouring one of your admirable pages of Cockney war stories.

Two modern young men, waspwaisted, weary, and wan, were discussing the very page that I was so keenly interested in.

One ventured the remark : ' Priceless lot of bilge ! '

If this was typical of present-day Youth, give me another war and put those two blighters in my platoon. —*V. G. Peer, 7 Elmhall Gardens, Wanstead,* E.11.

### Letter B.

## This New Vulgarity.

.     .     .     .

I was about ten minutes talking with my visitor, and when I came back the girl was sitting at a devastated table, eating very quickly, with a stump of cigarette by her plate, filling the room with smoke.

' Hallo, Coppie,' she cried, with her mouth full, ' I just could not wait any longer. Come along, I want my spot of salad. Do be quick about it.'

I am sixty, and I object to tobacco-smell during meals, and I loathe being called by this familiar handling of my name. I said so.

' You are quite a Victorian, you

old dear,' she replied unconcernedly.
' Take your pew and feed. That
salad is IT.'

The girl is really kind-hearted and
cultivated, but she affects—or has—
the rough ways of a blunt boy.

But one gets tired of meeting only
one sex everywhere, especially when
the new species refuses absolutely to
make itself agreeable to the remnants of a past era.—*Marguerite
Coppin, 42 Colville Terrace, Bays-
water*, W.11.

## Letter C.
### ' An Unbecoming
### Pompousness.'

A year or two ago I heard a sub-
ordinate in a railway office (not in
London) argue quite seriously that
the Lake District was in Somerset !

This may sound grotesque, and is
not typical of all people under
twenty-five, but it illustrates how
little the new-fangled education can
do with some of the young minds
of to-day.

It is a fact that the percentage of
candidates who fail at what is known
in the railway service as the Senior
Clerks' Examination is lamentably
high nowadays, when one considers
that the paper embraces little outside the three R's, and a smattering
of general knowledge.

Moreover, many of those who do
pass the education test soon begin
to display an unbecoming pompous-
ness. They try to patronise their
elders, and are peevish about their
own ambitions ; but they unmistak-
ably lack the powers of concentration and conscientiousness which
were demanded years ago, for much
longer hours—and for less remun-
eration—than is the case to-day.—
*R. E. Beech, 16 Ascott Avenue*, W.5.

## Letter D.
### The Fat Old Man.

Last Whit-Monday I visited a
town where, 36 years ago, I com-
peted in some athletic sports. As a
reminder of the old days I entered
for a couple of events. I found the
other competitors a pleasant set of
fellows, and in the dressing-room
their long, clean limbs filled me with
admiration.

Well, the time came to race, and
youth won, as it always will.
Imagine the contrast : I, a fat old
man, and these young fellows like
greyhounds !

But when, well-beaten, I prepared
to creep away I was met by all the
competitors, eager to shake my
hand, and the young people in the
grand-stand applauded me as
though I had won.

What do I think of Modern
Youth ? I think they are splendid.
—*J. C. Newman, 88 High Street,
Hoddesdon, Herts.*

## Letter E.
### The Men !—But Here
### is One Girl.

You masculine ' under 25's ' are a
sorry lot, I'm afraid—unstable,
conceited, self - opinionated, and
blasés. Another war would do you
good and take your minds off your
motor-bikes and your flappers, and
shake you out of your world of
jazz bands and iced drinks. But
probably you would ' come up
to scratch,' even as did your big
brothers. I wonder !

As for you bewildering short-
skirted ' kid sisters '—well, to an old
fogey of 32 you are a quaint mix-

ture, but I know you are all right underneath your flippancy and your make-up.

I know a girl who married at 17. She was a typical ' under 25 '—smart, super-sophisticated for her years, spoilt, pampered, and indulged all her short life.

She married a man 11 years her senior, in a good position and able to shower her with the pretty things she loved. That was three years ago. Lately her husband lost his job and all his money. Did the girl-bride run home to mother ? No, she got a job in a West End store and works eight hours a day for £2 a week to help keep things going. She hates every minute of the working day, but pretends to her husband that it is ' fun.'

She will be twenty on Friday, and I shall meet her in South Kensington and we shall have what she calls a ' small splurge ' to celebrate : I am the husband.—' *The Luckiest Husband,' London, W.2.*

## Letter F.

## A Word from the Man of Forty.

I am forty, and I served for three years in the trenches. My business takes me from London to Dublin, from Plymouth to Aberdeen, and I have had much opportunity of seeing To-day's Young Man in sport and games. And I can outplay him and outdance him.

It is not, therefore, jealousy which prompts me to say that, intellectually and physically, he is a seedy specimen. I wince at the thought that my generation might have been looked upon by its elders with the same contempt, but 90 per cent. of the boys in khaki surely did not consist of shallow-minded, pale, narrow-chested and spindly specimens of manhood.

But the girl of under 25 is a great improvement on her predecessor, and I have yet to meet the girl who does not prefer a man considerably her elder in years.—' *Critical, Brighton.*

## Letter G.

## When I Did His Job.

I was riding in a bus the other day when a fellow-passenger asked the young conductor if he were tired.

' Tired ? ' he replied. ' So would you feel tired if you were mobbed all the time by people wanting to get home. Why, it takes me all my time to lug 'em in and shove 'em orf, never mind about running up and down stairs a thousand times punching their tickets. No, guv'nor, I ain't tired,' he added, sarcastically.

How I ached to tell that young conductor that I had worked longer hours than he does, as conductress during the war, and if I dared to grouse I was at once reminded, by presumably well-meaning passengers, that the ' Tommies ' at the Front weren't grousing, so why should I.

When young men and women of to-day complain of their hard lot and criticise us, the women of 40, let them remember that the old-fashioned, narrow-minded fogeys got their eight-hour jobs for them.—*F. Darby, 87 St. John's Wood Terrace, London.*

# COMMENTARY UPON EXHIBITS

## 1 to 39

*Exhibit No.* 1.—This fragment is from a typical *age-war* article; it is a specimen of the hearty, kindly 'Old Stager,' called in to put his fellow-greybeards in their places—to slap 'Youth' very heavily upon the back and say, 'If the Old Buffers—those 'septuagenarian limpets'—won't *let you in*, my lad, why, *go* and '*kick in*' the door! It also contains the characteristic remark 'men should be paid *not* according to their years of service,' but their worth. This, in the vast majority of cases, and for all practical purposes, means according to their *freshness*. The 'Ten Thousand a Year Man' becomes a more fantastic myth every day.

*Exhibit No.* 2.—This is a typical 'Old Stager' (and 'White Guard') article. 'Bolshevism in the Drawing Room' it is sub-entitled. It is the 'Old Stager' laying about him, and fuming over 'Ill-bred' *vandalism* of the 'Young Pup.'

*Exhibit No.* 3.—The reader here is promised a gladiatorial play, in which all-conquering Critical Youth will duly 'wipe the floor' with all oil-painters, gravers, and sculptors over forty.

*Exhibit No.* 4.—Another Friendly-Uncle article (of Exhibit No. 1). All the woes of the time—the reason that England is on the down-grade—are due to 'The paralysing hand of Old Age.' There should be a retiring age in politics of Fifty-five. In general, however (just as in No. 1), the fallacy of the notion of *experience* is stressed. 'WE HEAR A GREAT DEAL ABOUT THE VALUE OF EXPERIENCE . . . MUCH OF IT IS FALLACIOUS.'

*Exhibit No.* 5.—Another 'Old 'Un - Good Sort' article. He is, he says, an octogenarian. But 'it is *the old*' like himself—not the 'mere grown-ups' (i.e. the villains block-ing up the Roaring Forties and the Whistling Thirties)—who are sympathetic and the friends of 'Youth.' The 'Mere Grown-Ups'—the middle-aged devils—hardly seem to care whether 'Youth' is made *free* or not. This is the typical article of the octogenarian agitator—designed to cause a warm feeling for all those with two feet and both legs in the grave, and stir up the hottest hatred for the 'Middle Classes' (i.e. the middle-aged).

*Exhibit No. 6.*—*Même jeu*—a repetition of No. 5 by the same hand, but agitating among the girls. 'I trust the young women more than the old ! ' this octogenarian agitator cries. '*Death to the Old Women !*' À la lanterne!

*Exhibit No. 7.*—Review of a play by Mr. Van Druten, which must have resembled *Three Score and Ten* by Mr. Alec Waugh. Terroristic tableaux of Parents and Children *s'entremangeant*—devouring each other, and then, when the son has killed the father, he 'reverts to type,' and the tragedy will be repeated in his case.

*Exhibit No. 8.*—Anti-ancestor-worship article, directed against religious teaching, and designed to cause 'Young' to repudiate all ancient forms of cult or ritual in favour of Progress and Modernity. (Thus: 'Shakespeare was all very well—a better poet than I am—but a live sparrow is worth more than a dead eagle,' etc.)

*Exhibit No. 9.*—'Whenever a bunch of parsons get together, etc.'—this is a bit of hearty, bluff, *anti-clericalism*. In this case it is the 'parson' who is to be the villain. Here are all the 'parsons' at a nice breezy seaside resort groaning over the 'restlessness of the new generation.' Again—'these parsons blame the Press, cinemas, novelists'! whereas, of course, it is in fact *themselves* they should blame for not being better 'parsons'—or at least so it seems to 'an ordinary sinner' like himself. What is implied, of

course, in all this is that 'the parsons' are blaming 'Youth'
for 'the Press, cinemas, novels, etc.' In point of fact they
are blaming, rather, the *promoters* of what is pushed in the
Press, Cinema, and in Fiction: and those promoters are
as even 'a parson' knows, scarcely 'Youths.'

*Exhibit No.* 10.—George Bernard Shaw here comes in for
a bit of insult. Shaw is in fact 'no good,' but just 'a foolish
old man.' And all Englishmen should thank the newspaper
in question for showing him up in his true light! An
essential part of the revolutionary Age-war propaganda is
that it should (mingling class-envy against the 'great' with
class-hatred of one age-class against another) give a good
kick as often as possible to the idols of the literary or artistic
world. Idols—'gods' in the vulgar jargon—are not in any
case *persona grata* with the political minds behind the
*class-wars.*

*Exhibit No.* 11.—The Truss-manufacturer and porno-
graphic chemist, unconsciously no doubt, take a hand in
depressing the OVER-FORTIES.

*Exhibit No.* 12.—'May I, as a *kid of 60*, be permitted to
join the Senior Section?'—Yes! 'Let them all come!' All
who are 'kids.'

*Exhibit No.* 13.—This is where the Age-war Racket
definitely passes over into the 'High-brow' field. The
extracts speak for themselves.

*Exhibit No.* 14.—Instead of paying a 'victim' to reply
a lady best-seller (who 'at the age of thirty' has just published her 'Confessions') steps into the breach, and defend
the 'great ones'—and then passes on to a few 'Lovely
Persons,' and ends up with 'the greatest intellect' of
the age.

*Exhibit No.* 15.—Here the *really discriminating*—and
properly 'youngergenerationconscious' reader—is offered

ne quite eccentric treat of a genuine member of 'the
eneration' telling of his fellow generos. But it is all
.instein's fault that the Thames Side Brights are faulty,
nd Einstein is, of course, not young. Which only shows
ou how 'Youth' can all be the result of something that
; not 'Youth.'

*Exhibit No.* 16.—Dean Inge provides the moral am-
nunition necessary.

*Exhibit No.* 17.—Here is the *Age-war* in full swing. In
ne letter the 'young men' have been ruined by parents
pending *too much* on their education. These are the *bad
,arents* (from the point of view of Big Business). In another
etter we are given an illustration of the *good parent.* 'My
,arents brought me up in the right way. *You've got to earn
your own bread and butter*, they said.' (Big Business will
;ee to it that such parents as these are encouraged.) Then
Middle-aged People' become, in a direct statement this
.ime, 'The Incubus upon the country.' It is they to whom
Youth' is being sacrificed.

*Exhibit No.* 18.—More varied propaganda. One letter
interesting for its statement 'it is obviously ten times more
difficult for the youth of to-day to reach the top of a
business,' etc. ('Youth' must sometimes be allowed to get
a dose of depression too. Later that will be handy.)

*Exhibit No.* 19.—The roguish announcement in the best
tradition of the 'Announcer' of the *Age-war* article. (A
photograph of that pioneer, Elinor Glyn, I unfortunately
was unable to use.)

*Exhibit No.* 20.—A hearty schoolmaster champion for
oppressed and vilified 'Youth.'

*Exhibit No.* 21.—'A successful young writer begins a
many-sided analysis,' etc.

N

*Exhibit No.* **22.**—Ursula Bloom, we learn, is not forty: but she will not 'find forty frightening.' She will at forty 'dare to admit' that she enjoys a hot bath. (At present, as it is left to us to guess, she would not 'dare to admit' that anything but—well, *love,* was either hot or agreeable.) 'If you are a serious thinker' you will have a little time after forty to 'appreciate good books, the best music, art, and higher thought.' (This is only if you are a 'serious thinker.')

*Exhibit No.* **23.**—'One of the very young said to me the other day, "*We don't think any more in terms of age*"'—or: 'One can't paddle all the years between six and sixty.'

*Exhibit No.* **24.**—Usual clarion call to revolution.

*Exhibit No.* **25.**—'Suburbia' rent in twain by Age-War.

*Exhibit No.* **26.**—'A sense of humour is a modern product.'

*Exhibit No.* **27.**—Greatness within the reach of 'Youth.'

*Exhibit No.* **28.**—Mr. Michael Arlen on 'The Young Men.'

*Exhibit No.* **29.**—Age-'Fear' complexes.—'We are in a period of the worship of Youth.'

*Exhibit No.* **30.**—'There never was a time . . . when chances for young men were so few as they are to-day.'

*Exhibit No.* **31.**—A good piece of 'shy-making' propaganda.

*Exhibit No.* **32.**—The burdens of Middle-age: 'Bath-Chair-article' for the Roaring Forties.

*Exhibit No.* **33.**—'We talk age, think age!' The newspapers follow suit—or is it us that follow suit? 'The very hoardings blaze with the horrid contingency!' The *very Press* expatiates very often upon the subject, too: but 'a woman *can* be happy at forty'—it is all right!

*Exhibit No.* **34.**—'Women of thirty-five are dowagers of the morrow!' *Remember*—souviens-toi—esto memor!

*Exhibit No.* 35.—'Thank goodness there is a revolt—for *her* sake!'—for the Woman of Forty-five—against 22-inch waists!

*Exhibit No.* 36.—Is 'a woman terrified of reaching thirty —or not?' Baroness Furnivall for her part 'rejoices that her *danger-spot* of eighteen is past.' Moral: Lucky Baroness Furnivall, of course!

*Exhibit No* 37.—Maugham 'will make people argue for months!' What about? Whether 'All middle-aged people should be killed painlessly off' or whether 'Any one over forty can find any joy in life.'

*Exhibit No.* 38.—Injunctions for a 'happy Old Age': (1) Never criticize anything that is done anywhere. (2) Be cheerful. (3) Approve rapturously of every 'new method.' Everything *new* is *good*. Remember!

*Exhibit No.* 39.—' BY PEOPLE OVER 25.'

*Letter A.*—Good one because it will stir up trouble in buses and Tubes between ex-Derby-Schemers and 'Under-Twenty-fives.'

*Letter B.*—Showing rearguard action between Old Female Has-been and a Jolly Modern Girl (smoking, cocktailing, and Old-beaning for dear life).

*Letter C.*—Good one, because it will stir up trouble among Railway Staffs, by way of inter-age-class vituperation and recrimination.

*Letter D.*—'I was prepared to creep away.'—'I was a fat old man of sixty!'

*Letter E.*—Great condescension to 'Old Fogey' of 32 on part of 'a Typical UNDER-TWENTY-FIVE!'

*Letter F.*—'I am Forty'—I am not jealous. You think I am? Never!

*Letter G.*—A bit of *sex-war* brought in to brighten up *age-war*. Old W.A.A.C. ticks off young Weary Willie of Under-Twenty-Five bus conductor. Another good one because it promotes bad feeling in public vehicles. Bad feeling—strong age-clashes—in public vehicles very important.

———

Having given you the first batch of numbered exhibits, and provided, at the end, a commentary upon each individual cutting, I will proceed to a short general statement.

First, in a book of this size, no idea can be given of the scale of the Headlines and weight of matter, and, however many cuttings were used, no adequate idea could be given of the profusion of such matter in the Press. (None of the cuttings are earlier in date than 1928.)

At least one thing, I think, must have been demonstrated, however, by this display, and that is that—as the writer remarked in *How to be Happy Though Forty*—'The majority of us talk age, think age,' if the Press is to be believed, and if we do not talk it and think it, the Press does that for us.

No one, I think, could deny that the sort of articles and pars. in question are calculated to promote goodwill upon earth. If *peace* at any price were our great object in life, then certainly it could never be said, could it, that we were defeating that end by publishing this order of inter-age, counter-generational recrimination and criticism! That it would be difficult to dispute—upon such a scale, so unceasing and in such volume—this sort of propaganda could not possibly give rise to friction and ill-feeling anywhere. 'Inferiority complexes' by the thousand are not created upon all hands: the natural envy that exists at the best of times between the more, and the less, fortunate at least will not be enormously intensified. That is quite sure.

The only question that remains is that question with which we started: is it done *on purpose*—that is to say, can such a phenomenon exist, upon such a scale, and can its promoters be *unconscious* of its existence? Is it certain, quite certain, that there is no political motive behind it? You know, of course, what my answer is. But I would prefer that the reader should arrive at his own conclusions, grounding his opinion upon the nature of the evidence, rather than allowing himself to be influenced by me.

# PART IV

# A NEUTER CLASS—SATURATED WITH SEX

IN Parts I–II, I have provided you with the evidence (which you can check for yourself by reference to current popular newspapers, etc.) showing set battle to be in progress at least as intense as that of Woman's Suffrage before the War. It has superseded the latter. But no movement of this kind can be taken in isolation. You must, in order fully to understand it, relate it to all those parallel movements of which it forms a part.

The 'Age-war' is really a Father-and-Children-war—not a Mother-and-Children-war—that is the first thing to note. On the one hand 'Youth-politics,' or 'Age-war,' is related to (1) our revolutionary life, which seeks to eliminate all those elements in politics likely to perpetuate traditional ideas: and, on the other hand, it is related to the abstract Might of Big Business and abstract Finance. The latter (in the process rather comically named 'Rationalization') seeks to break up the old *individualistic* spirit—indeed to remove all the privileges whatever of the individual, in the interests of the closest possible organization.

Perfect 'Rationalization' obviously does not end in the workshop or office—anything but. It passes over into, and regulates, private life. And all these little domestic islands —detached or semi-detached households—in villa, house, or cottage (and is not 'the Englishman's Home his Castle!')— all those individualist units, are economically wasteful. Therefore all that must disappear. Enormous 'cities' of dormitoried flats—with shops, a laundry, a central play-ground for the children, such as you find already in Austria and Germany—in the shortest possible time that must be put in place of these *separate*, individualist households. The 'break up of the Family' means merely that. And *one* of the reasons that Feminism received so much advertisement and support was with this 'break up of the Family' in view. Another reason was to obtain cheap female labour. Another was to take the starch out of the economically over-costly White European Man.

So Feminism—just like Age-war, or *Father-and-Children-war*—had both an *economical* and a *political* object.

But, lest I should get myself misunderstood, I must indicate my own attitude to the Feminist Revolution. Under present-day conditions it would have been impossible not to have the Married Woman's Property Act, radical revision of Divorce laws, and so forth (there should be a further revision now to liberate men as well). Many of the women who went in for 'Suffrage' were the best and most energetic types of women: such as were humiliated by being regarded as sweetmeats, as 'inferiors,' persons who wished to see abolished all those laws discriminating against the female sex, and so to acquire for it 'legal rights.' Why should an intelligent and sensitive woman be tied for life to a brutal and stupid man, after all—or *vice versa*, of course. But does not all that go without saying? Unfortunately not quite, for people get fanatical about these class-wars, and one has to supply a little credo (as above) if one is to discuss freely such a question as *Why did Feminism succeed?* For, obviously, a just cause does not *usually* succeed. It is the reverse. One has to make it clear that one does not mean '*Ought* it to have succeeded?' Those are absolutely distinct questions. In the latter we take practically no interest here.

It is especially to be remarked, then, that the Age-class-war is a Parent-and-Children-war in which *only* the male Parent is involved. And this fact exercises a great influence upon the situation that is developing as a consequence of this particular campaign.

This is the most complicated part of my essay to handle:

for, unless the reader is familiar with *The Art of Being Ruled,* he is liable at every moment to take for granted that I am arguing from another background of feeling or belief than that from which, in fact, all these arguments derive.

I will quote several passages from *The Art of Being Ruled.* These will provide you with the *backgrounds* that it is necessary to establish for a proper understanding of what I shall next have to say. These passages are from pp. 215-219—a chapter entitled 'The Meaning of the Sex-war':—

> The sex war . . . led off, naturally, as a war to free the woman. The woman was the chattel, or slave, of this terrible little despot, the Father of the Family. There were millions of such despicable little despots. Their power must be broken. The 'despot' smiled indulgently; he knew he was not much of a despot, he didn't know what all the fuss was about, but concluded that 'those women' had become possessed of some obstinate piece of illogic that they had better be allowed to 'get on with.'
>
> 'Socialism wishes to abolish family life, because it costs too much,' was Proudhon's explanation of feminism. . . . Feminism in that sense was simply the conscription, under a revolutionary egalitarian banner, of an army of women, for the purpose of the attack on and destruction of the home and the family. There is much more in the war in the family than the economic factor. But it is certainly the economic factor that persuades capitalism to favour the feminist movement and urge the conventional socialist to this form of 'war.'
>
> Men as a 'class,' the masculine class, have recently had to support a great number of wars all at the same time: the 'Great War,' which was of a traditional type, and yet very novel in its barbarity; the 'class war,' of course; and then a war that was regarded originally as a joke, the 'sex war.' All these wars are wars of freedom: but their ultimate objects are generally misunderstood. . . .
>
> How the sex war links up with the class war, the age war, and the war of the high and the low-brow, is as follows. 'The prevalent dominance of men' is a phrase used commonly. Man in himself is a symbol of authority. *Masculinity* (in a state describable as above) is in itself authoritative and hence arbitrary. The most miserable and feeble specimen of the male 'class' is in that paradoxical position of representing the

most devilish despotism and symbolizing brute force.  He
suffers from the accident that he symbolizes 'authority' in
an era of change and militant revolutionary revaluation.

So, in the sex department (conterminous with that of ad-
ministrative political power, or of the master-man relationship
in industry or in domestic life, and with the family relation of
parent and child), the revolutionary attack would, in its
most generalized form, have the character of an attack on
*man* and on masculinity.  For, apart from *man as father*,
or *man as husband*, or *man as leader* (in tribe or state), there
is an even more irreducible way in which man is a symbol
of power and domination.  *Man as man, tout court*, is an
anachronism, is 'unscientific.' . . .

The object of the capitalo-socialist promoters of the sex
war was dual.  One object was the quite temporary one of
discrediting authority, and reducing this smallest and feeblest
of kings, the little father of the family squatting rather miser-
ably in his shabby, uncomfortable little castle, like a 'king'
of *Alice in Wonderland*.  But the break-up of this expensive
and useless unit, the family, and the releasing of the hordes
of idle women, waiting upon little 'kings,' for industrial purposes, was the principal object.  Ten housewives daily per-
formed in the way of washing, cooking, and so forth, what
two could perform under a communal system of the Fourier
type, or that being introduced in communist Russia.  The
remaining eight would then be available for other forms of
work.  That is the economic object of the destruction of the
idea of the family and the home.  Incidentally, it will break
up and root out all those little congeries of often ill-assorted
beings; and terminate that terrible, age-long tête-à-tête of
the husband and wife, chained to each other for life for the
practical purpose of perpetuating the species, which could now
be effected more successfully *without* this often unhappy
union.

In the mind of the most villainous and black-hearted of
'capitalists,' no doubt, it presented itself solely as a problem to get hold of cheap female labour.  The hordes of un-
married women would be formed into a *third sex* like the
sterile female workers of the beehive.  This could not be done
without the displacement of an equal quantity of men.  So
a 'sex war' would be a good thing.  Funds were forthcoming
for feminist equipment.  Such an attitude did no doubt exist,
and does, among a certain type of men.  But that does not
affect the ultimate utility of the movement; nor is it any

reflection on the motives of such a man as Fourier, who recommended a social reorganization on these lines a century ago in his phalansterian system.

As a consequence of the 'sex-war' (the violent separation of men and women) that, among other things, an embitterment of all domestic life must ensue (an increased sexual tension between those men and women who had *not* already flown apart, but who continue to marry and be given in marriage), and secondly the formation of the nucleus (made up of recruits from both sexes) of a barren *Neuter Class*, seems evident. And a new Neuter Class, in its first phases, must still be saturated with the old sexual characteristics of inter-sex courtships and romantic love. Under these circumstances it is not to be wondered at if lesbianism, on the one hand, and homosexuality, on the other, should flourish.

But what we are particularly engaged in studying in this treatise is the Age-war—of the Father-and-Child-war, as it in fact is. And therefore the homosexual fashion is more important to us than is lesbianism. And to that I suggest we next turn our attention.

## CHAPTER II

# A VAST COMMUNAL NURSERY

'IN the contemporary world,' I wrote in *The Art of Being Ruled* (p. 244), '(homosexuality) is a part of the feminist revolution. It is as an integral part of feminism proper that it should be regarded—a gigantic phase of the sex-war. The "homo" is the legitimate child of the suffragette.'

But the homosexual is, of course, an imitation-woman—or at least the pathic is that. As such, he is subject to the same unkind sexual law as women—namely, that to be desired he must be young. His entire rationale is at an end when he ceases to be young. As a recognized and practising pathic he is already, at the age of twenty-five, discredited. But I will quote another passage from *The Art of Being Ruled* (pp. 307-308) upon the subject of male inversion, as practised by the Romans:—

> The wealthy Roman would have a harem of male slaves, which he called facetiously a 'paidagogia.' The boys chosen for this harem were called *exoleti*. The first step was to castrate them, as this 'exposed them to abuse the longer' ('Exoletos suos, ut ad longiorem patientiam impudicitiae idonei sint, amputant,' Seneca, *Controv.*, exc., x. 4). Some considerable trouble was also taken with their education; a certain literary polish was insisted upon, to render them more complicated objects of desire, upon the same principle that young ladies are taught to sing and paint, the mind thereby playing its part in the long civilized preparation for mating. If a closer contemporary parallel were desired, no doubt it could be found in that peculiar cultural furnishing, rather dainty, sickly, and smart, that an expensive modern university provides, along with aristocratic manners; and an inquiry as to how subsequently it was spent would usually elicit the fact that it served the same purpose as the matrimonial accomplishments of the middle-class girl—only, not so much in aiding simple Nature as in frustrating her.

206

With the roman *exoleti* 'all artifices were resorted to to delay the development of the child into the youth, and the youth into the man.' 'Decked out like a woman,' as Seneca says of one of these, 'he wrestles and fights with his years. He must not pass beyond the age of boyhood. He is kept back perforce, and, though robust as a soldier, he retains his smooth chin; his hair is all shaved off, and removed by the roots' (*Epist.*, 47). These epicenes were sometimes classed together by nations and colour, so that all were equally smooth and their hair all of one tint. That they might keep a fresh complexion longer, they were obliged, when on a journey with their master, to cover their face with a mask. It was thus that Clodius on his travels took his *exoleti* about with him as well as his women of pleasure. Tiberius, at Capreae, and even Trajan, kept such boys in droves, and in those days formal marriages between man and man were introduced, with all the solemnities of ordinary nuptials (Juvenal, ii. 117 seq.; Martial, xii. 42). On one of these occasions Nero made the Romans exhibit the tokens of a public rejoicing and treat his elect, Sporus, with all the honours of an empress (Döllinger, *Gentile and Jew in the Courts of the Temple of Christ*).

There again, in Seneca's account of the roman *exoletus*, who 'wrestles and fights with his years' because 'he must not pass beyond the age of boyhood,' we see the reflection of our time. The crowds of mild and veiled *exoleti* produce the impression of people 'playing children'—a childhood that is indefinitely prolonged, for none 'must pass beyond the age of boyhood.' The aged mind (with its devitalization, anxieties, and yearning for youth and its abundant freshness) is thus reproduced for the processes of this super-sexual obsession. It is thus that male sex-inversion contributes its share to the cult of *the child*.

And so, via the *exoletus* or the modern sentimental english version of that, we reach the *Cult of the Child*—of the child-art for instance of the German, Klee, or the gross and thunderous deliberate *naïveté* of Miss Stein, and all the other manifestations of the *Child-Cult*, artistic and otherwise (from Truex—'the most motherable man in London'—riding a rocking-horse, or Myra Hess being photographed upon the same nursery steed for *The Gateway*—the feminist weekly—down to the *childishness* of Charlie Chaplin—the little, down-trodden *child-man*—as 'motherable' as **Mr.** Truex, surely—or the fashion in Detective Stories among even the most elderly high-brows to-day).

But there is Mr. C. E. M. Joad, full of the Zeitgeist as a philosopher should be—he invades the 'Children's Pitches,' as witness the following extract from a report in the *Evening Standard* (March 18, 1931):—

---

# MR. JOAD HAS A GAME
# OF HOCKEY

---

## FINED FOR PLAYING ON A
## CHILDREN'S PITCH

---

Mr. C. E. M. Joad, author and lecturer, of East Heath Road, Hampstead, N.W., was fined 20s. at Hampstead Police Court to-day for playing hockey on a prohibited portion of Hampstead Heath. . . .

'HOW OLD IS THIS YOUTH?'

A heath keeper said that on January 18 he saw Mr. Joad and other persons playing hockey on the net-ball pitches on the heath. He requested Mr. Joad to desist, saying that hockey was not permitted on the children's net-ball pitches. Mr. Joad refused to stop and said: 'Take my name and address, and report me for a summons.'

The keeper said that he took these details, and Mr. Joad then said: 'Now I will continue, as I may as well be hanged for a sheep as for a lamb.'

The chairman (Mr. J. P. R. Lyell), referring to Mr. Joad, asked the keeper, 'How old is this youth?'

'About forty-five,' answered the keeper.

How all the fashions and 'class-wars' interweave and

fuse with each other should be evident enough to the reader by this time.

It is a 'motherable' world we live in—'Motherable' or nothing: the wise husband to-day attempts as far as possible to identify himself with his sons, so that a bit of 'mothering' should splash over on to him from time to time. And obviously in this nursery-world the *one* figure that is *de trop* and at whom every one, each after his manner, has a cut and does his or her best to drive at, is the MAN—the adult male, in short—the traditional Father.

But what are we to consider as essentially masculine—and if we are going to use these terms, masculine and feminine, intelligently, how shall we recognize (especially in the midst of the sexual merging and fusing in progress) what is a masculine attribute, what a feminine? For me, I see little essential difference between men and women. That distinction, that was formerly considered so absolute, is largely a matter of training and approach. Between a boy and a girl of ten, anywhere in the world, of a very rich and sheltered stock (not of a military, but merchant class) there is little essential difference. I should be inclined to say that there are only two radical differences between 'masculine' and 'feminine': namely, that 'masculine' suggests to us a larger physique, and also more personality or 'initiative.' But the former is very variable and depends upon occupation. And *personality* is infrequently met with anywhere, and is possessed as much by women as by men.

That we do mean something of a *superior* order by masculine is, I think, then certain. We simply mean personality, or creative initiative. But already in Part I of this essay the attitude of the 'Rationalizing' Business Power to personality was adequately described. And it would be as much resented, on principle, in a woman as in a man. That men have been supposed to possess a monopoly of initiative, creative genius, or *personality* is only because the political power was vested in their hands. They are also on the whole bigger and stronger, mainly because it was the tradition that they should be so. They *puffed themselves out*, as it were, physically, into *bigger* people. In a non-military race, like the jewish, or with the Hindu of merchant caste, there is not much difference physically. (The jewish cinema actors, men and women, are much of a muchness—or rather the men are less 'manly' than the Nordic Blond, and the women never so chocolate-boxily 'feminine' as their anglo-saxon sisters.)

But if *masculine* can be boiled down to a matter of *activity and initiative*—as a matter of mind rather than of muscle—so can feminine be boiled down to something not so much physical as mental. And an *inferiority* does go with it; what we agree to mean by 'feminine' is really little else than an absence of positive qualities, a receptivity, rather than activity: emotion, rather than intellect.

And it is in this sense that I propose to use it here. It has no other meaning for me.

Now a 'motherable' nursery-world, of 'motherable men' —feminine values everywhere in the ascendant, universities as forcing-houses for the nucleus of the great Neuter Sex of the future, in politics a toy-bazaar and puppet-show in place of the 'panoply of war' and the majesty of effective ministers of state; a cringing vulgarity upon the part of Princes, and *Child Cult* even among them—that is not exactly a good world for 'genius'—and I write, it will be remembered, *from the standpoint of genius*. The 'feminine' values are all the lowest, poorest-blooded—the most featureless, boneless, softest, the most emotional. And, of course, if it is a Matriarchy in fact that we are in, then it is in a *male-matriarchy*—not in fact a world ruled by an enormous Super-Mother, but by a ruling class of very *motherly-men*. For if 'feminine values predominate,' and if a Matriarchy is more than half on the way (as we are often told), it is feminine values promoted by men, and a pseudo-matriarchy (of a puppet-matriarch—a pantomime figure in the 'modernist' carnival) which conceals a figure (or a congeries of figures) in trousers.

But since 'feminine' in the only sensible way that one can use that term (and in this any intelligent feminist would be with me) is low-grade, second-rate, child-minded, mesmerically-receptive, dependent, etc., etc., etc.—then of course how this should come about is evident. For when you get government by Press, Radio, Film, and Fiction, which, in order to capture *every* Mrs. Everyman, has to be uniformly stupid stuff, you get also the glorification of every value that is feminine. You get (automatically) hatred for every value that is truly masculine.

The Family Circle—a small closed system full of the interference and despotism of brothers and sisters and unintelligent Authority, in the person of a dual-governorship of Father and Mother—is not an institution, *from the standpoint of genius*, that is very deeply to be regretted, should it be completely abolished. But *from the standpoint of genius* there might be no gain at all, but the reverse, if the world became one vast Nursery, reproducing, on a large scale, all the most oppressive and stuffy features of the traditional Family Circle. The old dispensation did at least leave open a hundred exits into the Public world *outside*. But if there were no *outside*, why then 'genius' would have nowhere to go at all, except out of the world altogether, if the domestic oppression and jealous interference became more than it could bear.

Such are the problems of Family Life, and post-Family state-domestication, *from the standpoint of genius*.

## CHAPTER III

# 'MOTHERING' AND MARRIAGE-STATISTICS

HAVING established just what is to be understood by 'feminine' (with no offence, the contrary, to any woman more than to any man), and having allowed that men and women in the lump are more or less feminine (and the creatures of those non-creative values), we can go on to evidence of one kind or another, to show how 'Youth-politics' are allied to the politics of Feminism. (For the exceptional 'Youth' ceases to be a 'Youth' in the invidious sense intended by the political boss with his eye upon him as promising cannon-fodder, just as the exceptional woman ceases to be 'feminine' in the conventional and derogatory sense.)

'In the last generation,' writes Ursula Bloom, '. . . *men were little gods:* in the nursery sisters gave way to them: in a career the man flourished.' (*Sunday Chronicle*, March 15, 1931. 'My Son—and Women.')

But one of the principal attributes of *a god* has always been that he did not grow old. And men, up till now, have shared that attribute to some extent with the gods. This 'seems unfair,' comments one of the lady writers brought in to discuss Age, in one of the 'Should a Woman Fear Forty?' articles.

Now it is only natural that a quite commonplace and not very intelligent type of 'suffragette' engaged in a 'sex-war' to liberate women from the rule of men (stirred up thereto by means of inflammatory appeals to her vanity and *amour-propre*) should very often be in no mood to associate (matrimonially or otherwise) with a member of the enemy-'class' —the hunnish, Fritzish male. The passions aroused in her bosom in the course of the political 'Suffrage' struggle

would make her so antagonistic to every one wearing the
hated trousers, emblem of the masculine prerogative and
despotic *rule*. But to this self-conscious 'class-warrior'
(her 'class' in this case merely her gender) a 'man' would
mean a 'Manly' man only—one of those disgustingly adult,
deep-voiced, domineering persons, who may have been
'born of woman' but have nothing much left to show for
it, and might really just as well have been *born of wolf,* or
suckled by one, like the founders of that super-masculine
state, Rome.

If, on the other hand, this particular woman we have in
mind should ever come to marry, it would be with the sort
of male who, in the Age-war, or the Father-and-Child-war,
would eternally be on the side of the Children, and could
be guaranteed, at least, *never* to become that most odious
thing, a Father—at least in appearance—at least, for a very
long time.

How it comes about that the type of man produced in
the more militant phases of the 'Age-war' should be rather
epicene is plain enough: and how it is that a certain sort of
woman, as an alternative to the masculine rôle in a lesbian
relationship, should choose occasionally the masculine rôle
in a marriage with an eminently 'motherable,' for preference scarcely more than adolescent, man, is also under-
standable enough.

In an interesting book entitled *Modern Germanies* (pp. 19-
20), by Cicely Hamilton, there is a very enlightening passage
upon the subject of *masculine baldness*. It is as follows:—

> I have always been interested in the phenomenon of
> masculine baldness—not the complaint, the actual falling of
> hair, but the masculine attitude thereto. The shamelessness
> of the male, with regard to alopecia, and the contrasting
> shame-facedness of the female. I know of only one woman
> who allows herself to be seen with a head that is really bald;
> and she belongs to a class which dislikes the cap, as a badge
> of servitude, and probably is not yet able to afford the de-

sirable wig. But I have only to look down on the stalls of a
theatre, or any other gathering where hats are removed, to
make the acquaintance of numerous male persons who are
not in the least abashed when they expose their expanses of
bald cranium.

*The reason for this indifference to personal defect is, I take
it, the masculine consciousness of dominance;* it has not been
rubbed into generations of men, as it has been rubbed into
countless generations of women, that it is their bounden duty
to make themselves look pleasant to the eye. *Constant preoccupation with personal appearance is the mark of the inferior,*
aware of the need to ingratiate. A young woman who went
about with a large hairless patch on the top of her head would
know she was damaging her chances of employment, as well
as her chances of marriage; but not so an equally disfigured
young man. If he were a first-class engineer, chemist or
accountant, his employer would not worry much about his
bald patch—and when his young man's fancy turns to
thoughts of love, he need not go to the discomfort of a wig
in order to obtain him a wife. Roughly speaking, the men
of all races are free of the need to ingratiate, that subjection
has laid upon women, and the German male, as regards sex
relations, is probably freer than most. Spite of women's
enfranchisement, or women's athletics, the tradition of masculine dominance is strong; hence the shameless ugliness of
the German shaven head.

The Germans, those past-masters in the cult of sheer
stark 'masculinity,' of keeping women women and men
men, in their unbounded insolence, and apparently to show
how little they depend upon the suffrage of the mere female
eye, actually go to the length of *shaving* their head, if it is
not bald already. Miss Hamilton is right. (Samson's locks
is a strange jewish folk-tale—it should have been told about
a woman.)

Now throughout all the past, up to this moment, it must
have been a source of envy to women of a certain order that
men possessed this curious prerogative, of gods and kings,
of remaining theoretically young—over against poor age-
complexed, age-sick woman. And one of the first things

that triumphant Feminism did was to proceed to reverse that superstition. (How perfectly that would fit in with the programme of Big Business there is no need to point out.) So the 'age of innocence' for man was past. He ate of these sour-grapes of Feminism—in the Garden of Eden of the New Age of 'Rationalization'—and (if he was a bald Adam) he 'knew he was naked!' And high time too! He has not yet proceeded to 'cover his nakedness' with a *toupet*, but will no doubt in time. Also he learnt that his privilege of 'eternal youth'—the Master's privilege—was no longer his. To-day honours—or dishonours—are about even. But already I think the woman has the best of it. A female at sixty is probably better off than the male of that age—that is, beneath the super-tax-class.

But this masculine privilege in the matter of age was attended by the right to marry at seventy a girl of seventeen (*en troisièmes noces*, for instance). And the age-discrimination against woman laid a woman open to attack and annoyance if she married a man even a year or so her junior. That wrong has been signally righted. This is well brought out by the following. (This cutting is from *The Observer*, October 6, 1929):—

---

# YOUTH AND AGE

### CURIOUS MARRIAGE STATISTICS

### REGISTRAR-GENERAL'S REVIEW

---

A surprising feature of the Registrar-General's Statistical Review for 1928, issued yesterday, is the large number of youths and men who married women much older than themselves. Twenty-one women of thirty, for instance, married youths of twenty, and one woman of thirty married a youth of seventeen, while another woman of thirty-eight was wedded to a youngster of nineteen. Two women aged forty and forty-one respectively married youths of twenty, and seventeen women between forty and fifty-one married men of twenty-two.

Still more astonishing are the following age discrepancies:

| Wife | | | | | Husband |
|---|---|---|---|---|---|
| 57 | . | . | . | . | . 24 |
| 55 | . | . | . | . | . 27 |
| 55 | . | . | . | . | . 29 |
| 63 | . | . | . | . | . 29 |
| 69 | . | . | . | . | . 34 |

Women of seventy and upwards married men of thirty-five, thirty-seven, forty, forty-four, forty-eight, and fifty.

These statistics from the Registrar-General's Statistical Review of four years ago indicate, I think, that the tide has turned. And the semi-incestuous is a common theme in a book or play. In this connection I may quote the following, which bears out the above:—

*Belfast. Friday.*
Miss Mary Borden (Mrs. E. L. Spears), the novelist, said to a woman's club meeting at Belfast:
'One way to make a success of a novel (in England) is to depict an elderly woman who inspires great devotion in a young man.'

## CHAPTER IV

# PRETTY BOY FOR 'PRETTY GIRL'

**T**HE statistics quoted at the end of the last chapter suggest the imminence of a reversal in the scale of age-values for men and women. This will be ephemeral, no doubt: it is an interim condition. When all the class-wars are won—or all lost, as may be—the whole sexual landscape will be transformed, we must suppose, as in the case of Soviet Russia. (I am not one of those who believe in the ultimate 'triumph' of *any* class in these class-wars. All equally will be defeated, I think.) But it is the *interim conditions*—the 'Transition'—that is occupying us here, nothing else.

This book is for popular sale, and it is impossible to define certain aspects of this transitional reversal too sharply: the hostile critic would certainly raise the cry that I had made use of 'repulsive phraseology' or something. So the imagination of the reader must be brought into play: all that need be said is that a 'mothering' is not a 'loving,' in the generally accepted sense. The *mothering-wedlock*—of a woman of fifty with an undergraduate, say—although un-objectionable (as Heaven would witness) does suggest a passivity on the part of the male, and, on the other hand, an unwonted activity on the part of the female. In all likelihood such is not a true marriage after all: a slightly incestuous mother-son relationship (in which there is no harm at all, and it is no one's business but the couple's, of course) ensues upon the solemnizing of the banns.

Such marriages, far out of the age-class of the dominant party, however, and in a reverse direction—of old widows or spinsters, for instance—do at least serve to emphasize the hostile cleavage between adult men and women. It throws into relief the issues involved in the age-cum-sex-class-war. Upon the one hand are the *Children* and their *Mothers*—or 'motherly' and 'mothering' persons. Upon the other stands the adult male, potentially or in fact the hated *Father*—standing beneath the full fanatical boycott of the anti-Father-principle.

How homosexuality comes into this is, again, quite clear. To be eternally 'children'—never to enter the category of 'Fathers'—that instinctively is what every sensitive, more or less educated, far-seeing young man of to-day must plan for himself.

But *the 'Pretty-Boy' state of mind* is not confined to homosexuals.  There is no occasion for a man to be actively homosexual for him to possess some of the eternal characteristics of the 'pathic.'  All young men now at universities and elsewhere are in contact with active and practising 'Fairies': it is unavoidable that at least some of the mannerisms and points of view of the homosexual should pass over into them (the 'B.M.s' or 'hearties').  So it is not unusual to find what is a homosexual frame of mind or outlook flourishing in a body that is in practice 'normal.'

What the homosexual habit of mind must be it is not difficult to see, for obviously (like 'the feminine') it is the result of a central habit (*sex*, firmly, freudianly, installed at the centre).  It is a *pseudo-function*, of course: and there is much romance, very much romance.  An imitation of the ultra-feminine—a being in that respect *plus royalists que le roi*—is what has earned for the homosexual in the rough frontier-jargon of the U.S.A. the term 'Fairy.'  But the traditional feminine obsession of 'Youthfulness' is not amongst the least of the female characteristics taken over, and exaggerated, by the homosexual.  And the Pretty-Boy state of mind in a general way reinforces the 'Fairy' element:  the bashful and dreamy, young-ladylike 'spoilt-child' has always, as a type, been an anglo-saxon speciality (the speciality of a 'spoilt' nation, in fact, softened by prosperity).

But these backgrounds are of the utmost significance for an investigation of 'Youth-politics,' as administered to the Anglo-saxon. For an attack upon the Father-principle it is clearly important that (1) the young males should not be, at the moment, in any tearing hurry to grow up and become sternly, adultly, masculine: or (2) that the young males should have too conspicuously set their hearts upon, at all costs, becoming 'Fathers' at all. And those conditions are, I think, satisfied to-day in Anglo-saxony, from San Francisco to the Goodwin Sands.

## CHAPTER V

# MAURIAC'S BABY-SNATCHERS

**B**EFORE leaving the subject of 'mothering' wed-
locks, or maternal 'pashes,' on the part of matrons
for very young males, I should like to draw the
reader's attention to a novel called *Destins*, by François
Mauriac.  It was published in 1928, I think, by Grasset.
This book depicts, with considerable skill, the infatuation
of a middle-aged peasant-proprietress for a very young
male.  If I spend some time in examining this book, it is
because a really thorough and meticulous examination of
one thing is better than a superficial glance at many;  and
this particular document may be taken as a summing up
for us of the tendencies in Western Society up-to-date—
though with especial reference to France, of course.  So
I will outline the whole story, with short quotations from
the text as I go along.  I am sure that it is worth the
trouble.

It is perhaps as well to say that Mr. Mauriac is a very
emotional christian (who seems consumed, however, with
a spasmodic loathing for christianity); and where he con-
trasts the *roman* strain in the famous gallic patriot-passion
for the mother-earth of France, with the romantic abstract
expansiveness of the celtic christianity, he gives the 'power-
complex' of the energetic roman strain no marks at all.
Mr. Mauriac does not say with his countryman Mr. Maurras,
'Je suis romain—je suis humain.'  He says, 'I am human—
I am *not* roman.'

His novel is a little epic of the break-up of France.  The
old peasant virtues that have endured for two millenniums
are seen in dissolution.  Some of this virtue disappears, as
far as *Destins* is concerned, into a trappist monastery, some

220

dissolves in sheer mediocrity and strong drink; but we are
left at the end of the book with the last representative of
the great 'kulak' families of Gornac and Lavignasse, a
woman, quite resigned for her part to all their properties
being broken up and the great names of Gornac and Lavignasse becoming memories. When her son, after many
hesitations, plucks up courage to tell her that he is pro-
posing to quit the world for good, and enter a trappist
monastery in Africa, and asks with anxiety what will
happen to their broad acres—vineyards, forests, and farms
—she only answers:—

> — Que veux-tu que cela me fasse? Crois-tu que cela ait la
> moindre importance?
> — Mais, Maman (he protests), songe qu'après toi tout sera
> vendu: j'aurai fait vœu de pauvreté; je ne veux pas garder
> un liard. Ces pins qui ont toujours été dans la famille, ces
> vignes que grand-père a plantées . . .

But his mother refuses to be moved by this at all; she
simply replies that if *he* didn't abandon and betray 'cette
terre,' why then his son, or his grandson, would—it would
be all one—it is all one!

> — Si ce n'avait pas été toi, c'eût été ton fils ou ton petit-fils.
> . . . Rien ne dure, rien n'existe.
> Elle répéta, presque à voix basse . . .
> — Rien . . . Rien . . . Rien . . .

Of this heracleitean, or shall we say this bergsonian,
attitude—the very unroman *laisser-faire*, the mystical
indifference to all that man builds up in defiance of Time,
in the teeth of Fate, Mr. Mauriac approves (being of a
mystical turn). But he sees the other side of the question.

Elizabeth Gornac—the last of her line—did not, however,
*always* feel like that. As a young woman she was a model
of french peasant energy. Prudent Gornac, her husband,
was a poor son for Jean, the superman, to have had, a
pleasant nonentity; so Elizabeth and her father-in-law,

Jean, managed between them all the Gornac vineyards and farms. She was a woman after the heart of the peasant superman, Jean Gornac, the king of this district of the Garonne.

'Ah! ma fille!' he exclaimed upon one occasion, as she sat, surrounded by account-books and correspondence— 'Ah! ma fille!—quel dommage que je n'aie pas été à la place de Prudent! Nous aurions fait ensemble de grandes choses!'

The *religion* that united Elizabeth Gornac to her father-in-law, Jean Gornac, the great peasant-proprietor—always improving his properties, acquiring new ones, and adding to his political prestige as well—was *not*, Mr. Mauriac tells us, the christian religion. It was *another* religion that united them.

> . . . une autre religion les unissait: les pins, la vigne—*la terre*, enfin. Ils communiaient dans ce même amour. Si on leur avait ouvert le cœur, on y eut trouvé inscrits les noms de toutes les fermes, de toutes les métairies, dont la possession les tenait en joie, les fortifiait aux jours de traverses et de deuil—empechait qu'aucun drame atteignit en eux le goût de la vie.

This 'taste for life,' this earth-love, as against human love—this Gornac 'religion' is the pagan one, of course. It was the religion of the superman Gornac till the end; when long past eighty he dies in the arms of his daughter-in-law Elizabeth.

But there are *two* loves. There are *two* religions. And that is where the drama lies in *Destins*. The daughter-in-law Elizabeth is after all *a woman*—this is Mr. Mauriac's point. And it is by way of the treacherous sentimentalism of *Women*, is it not, that this *other*—non-pagan, this anti-roman—religion enters into the world, and breaks up all societies however substantially built.

As a young woman Elizabeth Gornac was entirely pagan.

When her honest, timid, dull-dog of a husband (unworthy
offspring of the great Jean Gornac) was in the midst of the
tender midnight expansiveness of the nuptial bed (at his
breathless, silent devotions to that *other* god—the god of
women, not the god of men) Elizabeth would break out:
'Oh, remind me to ask you to sign that Lalanne lease
to-morrow! Don't forget!'

Elizabeth would say to her husband:

'I wonder you don't bore yourself—I don't know what
I should do here at Bos all the time if I hadn't got the property to look after!' And that poor underdog Prudent
Gornac did not dare to reply to her: '*Tu me suffis!*' in the
manner of that *other*—that non-pagan—sentiment, not
understood by his wife Elizabeth.

'— Ces sortes de gentillesses n'ont pas cours chez les
Gornac,' Mauriac writes. No: Prudent Gornac

aimait ses terres parce que, sans elles, il n'eut pas épousé
Elizabeth, mais il en était jaloux: il souffrait de ce que la
nuit, alors qu'une profonde émotion lui défendait toute parole,
soudain s'élevait, dans l'ombre nuptiale, la voix d'Elizabeth:
'*Fais-moi penser, demain matin, à te demander ta signature
pour le bail Lalanne!*'

But this poor devil, Prudent Gornac, died. And his
father Jean Gornac, and Elizabeth his widow, went on
building up and extending the Gornac properties as before,
as happy as sand-boys, in the grip of the peasant 'power-
complex,' and also in the grip of the slightly mystical
(though hardly respectable according to the canons of
that *other*, hostile, 'love') religion, that of the soil—*la
terre*.

But *Destins* is the account of the debacle of Elizabeth—
of the triumph of the other love over this pagan one. The
poor woman is after all *only a woman*: she is susceptible,
as are all women, to the bow and arrow of Cupid. ('Vous
êtes bien toutes les mêmes, ma pauvre fille. Quand on

connaît l'une de vous, on vous connaît toutes!' her con-
fessor tells her afterwards.) Her husband Prudent, he
meant nothing to her, it is understood: she was a splendid
roman woman—up to the age of forty-eight (a late climac-
teric?). Then comes the horrible debacle. This is at least
Mr. Mauriac's reading of human life and destiny. Elizabeth
Gornac, at forty-eight, suddenly falls the victim to an
atrocious 'letch' for 'le petit Lagave'—a sort of Cupid-in-
person, and a homosexual into the bargain, to make destiny
more complete, as it were—and of course to provide us with
the full illustration that we require of the operations of all
those tangled interests and counter-interests.

Bob Lagave was twenty-three years old, but 'Son visage
n'était pas . . . celui d'un homme de vingt-trois ans.' He
did not look his age—he seemed a mere gossoon. His voice,
even in making the most ordinary remarks, charmed on
account of 'une fêlure légère, comme si elle n'eut pas fini de
muer.' His voice had not properly broken, it only had a
half-crack, and he was a semi-choir-boy, to all intents and
purposes. His blond cheeks were hairless as a woman's—
with a red colouring, 'd'un sang trop vif.' But, *above all,*
he had abundant baby-eyelashes, 'des cils d'enfant longs et
touffus.' That was what more than anything did it. These
languefied and weighted his eyelids—so that 'he honoured
with the same languorous attention' cow, tree, or man.

When Bob was a small boy he was not very intelligent:
'he did not marvel' at all that everybody should melt at
his approach, and pat him on the head.

'L'indolent écolier trouvait tout simple de ne pouvoir
lever la tête vers les grandes personnes sans qu'une main
aussitôt se posât sur ses cheveux.' It was relatively late
on that he began 'exploiting'—but quite nicely—all these
natural advantages.

But if Bob is slow in learning about the advantages of
the infantile, once he has grasped the point he becomes

xpert. Also he becomes bitter. At twenty-three he is in he bohemian post-war *monde* in Paris—the apple-of-the-eye of a circle of rich infant-adoring, eyelash-loving persons, ranging from american millionairesses to homosexual polish Jews. He is very, very successful, and decorates everybody's flat, both male and female, for he is an artist. He doesn't mind whose flat he decorates, and he is very popular.

'Il croyait en son corps comme en son unique dieu.' But his 'god' catches cold, he has a very high temperature, and all the great rich 'rastas' to whom he has recommended himself—in some cases he has had to be homosexual in order to climb, that was unavoidable—flock to his parents' flat to visit him and bring him flowers (much to the annoyance of Papa, but to the great delight of Mama). 'Des êtres, dont Bob était le tourment et la joie, inquiets de demeurer sans nouvelles,' brave the ogre, the bourgeois father of Bob: and the mother lets them in. His bedroom becomes full of them and the perfumes of their clothes and turkish cigarettes.

Here is the account of these events. The mother of Bob sits in the next room, full of maternal pride and astonishment. She—

de la chambre voisine, elle les entendait rire, et respirait la fumée de leurs cigarettes. A travers la serrure, ou par la porte entre-bâillée, lorsque la bonne apportait la collation, elles les voyait assis en rond autour du lit de Bob: la princesse, une autre femme blonde, et ce jeune homme échassier avec sa trop petite tête sur des épaules d'égyptien; puis, le juif polonais, laineux, la lèvre inférieure pendante. C'étaient les fidèles; mais des visiteurs moins intimes se joignaient souvent à eux. Tous se ressemblaient par un air de jeunesse: jeunes gens, jeunes femmes quadragénaires, ils couvaient du même regard maniaque un Bob agressif, rétif, insolent—tel que sa mère ne l'avait encore vu. Ils riaient de ses moindres mots. Mme Lagave n'aurait jamais cru que son petit put avoir tant d'esprit. D'ailleurs, à peine aurait-elle reconnu le

P

son de sa voix: un tout autre Bob, en verité, que le garçon taciturne qui s'asseyait à la table de famille. C'était incroyable à quel point ces gens du monde l'admiraient. Il fallait que Bob eût quelque mérite extraordinaire, songeait Mme Lagave, pour que ces personnes difficiles le dévorassent ainsi des yeux. Elle ne savait pas qu'ils chérissaient en son fils leur jeunesse souillée, agonisante ou déjà morte,—tout ce qu'ils avaient à jamais perdu et dont ils poursuivaient le reflet dans un jeune homme éphémère. Une religion les rassemblait ici, un mystère dont ils étaient les initiés, et qui avait ses rites, ses formules sacrées, sa liturgie. Rien au monde n'avait de prix, à leur yeux, que cette grace irremplaçable qui les avait fuis. Et les voilà assis en rond autour d'un corps que la première jeunesse, pour quelques jours encore, embrasse. La maladie qui l'altère à peine les rend plus sensibles à cette fragilité, à cette fugacité. Peut-être Bob sent-il qu'il n'est rien pour eux qu'un lieu de passage où, quelques instants, se repose le dieu que ces fanatiques adorent. Peut-être pressent-il que ce n'est pas à lui, dénué de naissance, d'argent, de talent, d'esprit, que s'adressent leur adorations: de là, sans doute, cette humeur méchante qu'il oppose à leurs louanges, ces caprices de César enfant. Avec quelle affectation il se fait servir par eux!

Un jour, le juif de Pologne s'étant excusé de n'avoir découvert nulle part les pamplemousses dont Bob avait envie de goûter, le jeune homme eut le front de lui faire descendre quatre étages et lui enjoignit de ne reparaître qu'avec les fruits dont il était curieux.

Here is *another* religion. And it is, of course, that religion that we are attempting to define in this book. As seen by Mauriac, these 'fanatics' sat round the beardless Bob in bed, 'devouring him with their eyes.'

All these people who flocked to the bed of the convalescent idol, Bob, had one thing in common—'un air de jeunesse'—*a look of youthfulness* characterized all these 'forty-year-olders,' who with 'the same maniacal air' sat round the insolent 'Bob.'

'A religion brought them all together here, a mystery of which they were the initiates, and which had its rites, its sacred formulæ, its liturgy. Nothing in the world had any

value in their eyes, except this irreplaceable grace. . . .'
'A body in its first Youth' was the ineffable magnet.

But 'Bob,' though a slow learner, has learnt well: and
when they have left, he says to his mother:—

'. . . j'ai horreur de ces gens.'
'Ils ont été si gentils pour toi, Bob; ce n'est pas bien!'
'Ce qu'il y a de plus vil, mère: des gens du monde, qui ne
sont que cela.'
Entre les cils, il regardait sa mère.
'Papa a raison . . . Ils sont à vomir . . .' Quelle rancune
dans sa voix!'

Bob was a slow boy, and a sentimentalist too: once he
understands, he grows very anxious about his *Youth*: 'il a
. . . besoin . . . de cette atmosphère d'adoration dont ses
amis parisiens l'empoisonnent': and he lives in constant
dread of the moment when 'the god will depart'—when he
will be no longer worshipped for his Youth: and, at twenty-
three years old, he watches his face in the glass like a cat
a mouse.    Here is the description of him while he is con-
valescing at his grandmother's farm in the Garonne:—

. . . Il mesura d'un œil desolé ses jours futurs, aussi déserts
que cette plaine livide et endormie sous un ciel de ténèbres, un
ciel de fin du monde que des éclairs, à l'horizon, brièvement
déchiraient.    Il faudrait s'enfoncer dans ce désert, être dévoré
par les autres et, à tout instant, se sentir un peu moins jeune.
*A vingt-trois ans, il souffrait déjà, et depuis sa dix-huitième
année, de vieillir.*    Aux anniversaires de sa naissance, parmi
les rires de ses amis, et à l'instant des coupes levées, il avait
du ravaler ses larmes.    Ceux qui l'aimaient connaissaient
bien moins son visage qu'il ne le connaissait lui-même.    Le
matin, dans son miroir, il épiait des signes imperceptibles
encore, mais qui lui étaient familières; cette petite ride entre
les narines et la commissure des lèvres; quelques cheveux
blancs arrachés sans cesse et qui reparaissaient toujours.
Auprès de Paule seule, il eut consenti à vieillir.    Aux yeux de
Paule, il sait bien qu'il fut demeuré jusqu'à ses derniers jours
un enfant, un pauvre enfant.

Here you have the same sensations as those we are told

the roman 'exoletus,' or joy-boy, was afflicted with: a precocious terror of ageing. An old and fatigued civilization, in erecting this supreme value, 'Youth,' and charging the young mind with its mysticism, turns something charming and unconscious into something suffering and conscious, so that it becomes the Tom Thumb victim of this Youth-worshipping 'ogre,' which abandons it upon the instant once it is no longer 'Youth'—that is the idea.

Mr. Mauriac is sentimental, that is true: but his book is instructive because of the scene chosen, and of the underlying truths which, although he is apt emotionally to distort them, still keep their place in his recital, and retain a good deal of their original character. Bob reflects upon his homosexual slips, for instance:—

'Ma vie . . ., murmura-t-il, Ma vie . . . Il n'avait que vingt-trois ans. Entre toutes les actions dont le souvenir l'assaillait, qu'avait-il voulu? Qu'avait-il prémédité? Bien avant qu'il connût ce qui s'appelle le mal, combien de voix l'avaient de toutes parts appelé, sollicité! Autour de son corps ignorant, quel remous d'appétits, de désirs! Il avait vécu, dès son enfance, cerné par une sourde convoitise. Ah! non, il n'avait pas choisi telle ou telle route; d'autres l'avaient choisi pour lui, petit Poucet perdu dans la forêt des ogres. Son tendre visage avait été sa condamnation . . .'

It was his little blond face that was his ruin! says Mr. Mauriac. Poor little lost Tom Thumb, lost in the 'forest of ogres'!

While at his grandfather's, still not very strong, his grand Paris friends—the 'Youth-worshippers'—visit Bob. They have a shock! He is twenty-three—he has had an illness. *He is no longer quite so pretty.* While he is out of the room they discuss his appearance:—

Ils mirent à profit la courte absence de Bob:
'Il a une sale tête, vous ne trouvez pas? . . .'
'Bob est rudement touché, vous ne trouvez pas? Certes, il a toujours son charme . . .'

'Le charme de ce qui est déjà presque fini . . .'
'Les restes d'un déjeuner de soleil . . .'
'Attention! Le voilà!'

Here are the 'ogres' at work, preparing to drop 'Tom Thumb,' whose looks are on the wane.

A few weeks after this Bob (who has taken to drink, 'Youth' being altogether too much for him) is killed in a motor accident.

But not only Mr. Mauriac, also (as I have said) the staid and steady middle-aged matron, Elizabeth, is struck down by the darts from Bob's cupid-eye. Like an ageing cow, she falls into a bellowing romantic eclipse at the sight of Bob's eyelashes: and when finally Bob lies in state at the local church, after his body is brought back, she fills the House of God with her distraught roarings, and has to be carried out by her horrified son. Such is the end of the race of the Gornacs, and of that of Lavignasse! That that is too pat and symbolical, and, like the other, smacks too much of the moral-tale, is true. Also (though here you must allow for my prejudices, all of which are entirely pagan) the contrasting, by Mr. Mauriac, of *those born for love* and *those born for power*, is spoilt by the same sugar that sweetens too much everything that he touches. On the one side he shows you the ambitious, energetic peasant, Jean Gornac, 'impropre aux passions de l'amour'—one of those 'hommes non créés pour aimer': and such men 'despise and hate,' he tells us, an 'être de la race hostile.' Bob is a member of this 'enemy race.'

But what is this 'enemy race'—'born for love' and so on, as opposed to the ambitious, energetic, *roman* natures of these fine French peasants? What Mr. Mauriac certainly means is not so much *race* as *class*. And the *class* in question is certainly—in the mystical *age-war* (of which the novel is a reflection in the field of creative fiction)—the class of *The Women and Children*. And it is beyond question that that 'race' of people 'impropres aux passions de l'amour,' or not 'born to love' (but born to amass wealth and power, to *work* in whatever manner it may be)—that is simply the *Adult Male* of the species. *For man love is a thing apart—'tis woman's whole existence*—this saying of Byron's is the burden of Mr. Mauriac's song (and to the feminist it would sound both stupid and offensive). But I have given you, at considerable length, Mr. Mauriac's message for whatever it is worth, and what it may bring in the way of grist to this mill we are busy operating.

## CHAPTER VI

# THE 'CLUBMAN' AS VILLAIN

THE *duty* of man *to love*, in the feminine manner—and give up all those repulsive masculine habits, such as clubs and pubs (according to social status)—was well expressed by Mr. Michael Arlen in an article entitled—

> # DOWN WITH THE GOOD FELLOW!

It appeared in the *Daily Express* (December 15, 1930). By quoting a few passages we will obtain, in a peculiar purity, the view of masculine duty as held by the more fanatical members, I suppose, of any american WOMAN'S CLUB. Here is some of it:—

LUCIFER was not expelled from heaven because he was a bad man, but because he wanted amusement. Lucifer was not the Prince of Darkness, but the Prince of Good Fellows. And what he wanted was to get together with other good fellows.

Looking around him in heaven, at the cohorts of angels and the choirs of cherubim, he found there was scarcely one among them with whom a fellow could have a drink. But at last he found several discontented archangels, and he said to them: 'Have you heard this one?'

When they looked expectant instead of bored, as all the other angels did, he suggested to them that what they needed in heaven was a club. He said to them: 'I'll show you.'

And he showed them. And it was a good club, and they could not be persuaded to leave it. And it was called Hell.

Mr. Arlen comes up from the biblical nether regions into English Clubland: we breathe the perfumed atmosphere of Mayfair.   But, behold, we are at the funeral of a 'Club-man ':—

> Now I knew this man.  And I knew him well.  And I knew, too, that quiet and gracious lady, his wife.
>
> This man, this boon companion and good fellow and loyal friend, was in his home life a liar, a thief and a cad.  But, of course, in a charming way, for he was also a hypocrite. . . .

(The employment of the epithet 'cad,' as above, is for some people a source of almost supernatural enjoyment!)

> His wife (he goes on) married when she was a girl of twenty-two.  In the first two years of their married life she bore him a son and a daughter.  She loved her husband, and he was favourably disposed towards the mother of his children.
>
> After his second child—the son—was born, he found he was out of the habit of making love to his wife.  He found he didn't want to make love to any one.  So he didn't.  And he would say, in the company of other men, nodding his head wisely: 'There are other things in life besides love-making.  All these novels about love and sex!  There are bigger things in life, things that really matter.'
>
> It appeared not to occur to him and his boon companions that it matters a little to a woman of twenty-five to be for ever deprived of the tenderness and ardour of love.  It appeared not to occur to these good fellows that a woman who wishes to live as a nun will go into a convent and not get married.
>
> This lady brought up her children.  She devoted the best years of her life to bringing them up.
>
> There they were at last, the girl nineteen, the boy eighteen, the mother still a young woman, the father the most popular man of his time in London.
>
> The lady had promised herself this: her children, once they were grown up, would be her companions.
>
> Unfortunately for her, their father discovered them.  Still more unfortunately for her, her children discovered their father.
>
> .        .        .        .        .        .        .
>
> He had always been there, of course.  They knew him slightly, this popular father, who used to come in and go out, always with a charming smile and a pleasant word.  But now

they discovered that he was an amusing fellow. Their mother
wasn't amusing, she was a habit.

Their mother had been saying 'Don't' for the greater part
of their lives, but their father had never said 'Don't'—for
the simple reason that he hadn't seen enough of them.

And so father and children got together. And the mother
developed a capacity for smiling sympathetically. She had
plenty of time for it.

.    .    .    .    .    .    .

This man, this charming fellow who never thought of giving
his wife a fair break, is held up by his mourning friends as an
example for their sons. Well, so things go!

Let us suggest this epitaph for our lamented friend:—

*Here Lies A Man With A Gap Instead Of A Heart.*
*Into This Gap He Spent Fifty-Five Years Of A*
*Popular Life In Putting, Cigar Ash, Golf Balls,*
*And Brandy.   For He Was A Jolly Good Fellow.*
*May God Have Mercy On His Soul.*

But, do you know, I rather hope He won't.

Copyright by Michael Arlen in U.S.A.

'Copyright in U.S.A.'!—of such stuff was 'Prohibition'
made! Well, I suppose we must give Mr. Arlen a 'fair
break.' That this dismal personage should scold 'Clubmen'
and display himself as the eternal friend of 'the ladies,
God Bless Them!' (the 'gracious ladies' knitting at home
while the 'Clubmen' in their cock-clubs, from which 'hens'
are excluded, indulge in a devilish masculine freemasonry—
a sweet, a 'gracious,' a victorian picture, indeed, but
characteristically spurious—all that is but too natural.
It is singularly inevitable. But heaven knows to what
public it is addressed—for no public-with-a-Club, or with
a wife, to-day would understand it, it is so false to life. It
is, however, useful as revealing—as you see in the disarming form of a mere practical joke played by one 'Good
Fellow' (or *Faux bonhomme*) upon another, or upon his
class—the type of agitation that resulted in the Volstead
Act. If such a thing as Prohibition were put across here

it would be done in a joking 'Good Fellow' manner—and this tawdry gentleman sporting the christian name of an eminent archangel, and cracking his jokes about some old Lucifer, would hurl his once heavily-boosted pen, no doubt, at some notorious Clubman (whose wife was at the moment with child) as he was in the act of smacking his lips over a Scotch-and-splash—with his eye on the clock that forbade him to drink in his own club after it had hammered out (by that time, we will suppose) eight or eight-thirty time-beats. There, anyhow, you have the case against the adult male privilege and right of meeting in Club, Common-Room, or Saloon Bar. And with it you have the American Clubwoman's view of the male duty to love ('there are other things in life besides love-making,' indeed!) and not to drink.

## CHAPTER VII

## LYTTON STRACHEY'S 'MATRIARCH'

THE religion of feminine 'love,' as advocated by François Mauriac, can be more easily imagined if we present to ourselves the position of the adult male in America to-day; and for that purpose I will quote from a popular article (August 16, 1929) which appeared in the *Telegraph* or the *Express*. It was entitled:—

---

# THE NEW AMERICAN SEX ARISTOCRACY

## By CONSTANCE EATON

---

Nominally (says this writer) America is the greatest experiment in democracy that the world has ever known. Actually, however, it is working out into something quite different. It is becoming an aristocracy along rigidly drawn lines.

Two distinct classes are evolving, one inferior and the other superior. To the former belong all men, and to the latter belong all women. The distinction is not overtly discussed: it is rarely thought about: it is simply taken for granted. Owing to this conspiracy of silence the dividing line is growing sharper every day. Herein lies the insidiousness of this change that is coming gradually over the face of American democracy . . . idealization of woman is one of the most characteristic qualities of the great Western Republic. It has become organized almost into a religious cult.

MYSTERY AND POWER.

. . . What this new aristocracy in America most nearly approximates to is the caste system of India. The United

States is becoming a two-caste country, the distinction based not on class but on Sex, the higher caste being formed by its women.

Only the 'homme propre à aimer,' in the fanatical woman-serving sense of Mr. Mauriac, would be allowed to exist in such a caste-system as that indicated by Miss Eaton. As a matter of fact, of course, the revulsion against this is absolute in America—Miss Eaton is speaking, I think, of a phase of american life that is rapidly passing away. And, as I have emphasized throughout these pages, the 'matriarchate' that we hear so much about would be of very short duration; and even then it would be more a *male-matriarchate*—or rule by energetic, very feminine men. Women will merely be the tools employed in the operation of changing our individualistic society into a communist society. Once more, it is *the transition* we are studying.

But whether in *transition* or *post-transition*, feminine values will largely prevail, even if administered by *male-matriarchs*—who in fact are physiologically male, though very feminine in outlook—not warlike masters like the Normans, or Manchus, but more like a sleek and subtle theocracy—for machines have entirely put out of date the warrior-type—there can be no Siegfrieds (except a Siegfried Sassoon) when there are tanks and poison-gas. But imagine a male-matriarch upon the lines of Queen Elizabeth if you like.

In the universe as conceived by Mauriac, his Elizabeth Gornac would, at fifty, have wedded the 'gigolo' Bob: she would have administered the Gornac estates, 'Bob' would have lain in a scented hammock in the back-yard. It would have been what we call a 'matriarchate.'

The 'Matriarchate' of the great masculine Tudor (almost a male-matriarch) was different to what is meant by 'matriarchate' generally, of course, since there was only *one* woman, and it was, otherwise, a man's world. But—

to employ Mr. Lytton Strachey for this purpose (*Elizabeth and Essex*) and he is peculiarly adapted for throwing into high relief such a situation—it was an administration in which the officers of state and generals were chosen on account of their *calves*—the Queen-mistress being very *friande* (according to Mr. Strachey) of the male calf. (You have to imagine tights in place of trousers.)

A ring of mediocrities, with enormous calves, would, in such a state, surround the Matriarch — the Queen-bee. And the more advanced in years the Matriarch became, the younger her ministers of state would become, in the nature of things. She might even (if her reign were long, as with Elizabeth) take at sixty a consort in his teens (whom she would behead at twenty-one and replace by another adolescent).

In her heyday the great historical matriarch of England was, in Mr. Strachey's words, 'an old creature, fantastically dressed, still tall, though bent, with hair dyed red above her pale visage, long blackening teeth, a high domineering nose, and eyes that were at once deep-set and starting forward—fierce terrifying eyes, in whose dark blue depths something frantic lurked—something almost maniacal.' Elizabeth's Court was a menagerie of strong-limbed youths whom the Queen-bee would push into 'embrasures' (embrasures, we gather, were particularly numerous in the Tudor architectures), and tap with her bejewelled antennæ, having first examined the 'Youth' to see if his calves were big enough. 'She was filled with delicious agitation by the glorious figures' of all these big-calved court bumpkins, with whom she chatted amorously in the 'embrasures.' 'She loved them all!' cries Mr. Strachey ecstatically.

When Elizabeth met Mr. Strachey's hero and hers, Elizabeth was fifty-three—Essex was not yet twenty: 'a dangerous concatenation of ages.' As he bent down his 'auburn' head, she gloated down upon his calves, she loved him; and so he became generalissimo and admiralissimo, Lord Deputy, Earl Marshal, and Master of the Horse (of course a Knight of the Garter—all such Calves as *he* had Garters before they walked a dozen steps in the Palace of Queen Bess). He was a very bad general. But he luckily grew old—he was soon twenty-four—before he could do much harm. 'The Spring of Youth was almost over: in those days, at the age of twenty-five, most men had reached a full maturity. Essex kept something of his boyishness to the end, but he could not escape the rigours of time . . .' (p. 40, *Elizabeth and Essex*). And so, to cut a long story short, after causing a great deal of trouble, this calfiest of the calfy had his head chopped off a few years after this: he was nearly thirty (the Court was full of new-born Calves) and it was high time.

That is Mr. Strachey's Elizabeth and Essex, *en raccourci*, it is understood, but substantially the tale conveyed by the text: read in conjunction with the Registrar-General's Statistics of Marriages for 1928, and Mauriac's narrative dealing with the religion of 'Youth,' this should enable us to effect a flank attack upon the problem of 'matriarchy.'

Raleigh—in what I should venture to call this spirited *Fairy-story* of Mr. Strachey's—of 'calves,' of 'auburn hair,' of 'divine madrigals' sung to lutes by 'bewitching boys'— Raleigh, in the midst of all that, becomes a most sinister figure. It is really worth while having a look, before we drop the subject, at the figure Raleigh cuts, it is very peculiar. Here he is (pp. 29-30) :—

> The summer idyll (that of Elizabeth and Essex at fifty-three and nineteen respectively) passed smoothly on, until, in the hot days of July, there was a thunderstorm. While the Earl conversed with the Queen in her chamber, the Captain of the Guard stood outside the door on duty: and the Captain of the Guard was a gentleman with a bold face—Sir Walter Raleigh. The younger son of a West Country squire, the royal favour had raised him in a few years to wealth and

power: patents and monopolies had been showered upon him: he had become the master of great estates in England and Ireland: he was Warden of the Stannaries, Lord-Lieutenant of Cornwall, a Knight, a Vice-Admiral: he was thirty-five—a dangerous and magnificent man. His splendid bearing, his enterprising spirit, which had brought him to this unexpected grandeur—whither would they lead him in the end? The fates had woven for him a skein of mingled light and darkness! Fortune and misfortune, in equal measure and in strange intensity, were to be his.

The first stroke of the ill-luck that haunted his life had been the appearance at Court of the youthful Essex. Just as Raleigh must have thought that the Queen's fancy was becoming fixed upon him, just as the decay of Leicester seemed to open the way to a triumphant future—at that very moment the old favourite's stepson had come upon the scene with his boyish fascinations and swept Elizabeth off her feet. Raleigh suddenly found himself in the position of a once all-conquering beauty, whose charms are on the wane. The Queen might fling him three or four estates of beheaded conspirators, might give him leave to plant a colony in America, might even snuff at his tobacco and bite a potato with a very wry face—all that was nothing: her heart, her person, were with Essex, on the other side of the door. He knotted his black eyebrows, and determined not to sink without a struggle.

Although thirty-five (he had been 'mature' for a decade —the reader cannot but shudder involuntarily at the thought of the dangers he must have already run) Raleigh determines not to be beheaded 'without a struggle,' in spite of his age. We see Raleigh (in the mirror of Mr. Strachey), 'a once all-conquering beauty,' standing outside the door of the Queen—like a sinister, armed footman, or detective-inspector—and listening at the keyhole while 'the daring youth ' inside flings himself about in a tantrum, and violently abuses the veteran 'beauty' outside to the melting Matriarch—and afterwards, the eavesdropping *has-been* steps hastily aside in order not to be trodden on when Essex, 'flinging himself from the room,' disappears in a storm of petulant highschoolgirlish rage because the Queen *will not*—even with such calves as *he* has—behead upon the spot the old 'beauty' at the keyhole! And facing page 29 there is a portrait of this same bald old 'beauty' (once 'all-conquering') with large ear-rings, and a hunted look. The picture speaks for itself—he evidently knows his number's up, and is getting ready for the block.

It is a great temptation to linger over this fascinating department of our study; but I think that enough has been said to have established firmly the sort of problems that are involved in all administrations, autocratic or otherwise, where the sexes, *upon the old terms of romantic love*, are combined, and the uneasy character of an executive composed according to the values inherent in that passion —and that applies as much if the balance of power is upon the one side or the other. Only in *A Land of Love Locked Out* would these rather comic paradoxes not ensue—the 'Loveless Land' being Russia, where romantic sexual love is, we are told, discouraged. I will quote from an article by Mr. Joad to make clear what I mean (it is about a visit he paid to the U.S.S.R.):—

> I was a frequent visitor to the cinema: in all I must have gone a dozen times. The Russian films had all the vigour and novelty of technique for which they are justly famous, but never once was there an introduction of what one calls the sex *motif*. The only kind of love whose existence was admitted was mothers' for their sons, parents' for their children. On no single occasion during my stay in Russia had I been reminded of the fact that young men and women could be attracted to each other: that love, in fact, was an important thing. People might be born in parsley beds and live like hermits for all the suggestion in Russian life to the contrary.

And in an interview with Mr. Shaw, entitled 'Love' (*Sunday Express*, Nov. 10, 1929) the following piece of dialogue occurred. Shaw is replying to the interviewer:—

'You will find that in all my plays I look at love in the proper perspective. Most writers are unable to emancipate themselves from their personal Sex obsession and from the sentimental rubbish of love-lorn poets.'

'Your attitude is not unlike that of the Bolshevists. They, too, look upon love as an impersonal passion.'

'I should not be surprised at all,' Shaw replied, 'if Bolshevism succeeded in evolving a more civilized attitude towards sex and life. . . .'

If ultimately human society results in a state having much in common with contemporary Russia (though, we must hope, not in everything), and if a 'more civilized attitude' towards love is, as Mr. Shaw believes, evolved, then all that we should have to consider regarding 'matri-archates' to-day would happily be obsolete. The Fairy-tale of Mr. Strachey would be a *Fairy-nightmare* merely. But in the *transition* all these things have to be dealt with. And 'Youth-politics' to-day repose upon a very traditional basis of highly-coloured, and indeed garish, emotionality. So, if our survey is to be a thorough one, all that must be taken into account. That is why I have been interrogating the pages of Mr. Mauriac and of Mr. Lytton Strachey in such detail.

Q

# PART V

# CONCLUSION

## CHAPTER I

# POVERTY, CHILDISHNESS, AND MARIOLATRY

I WILL now review some of the ground covered in the present investigation up to date, and so bring it to a close. For the last few chapters I have been busy with the question of the two ideals, the masculine and the feminine (those terms employed in an unrestricted sense—not skirts and trousers). I should be sorry to be accused of believing that the collapse of Elizabeth Gornac (in her one wild last grab at the *Baby-Man*—half-Child, half boy-beau) was a final picture of women: I mean that discipline and energy are good, and the romantic and frantic abandonments held up by Mauriac as desirable are not: but that women as much as men can be starched up against false or destructive passions. To-day it is the dregs of the female nature, all that is stupidest in the mere *being a woman*, that is stimulated, and allowed to triumph (to force our society into a rapider disintegration): it is the dregs in everything whatever that is encouraged (male or other) as our democracies become more and more enfeebled: and, with the female, emotion is nearer the surface—that is all that is meant by 'feminine.'

Because of what is now cultivated, beamed upon, and brought triumphantly to the top, you must, as a matter of course, arrive at the sort of thing indicated in this cutting from *The Daily Telegraph*:—

---

## PARIS DAY BY DAY

---

### THE FRENCHWOMAN'S HEROES

#### MEN OF ACTION

---

245

PARIS.

A French literary weekly journal which is largely read by women appears to have established that woman's taste in heroes has changed considerably since the war. Women readers were invited to elect an ideal Académie française, but that which has emerged as a result of their vote is as unlike the present company of 'Immortals' as it could be.

The women's list includes only one writer of poetry, the Comtesse de Noailles, and not a single novelist. But it includes airmen, racing motorists, explorers, and soldiers. The inference drawn by the *Journal* is that the time has gone when women sighed in love and admiration of those writers, actors, and artists who inspired romantic dreams.

Their affection has swerved from *romance* to *action*, and it appears that an Academy elected by women would be composed almost entirely of such men as Marshal Foch, Marshal Lyautey, the airmen Fonck and Pelletier D'Oisy, the lonely voyager, Alain Gerbault, and the Polar explorer, Dr. Charcot —all of them men who chose perilous professions. The pale hero of the library or the laboratory has gone out of fashion.

Needless to say, 'The Frenchwomen' involved (supposing the responses to be not entirely faked) are sedulously taught what sort of 'hero' to admire by the Press, day in, day out, for many years (Press, Film, and Novel monotonously insist upon Action, Action, Action) before the questionnaire is sent to them upon the subject. So their answer is a foregone conclusion. But the *Académie française* being founded in order to organize learning, and intellectual distinction, it would be a mistake to convert it into a 'crack' tennis club, or an exclusive circle for flying aces, or a rendezvous for Valentinos, selected according to 'box-office appeal.'

Let us turn from France to Germany. I will take *Lill*, a Berlin best-seller of two or three years ago. The *best-seller* (regarded as a social document) is like the camera, it cannot lie. This narrative deals with the attitude of the post-war German to Sport.

In Germany the tide has now turned against this obses-

sion. (Sport involves *capital*, to start with: the Aussems—
as the Helen Wills—are rich, first, else they could not be
'cracks.') The *Nazi* has effected this change in the german
conscience. The *Asphalte-Presse*, as the Nazi calls it, still
fills its pages with Crime and Sport. But the german
Youth has turned away from Gunmen, Poisoners, and
Squash-racquet Cracks, to topics of greater immediate interest. So *Lill* is out of date. But still it represents a germ
of teuton decadence not by any means purged out of the
masses—perhaps already too far entered into their blood to
be expelled at all, during the 'Transition'—though I do
think that the Germans stand a chance of passing through
the 'Transition' without sinking to such depths as the
Anglo-saxon.

The whole german world (says this german best-seller)
has turned away from all that formerly it regarded as
worth-while. The best-seller deplores this: which shows
that at least his public are not like ours: which would not
demand that of a best-seller. Despair has seized upon the
German: he has turned from the reality to a *Scheinwelt des
Sports*, says the best-seller. He can no longer bear even to
think of all those formerly momentous things, of culture
or politics: they spelt disaster, they are popularly discredited.

The hero of *Lill* is represented as the incarnation of post-
war german Youth. (He is not—he is in fact only that of the
youthful hanger-on of the *Schiebertum*: but that does not
matter.) He is a boxer, dirt-track racer, mile-runner, tennis
'crack' (as the German calls a record-breaking sportsman),
et cetera; in all these sports he excels. In his personality he
has 'die sorglose Miene der neuen, jungen Männer Deutsch-
lands, die den Krieg nicht mehr mitgemacht hatten—die
nichts mehr von Sterben und Blut, sondern nur von Leben
und Schweiss wussten—denen die Vergängenheit nichts,
der Sport alles war.'

And elsewhere in the book is the following passage, intended to throw a light upon this situation:—

> Ihr tanzt. Ihr tanzt überall in Europa. Ihr tanzt auf Gräben und wisst nicht, was darunterliegt. Wollt es auch gar nicht wissen. Aber Ihr habt doch eine Ahnung, dass viele schöne Dinge nicht mehr da sind und die Welt nicht mehr schön ist. Das geht allen Leuten in Europa so. Und darum schafft Ihr Euch überall in Europa eine Scheinwelt des Sports bei Tag und des Tanzes am Abend und nehmt diese Welt so wichtig, dass es wirklich Eure Welt wird, in der Ihr lebt. . . .

That is the account of things given by the german best-seller in *Lill*. And what is that *Scheinwelt des Sports* but the *Scheinwelt* of the schoolboy? It is the civilization of the anglo-saxon schoolboy, who invaded half the earth and is so stupid he now is losing it. (How could a mere Public schoolboy do otherwise?) With that is interbred and crossed the melancholy hysteria of the american negro, and the communistic mystics of his african music.

As I have taken it to be axiomatic that the best-seller, like the camera, cannot lie, I will quote a little more from Stratz.

The super-sportsman takes his sports-girl to a lecture. There she hears from the lips of the famous mental specialist the following discourse.

Eventually this lecture puts her off dirt-track racing and tennis altogether. Lill is never as good a sports-girl again. The Irrenarzt had done the trick:—

> 'Denn sobald wir, wie jetzt, dem Körper den Vorrang vor dem Geist einräumen, verzichten wir auf unseren eigenen Vorrang gegenüber der übrigen belebten Welt. Mehr noch: wir verzichten auf den Vorrang der höheren Menschenrassen von den niederen. Und dieser Sklavenaufstand der Kultur war immer noch das Zeichen einer sterbenden Epoche! Diese Epoche heisst seit kurzer Zeit—seit etwa zwei Jahrtausenden—Europa. Der Fall Europas ist es, der uns letzterdings heute hier beschäftigt. Denn jeder von uns ist Europa. . . .
> 'Europa ist der weisse Herrland. Alte Sünden der Jahrhunderte rächen sich an uns weissen Menschen. Wir ver-

gessen, dass Geist verpflichtet. Wir haben den Geist nicht zum Mitleid, sondern zur Macht gegenüber den anderen Menschen missbraucht. Nun schrauben wir und freiwillig auf die Stufe hinab, auf der diese primitiven Menschen stärker sind als wir auf die Leiblichkeit als Selbstzweck und Ding an sich. Wir bewundern die harte Hirnschale, die dem Faustschlag trotzt, ohne uns zu sorgen, was unter dieser Hirnschale wohnt. Der Neger kriecht in unsere Seele.'

This is from the discourse of the Irrenarzt: but by Lill's side the 'Crack'—the super-sportsman—is there too, and he objects strongly to all these remarks. He takes up the cudgels for *the body*, as it were, against the *Geist*. Putting questions to the lecturer, he asks whether swimming records are matters of no importance—whether the Half-mile is not *something* after all—and how about Ju-Jitsu? At all these physical feats animals far excel men, the lecturer has no difficulty in showing: and when the spokesman for *the body* against *Geist* exclaims:

'But how about *jumping*, Mister Doctor!' the Herr Doktor replies:

'Ich wurde gegen Sie auf jedes Kanguruh wetten! . . . Oder meinen Sie einen Sprung in die Höhe? Da hält nun der Floh die Weltmeisterschaft. Er hüpft, in Verhältnis zu seiner Grösse, wie ein Mensch bis zu einem Kirchturmknopf.'

This Berlin best-seller suggests, in short, that the White European is being in the most absolute sense disarmed—by way of Sport and by fanatical body-worship. Driven away from the principal instrument of his former power and success, namely, his intellect, what is left him?—except what the savage has (only more of), feats at which any insect can beat him? Systematically discouraged from using his head (by rulers who desire him to be as politically malleable as possible), he is given a hundred mechanical toys to play with: an extreme brutish childishness must supervene. In process of being systematically discouraged from using his head (which will make him easier to govern as a fool is

always easier to rule than an intelligent person, and an un-
taught child than an adult, who has had a little time to
reflect about the things that have happened to him) the
European is being systematically and tirelessly encouraged
to absorb himself in the study and enjoyment of mechanical
toys; in Sport and by way of mass-amusements of all sorts,
from community-singing to mass sun-bathing (*Nakt-Kultur*)
he is being imperceptibly thrust back to the condition of
stone-age man. And the droning and rapping of the mass-
music of primitive tribes is there to hypnotize him into
acquiescence.

*Charlotte Etwas Verrückt* (by Speyer) was a sort of german
'Gentlemen Prefer Blondes': I refer the student to that for
further german best-seller enlightenment. It tells the same
tale as *Lill*—only Charlotte is never disillusioned.

With all this account of conditions in Europe, I of course
agree, as far as it goes. The sun-bathers stretched out at
full length all over our Continent in the summer months—
they *are* the first instalment of a predestined savagery.
Just as much as Al Capone and 'Legs' Diamond (or for that
matter the poor huddled, mud-caked, half-starved savages
called 'Fritz' or 'Tommy,' 1914-1918) that is so.

Here is an account of a Baltic watering-place, for instance,
called Ostseebad Brunshaupten (a cutting of recent date):—

The beach presents to unaccustomed eyes a very strange
spectacle. It is covered with a growth of objects which at
first sight you take to be wigwams of some primitive tribe,
but which prove on closer inspection to be huge basket chairs,
roofed over for protection from the sun, most comfortably
upholstered, provided with telescopic foot-rests and adjust-
able to any angle required. Each of these beach baskets is
romantically constructed for a pair of occupants, but usually
each family hires one for a few shillings a week and uses it
prosaically as its bathing headquarters.

The beach-master allots you a pitch for your Korb, and
round it you are expected to build for privacy a rampart of
sand, known as a Strandburg, or beach fortification. This

fortification is an officially recognized institution, and a printed notice solemnly informs you that by order of the Bade-Verwaltung, or Resort Authority, no Strandburg may exceed five metres in diameter. Burge and Korbs are decorated with flags of all kinds.

I do not know Brunshaupten: but transport the 'Kaffir Village' of Brunshaupten anywhere to the torrid coasts of France in August, where hundreds of thousands of persons are burned to a negro mahogany yearly, from toe to crown, and you might get the illusion, I suppose, of a veritable primitive negro community. This, it must be allowed, would harmonize with the Jazz that hums in their heads, those airs to which they nightly stalk and shamble.

That the mass of people should be taught to do without clothes, or without too much food, or alcohol, or *anything*, may not be bad. If Everyman became a Kaffir, well, what then? Luxury is not good for us, certainly. It is only necessary to remember that the tendency is to deprive people of everything, and to head them towards a universal, artificial state of want, and to recognize what that signifies. Would it matter if they had *fewer cars* in England? Not that I can see! But if suddenly they were ordered to leave off buying them, still it would be wiser to ask *why?* For millions of people are without work—are ready to construct them, buy them, and use them. There is plenty of stuff to make them with. It is the importance of *question-asking* only that I stress—that the 'élite,' as Guénon calls it, should retain its question-asking habits.

The final downfall of Western riches and power is imminent. Have those riches and that power been enjoyed wisely and well? Of course not. What power ever has been? But that is no reason for the European (spasmodic and imperfect sentimental Christian that he is) to rejoice too stupidly. Our 'White Epoch' is, doubtless, doomed. But do not let us be *too* enthusiastic over that, any more

than too sad.  But hear Miss Cicely Hamilton upon Modern
Germany and its cult of the naked.  (I quote again from
her excellent book, *Modern Germanies*, p. 16):—

> And this bathing-kit fashion is not only a blessing to the
> Children who follow it: it must also be a boon to their
> parents.  *Think of the saving in cost of dress material*: think
> of the saving in time and the weekly wash!  When a bathing-
> dress is grubby all you have to do is, give it a dip and then
> hang it out to dry in the sun.  No scrubbing, no careful
> ironing and folding!  A fashion *entirely of the twentieth century
> and springing, perhaps, in the beginning from sheer poverty*—
> like many another good custom.
>
> It is of set purpose that I have headed this chapter the
> Cult of the Bare and not the Cult of the Nude: because, as
> I suggested a page or two back, scantiness of clothing is not
> an isolated phenomenon.  It is one of the symptoms of a
> tendency widespread and strong, one of the manifestations
> of the modern German *spirit of economy*.

It is not, I think, necessary to underline this any more
than I have done.  That 'modern German spirit of
economy' is so strangely coeval with *modern German
poverty*—an unprecedented poverty—that there is no
occasion to speculate whether they *might* not—*perhaps*—
have influenced each other!  And the material of that
syllogism being only too palpably present, I need not
formulate it for you.

But all these contributory tendencies of a central,
rapidly-gathering barbary, a Dark Age, I need not
enumerate.  Let us take, however, that most significant
fashion of the intelligentsia—the 'detective story.'  In
England and America, for several years, it has been a cult,
of an intensity of the first order.  But these detective
stories are in no way different to what detective stories have
always been.  The only difference is that formerly they
were read by schoolboys and uneducated people, and no
'grown-up' or 'educated' person, male or female, ever
experienced any desire to read them—indeed *could* have

read them, had they tried ever so hard. But to-day they have become their *livres de chevet*. One of the well-known 'high-brow' reviews in London is practically run to advertise and discuss this type of literature.

I will reproduce the 'blurb' (inside the dust-jacket) of one, namely:—

# THE  DEATH  GONG

By

### SELWYN JEPSON

Author of *Rogues and Diamonds*, etc.

The scene of this swiftly-moving thriller of love and adventure is laid in Italy and North Africa. The story is concerned with a Chinese Gong which legend claims was used by the priests of Quen-Ki-Tong three thousand years ago to kill their enemies by its vibrations. Sir John Perrin, who tells the tale, becomes involved in the hunt for the gong, and narrowly escapes with his life from mysterious happenings in the Arab quarter of Tunis, when he succeeds in rescuing the girl he loves from the machinations of her brutal husband.

With many a Bloomsbury smirk and giggle (at the thought of the signal *Intellectual naughtiness*, as it were, of displaying an *intellectually immoral interest* in such 'low-brow' confections) this sensational crime-literature is eagerly canvassed.

But the *Child* and the *Primitive* are never far apart: and the one opens the door for the other—especially when it is not a real, physiological Child—but a *Faux-naïf*—and when it is not a technical ignoramus or tyro because of a lack of cultivated training, but a *savage on purpose*.

In a very tub-thumping sort of article on 'The Risen Lord' (in answer to a question as to his proposal for the correct 'Religion for the Young') D. H. Lawrence divided the world into three distinct age-classes. First there were those who were over age at the time of the War: they still hold to the picture of 'the Christ-Child'—happily sitting upon the knee of the Virgin Mary, beneath her protection. Second, there are the soldiers: their Christ is 'Christ Crucified.' The 'Christ-Child' image was 'smashed' for them in the War. (No woman came forward to save them from death by shell-fire.) Then there are the post-war 'Young.' Neither of these first two images are believed in by the post-war 'Young': 'Christ Risen' *should* be their image.

In the Catholic countries (he wrote), where the Madonna-and-Child image overwhelms everything else, the man visions himself all the time as a child, a Christ-Child, standing on the lap of a virgin mother. Before the War, if an Italian hurt himself, or suddenly fell into distress, his immediate cry was: '*O mamma mia! mamma mia!*'—O mother! mother! The same was true of every Englishman. And what does this mean? It means that the man sees himself as a child.

A chicagoan, jewish journalist of my acquaintance—an intelligent, placid, middle-aged 'columnist'—has assured me that 'he always thinks of himself as seventeen.' He always sees himself, in his mind's eye, as he was then. I am sure he does. But I am also quite sure that D. H. Lawrence is wrong about the 'War-generation.' Far from *giving up* the 'Christ-Child' image, they embraced it after the War *en masse*, in a most remarkable way, and only talked about the 'crucified self' on occasion, to turn an honest penny. People who, I am sure, had never regarded themselves as 'Christ-Children,' or any other sort of *Child*, before the War, became—with a fanatical obstinacy—*Children*, after the War. D. H. Lawrence was taken in, I am afraid, by War-generationism. And as to the 'Risen Lord' —that is another illusion of Lawrence's (and 'Mammon' was another conventional tub-thumper's facile imagism).

## CHAPTER II

# THE *SCHEINWELT* OF THE TRANSITION

TURNING to what is more particularly the subject of this book—the technique of the 'Politics-of-Youth'—the effect of those politics upon the popular plane is often productive of the most barbarous anomalies and patterns of fantastic vulgarity. In a general way, the 'Politics-of-Youth' is not designed to affect the upper social layers, as at present constituted. Obviously the supreme leaders of the world (still less the powers behind the throne) will not ever be blushing schoolboys, or coy maidens, at any time. The Popular Press is strictly reading matter for wage-slaves ; it is the bulletin for the slaves. And the 'Politics-of-Youth' is hypnotic instruction for cannon-fodder, the servile masses—that is clear.

But, in Western Democracy, since the submerging and disappearance of the privileged families—the old 'ruling class'—the slave-consciousness, and slave-manners, has invaded every circle of the plutocracy. There, in Mayfair or Long Island, the manners, the vernacular, and the attitude of mind, on the surface, is very little different to that of Broadway or Commercial Road. Under these circumstances (with an exceedingly important difference) the 'Politics-of-Youth,' intended for the servile-circles (for Workshop and Factory), also gives its colour to the lives of the gilded, super-tax circles as well. The *important difference* mentioned above is, of course, that whereas for the workman these effects are a matter of grim earnest, for the more fortunate plutocratic minority they are not. The latter patronize the fashions of the Underworld. They sing the slave-songs of the industrial serfs of the metropolis (their sobbing factory-folk-music). But all that is borrowed, in this way, from the arts and manners prevalent in the Heartbreak House of the Underdog, is taken up in a spirit of light-hearted cabotinage.

Although nothing vital is really at stake, however, the *passage-of-the-years* (grey hair, pop-bellies, and wrinkles) *is* a humanly stimulating topic (it is a best-selling topic for a book, I hope—the Old Adam apart from Youth-politics has a tremor at the thought of baldness, deafness, and gout). So the *Age-war* raging in the jungle down below—a matter of life and death for the small employee—is, up above, among the plutocratic Olympians, often a (very venomous) sham-fight.

We now are all *class-warriors*, are we not, more or less, just as in the old Christendom the Royal Courts maintained at least the outward show of devoutness? Every *class-war* is dutifully reflected from beneath upon the gilded surfaces up above. But homosexuality has also been a master-fashion for some time : and homosexuality more than anything breeds age-consciousness. The pathic and old homosexual beau (or 'Aunt Mary') takes to age-class-war as a duck does to water.

The age-values imposed upon the popular mind thus obtaining, in a playful form, in fashionable-bohemian circles (the World of Ritzes and Rivieras), the 'Youth' up there does not of course *get the sack* at the end of his Ten Years, but something mildly analogous happens to him. The eclipse of the 'Youth'—and his violent transformation, resembling in its abruptness the transformations of insects, into an 'Ex-Youth'—is often very sudden. It is not with such a sickening bang as the *sack*—as with a deadly dismissal in the slave-world : but there is a *smothered report*, as it were. (In Mauriac's *Destins* we saw 'Bobby' being practically executed at twenty-three by his gilded patrons —as the first specks and frecklings of *age* became apparent upon the surface of the fruit, as it were.)

No rules can be laid down—pronounced homosexual habits, for instance, will make a great difference; but in the ordinary way an individual, who thinks himself somewhat of a great guy and has money, may announce to his friends 'I will give myself another two years'—or he may say 'eighteen months.' That means that after that period has elapsed he will be no longer 'young.' It will be in the nature of a promise to put up the shutters and retire from active life. He may subsequently—if he has a great deal of hair (and if his efforts to remain 'young' have not sprinkled it with unpigmented strands of a disgusting silver) and if his stomach is in place and does not out of reason protrude, and if he is rich—give himself another twelve-month. It will depend what his friends say. But at last he will take himself for a ride (go a long sea-trip), or put himself, so to speak, 'on the spot.' Publicly he will pass over into the Elder Half of the World.

There (if he is rich, again) he will proceed to make himself comfortable. (With a woman this is all managed differently; I am confining myself here to the description of the male dying—or burying his 'youth' rather, with an unhappy pomp.)

In artistic circles, of rich amateur, or bourgeois-bohemian life, in order not to lay himself open to ridicule, this 'deceased' person must go the whole-hog at once—there must be no half-measures. If a wealthy bachelor, at once an enormous pair of slippers (such as belong to the 'lean and slippered pantaloon') must make their appearance. He must never move too quickly up or down stairs, in however great a hurry (although in point of fact he is by this time—should he have 'carried on' till nearly forty, say— usually quite unable to), lest his friends should whisper that he is affecting 'youth.' He must rise slowly from a gigantic sofa of a chair, and for preference carry his hand to the lumbar region, to suggest lumbago. If he has a bold bald

R

patch, he must make the most of that. Then with a painful ostentation he must for preference converse of events that occurred twenty or thirty years before. This last point is exceedingly important: it must be clearly understood that he is in fact dead—that openly (and loyally) he lives with the Past (with Death in the form of Chronos).

## CHAPTER III

# A COMMUNITY IS RULED BY SNOBBERY

AN 'Atmosphere'—a *Stimmung*—is created by means of the 'Youth-politician,' and a very oppressive atmosphere it must be, from thirty upwards, in workshop, office, and factory. What must inevitably be the outcome is an *inferiority-complex* on the part of all those people unable to call themselves Flaming 'Youths.' And how exceedingly useful this must be to the Big Business directorate has already been pointed out. A man with an acute *inferiority-complex* because five years has passed over his head since his last rise in salary, is scarcely likely to be a very difficult customer to deal with when it comes to discussing perhaps a *reduction*, rather than a rise—with the black spectre of Unemployment in the background.

A girl clerk starts, I suppose, at fifteen, at 7s. 6d. a week. Being under age, that is all she gets. But to-day she is apt, in time's revolutions, *to come back to that 7s. 6d.* if she stops on the job long enough. Large businesses are at present using quantities of cheap *old labour*—just as they have always used cheap *child labour*—*paid at the lowest rates* : the child of fifteen and the crone of fifty are in the same *minimum* category. One hears of squadrons of superannuated typists, between forty-five and sixty years old,, working in invoice departments at 10s. or less a week.

*Inferiority-complex* is a term that has not been current for longer than twenty years or so. *But all government has been conducted since the world began* upon *a solid basis of 'inferiority-complexes,' as much as upon a basis of armed force.* Make a person feel *small*—that is, give him an '*inferiority-complex*'—and he is in your power. Even though you yourself are unarmed, he will not dare to touch you. In the heyday of kingship it took a very original and independent fellow to pluck up his courage to lay a finger upon 'a king'—even if he and the king were alone, and the king unarmed, old, and feeble.

A *History of Inferiority-complexes* would make a most interesting book. Until very recently there was in Europe a standing example of this *spell*, as it were, of 'inferiority,' namely in the spell that had been put upon the Jew. Fifty years ago to have been 'a Jew,' that would have been a very strange sensation, I should imagine. This terrific superstition has been extirpated from mankind—within, as a matter of fact, a very few years, almost as if by magic. And in England the superstition of 'birth'—of the 'upper classes' being of a different clay—that was a tremendously powerful superstition as well. The 'inferiority-complex' of a 'common' man or woman, under Victoria, that must have been a very intense sensation—though of a different and less absolute order than all that was suggested by the word 'Jew.'

No sooner than one superstition is overcome, however, than another takes its place. For mankind is inveterately snobbish and superstitious. It *must* have these spell-binding superstitions—the mystical-values. And I do not think that the intensity of the old 'class' superstition (now long dead) of the 'gentleman' or 'lady,' and the men and women who were distinctly *not*—even that would not outdo, I think, the superstitious values of the *age-snobbery* now in process of crystallization.

It is by Snobbery, in fact, that a community is ruled: for if you say that it is by means of carefully-fostered 'inferiority' and 'superiority' complexes, that means the same thing. If you wish to get the better of a man in any field whatever, in whatever matter you may be competing with him, *get him feeling 'inferior'* and you cannot fail to overcome him.

That, then, is the principle at the back of all 'Youth-politics'—both upon the economic and upon the political side—in our Western Democracies at present.  Once you have seized firmly this key to an at first sight complex situation—or once you have entered into possession of *the whole bunch of skeleton keys* with which, in fact, I have provided you in this book—why, then, you will really have (mentally at all events) the freedom of this 'transitional' dream-city—this paper *Scheinwelt* of ours—and go where you will.  There is only one door I do not recommend you to use your skeleton keys on.  But there are some things, after all, you must find out for yourself.

# CHAPTER IV

# YOUTH, LIKE SEX, IS TO BE ABOLISHED

IT is not in the least to reverse what we have just been saying to assert that there has probably never been a period less superstitious than the present (whether as regards rank, race, age, or any other superstition) among those people really possessing political and social power. *The superstitions are all for the underdogs*—those in very fact *inferior*; such as are unable to see through, or to shake themselves free of, superstitions. The conspiracy of power to-day is—as Mr. H. G. Wells has called it—an open conspiracy. It is all fair, square, and above-board! There is no excuse for any one at present not to be politically enlightened. Yet there have never been so many people entirely ignorant of everything that is happening to them. Which only shows that 'openness' is the best policy. If Guy Fawkes had explained publicly to all the citizens of London exactly what he intended to do, then probably the Gunpowder Plot would have been a signal success. (For is it not only 'madmen' who carry out their destructive designs openly?)

As to the *Age-complex* again (manufactured, for commercial and political reasons, expressly for use against the emotional herd, for *class-war* purposes—to take the starch out of the european adult—by discriminating against him in favour of Women and Children—to soften him at the core with a novel 'inferiority-complex,' and so on): it would be true to say probably that among an enlightened minority *less* meaning is attached to mere physiological age than at any other time. But that only applies to a small percentage. Feminism having in large measure destroyed 'sex' (in the old, romantic, overheated sense), the *age-bogey* with woman

262

(which was a sex-bogey, of course) has disappeared: as a consequence the small minority of intelligent and active women take as little notice as did formerly men of the age-classification.   But those women are still the exceptions.

To bring home the great advance in civilized standards that the last twenty years has witnessed (always at the top in the civilized and leading classes, not throughout the masses), let me cite the attitude to 'beauty,' as that applies to the faces of women.   At this moment there are great numbers of women going about with great reputations for 'beauty,' who would have been compelled under Victoria to hide their heads and creep away into a corner and die, shamed by their repulsive 'ugliness.'   They would have had to resign themselves never to marry, for they would have been labelled—with that deadly victorian label—PLAIN. No side-whiskered Victorian (however 'homely' himself) would have dared to 'take them to the altar.'   He would have been eternally shamed had he done so.   Their faces failing to conform to any recognized chocolate-box canon, thousands of women far better fitted to continue the race than the indolent characterless chocolate-box-faced monsters of 'prettiness' in vogue at the time must have been practically sentenced to death, or at all events (for it was the race more than they who would suffer) condemned to barrenness.

This does testify to an enormous advance *somewhere* in the taste and intelligence of the community.   A woman with an exquisite parchment-coloured face, or one of an attractive mildewy wax, is not damned with the silly word *sallow*—because she does not sport a complexion of mono-tonous roses, or one of crushed strawberries and cream. What is more lovely than *sallowness*?   That to-day is fully recognized in those quarters where such recognition is most important, namely, the richest and most powerful.   'Chinese eyes,' again, do not cause a woman to be an outcast:   thick lips relate her to the much-honoured types of Africa: and a large boxer's hand and iron jaw bring every pathic to her feet.

The tables have been turned in a most thorough manner, everywhere, upon the 'chocolate-box': and if this catholicity brings in with it a certain number of abortions—who under the Prince Consort would have been strangled out of hand at birth—the gain is very great. With the opening up of the meaning of the word 'beauty' a very foul superstition has been exploded. *At the top*, at all events, we can all breathe freely again, if we are women, whatever our faces (with their features and organs and skin-covering) may be.

Now 'Youth' was—or it came to be—a superstition as pronounced as any. And in most respects the doom of 'Youth'—its suppression, at the hands of the 'Youth-politician'—is (or will be) a notable achievement. That, too, will find its way to the Waxworks, the historical museum, where in the future all these classes of superstitions will be classified and exposed to the gaze of the sightseer.

To abolish the prolonged period of ignorance and primitiveness artificially maintained at great expense, for twenty years or more, at the beginning of life, is surely an excellent policy—something like 'daylight saving,' and the adjusting of the clock to suit the seasons. It is not only unobjectionable, but a welcome innovation, to eliminate the 'childish' child—either lisping dreamy-eyes, or pulling legs off frogs and behaving like a miniature savage.

And if the 'doom of Youth' ('Youth' according to the old, sentimental conception) also means *the doom of Sex* (and all its old superstitious romantic attributes) rather upon the lines occurring to-day in Russia ('The Land of Love Locked Out')—well, would not that be a very good thing too?

But I have now enumerated all the problems involved in

this proposed readjustment, I think.  Really what the 'doom of Youth' means is the erecting of 'Youth' into a *unique* value, and by so doing abolishing Youth altogether. For something that is *everything* in human life cannot be anything so limited as 'Youth' as understood upon the merely emotional plane.

A 'Youth' (Peter Pan) that *never can grow up*—that is the *all-youth* of the super-sentimentalist.  For him there is nothing whatever in the world of any value but 'Youth' in the traditionally romantic, the sugar-and-spice sense. 'Youth-politician'—that is diametrically the opposite to Sir James Barrie's sickly variety, or the bogus and lisping species that is peculiar to the Invert's paradise.

For the 'Youth-politician' there is, strictly speaking, *no youth*.  There are only different degrees and powers of an abstract energy.  There is one long *adult life*, if you like. No life is worth considering, for the 'Youth-politician,' except adult life.  And adult life is not worth while, of course, once the person is no longer active and capable of creative or at least of useful work.

This appears to me to be not at all a bad ideal.    On the other hand, the use of the term 'Youth'—as a result of the technique of 'Youth-politics'—for this *inclusive* valuation, is confusing.  But as interpreted by a stupid person, anything at all becomes stupid.

It is quite clear what is intended, and what is destined to come about.  'Youth' is to be abolished altogether (just as the old 'sex' conception was wiped out by Feminism). And it is also quite certain that it is the very reverse of that (to the mind of the simple Everymans) which is on foot: nothing but endless, irresponsible, something-for-nothing 'Youth' is their *simplest* of 'Youth-politics.'  And, of course, for the *Everymans* it *will* be the reverse.  I have said that I was a prophet.  And I prophesy that two centuries hence a long and sweeping snow-white beard will be an emblem of aristocratic privilege (no 'Everyman' will live beyond twenty-nine and a half)—just as long skirts returned to us—but as a token of social distinction, on the principle of long finger-nails in China. Obviously *long* skirts suggest that the wearer *does not work* : long finger-nails the same. The long white beard will be the supreme token that the person possessing it belongs to the ruling-class—that he is a member of that super-class who do not die, like dogs, after ten years of active life.